Mastering LibGDX Game Development

Leverage the power of LibGDX to create a fully functional, customizable RPG game for your own commercial title

Patrick Hoey

BIRMINGHAM - MUMBAI

Mastering LibGDX Game Development

First published: November 2015

Production reference: 1241115

Published by Packt Publishing Ltd.
Livery Place
35 Livery Street
Birmingham B3 2PB, UK.

ISBN 978-1-78528-936-1

www.packtpub.com

Credits

Author
Patrick Hoey

Reviewers
Jason R Chandonnet

Richie Heng

Commissioning Editor
Veena Pagare

Acquisition Editor
Reshma Raman

Content Development Editor
Athira Laji

Technical Editor
Taabish Khan

Copy Editor
Trishya Hajare

Project Coordinator
Bijal Patel

Proofreader
Safis Editing

Indexer
Priya Sane

Graphics
Kirk D'Penha

Production Coordinator
Shantanu N. Zagade

Cover Work
Shantanu N. Zagade

About the Author

Patrick Hoey is a software engineer with over 15 years of professional experience, contributing to the success of organizations from Fortune 500 companies to startups. While working full time, he completed his master's degree in computer science and then went on to graduate from law school, passed the bar exam, and became a licensed attorney. He has also donated his services as a director at a non-profit company.

Patrick started developing video games from the age of 12. The first video game that he created was a crude hangman game for the Atari 800 home computer written in Atari BASIC. He has developed demo programs throughout the years that demonstrate certain features or exercise certain APIs of interest at the time, such as OpenGL, DirectX, SDL, Allegro, Cocos2d-x, and recently LibGDX.

For entrepreneurial endeavors, Patrick ported video games to mobile phone platforms. His latest adventure with LibGDX started in 2013, creating a game that he always wanted to play called CityPunk: A Hacker's Story.

Patrick's research interests include game development, graphics programming, intellectual property case law, data visualization, microcontrollers for embedded devices, and machine learning.

Patrick loves photography, hiking, traveling, and creating short films.

Find out more about Patrick on his personal blog at http://www.patrickhoey.com.

Acknowledgments

I would like to thank my loving mother, Jean, for being my biggest fan, for being the light when all was dark, and for instilling in me a strong depth of character that has enabled me to overcome all challenges. For these gifts, I am eternally grateful. I would like to thank my wife and best friend, Samborn, for helping me realize another dream with unending support and love. I could not ask for anything more than to share this adventure called life with you. I would also like to thank my good friends, Jason and Richie, for having unyielding faith in me and for joining me on this amazing journey as technical reviewers. I would like to thank Reshma, Ajinkya, and the rest of the great team at Packt with all their help, patience, and resourcefulness throughout. Finally, I would like to thank Andrew Rios for creating the DawnLike tileset, as well as the greater community of video game artists and musicians contributing fantastic art and music under the Creative Commons license.

About the Reviewers

Jason R Chandonnet is a software engineer with over 15 years of professional experience. While working full-time, he completed his master's degree in computer science. He was an inventor on several patents and started an independent website development and hosting business. He also spent many years on the board of Rebuilding Together Lowell, a non-profit organization that renovates houses of people who are unable to pay for essential home repairs and much-needed updates.

Jason has been tinkering with computers and electronics since a very young age. As soon as he was able to read, he would spend hours entering programs from books and magazines on a Commodore 64. At age 11, he created a simple shoot-em-up game on the Commodore 64 in BASIC. Here he learned the joy of reading and writing registers to make the computer do what he wanted. He also was infamous for his electronics experiments that were often a means to generate high voltage.

While in college, Jason started building websites and web servers. This led him to join an IT sales and service company to develop a product catalog web application. While there he took on computer repair, UNIX system administration, and networking before officially moving into software development. Over the years, he has worked on data collection and processing systems, embedded systems, robotics, medical devices for image-guided surgery, supported clinical trials, and cadaver studies. More recently, he has been working on embedded Android devices customizing Android, as well as designing and developing the suite of applications.

Jason loves the outdoors, hiking, traveling, raising poultry, playing music, volunteering, and, of course, playing with microcontrollers, embedded systems, or other gadgets.

Richie Heng is an information technology specialist living in the United States. After finishing his bachelor of science degree in computer science from Seattle University, Washington, he worked for both the private and public sectors. With over 10 years of front and backend experience, he is currently working with the government developing data visualization applications that impact legislative decision making. Among his many projects, his favorite project is a Windows application written in C# that captures immigration clients and their activities. In his spare time, he likes having fun with his family, petting his dog named Onion, playing chess, camping and hiking, and travelling.

I would like to thank Mr. Patrick Hoey for writing this book, and my family and friends for giving me the support through the years.

www.PacktPub.com

Support files, eBooks, discount offers, and more

For support files and downloads related to your book, please visit www.PacktPub.com.

Did you know that Packt offers eBook versions of every book published, with PDF and ePub files available? You can upgrade to the eBook version at www.PacktPub.com and as a print book customer, you are entitled to a discount on the eBook copy. Get in touch with us at service@packtpub.com for more details.

At www.PacktPub.com, you can also read a collection of free technical articles, sign up for a range of free newsletters and receive exclusive discounts and offers on Packt books and eBooks.

https://www2.packtpub.com/books/subscription/packtlib

Do you need instant solutions to your IT questions? PacktLib is Packt's online digital book library. Here, you can search, access, and read Packt's entire library of books.

Why subscribe?

- Fully searchable across every book published by Packt
- Copy and paste, print, and bookmark content
- On demand and accessible via a web browser

Free access for Packt account holders

If you have an account with Packt at www.PacktPub.com, you can use this to access PacktLib today and view 9 entirely free books. Simply use your login credentials for immediate access.

Table of Contents

Preface

"It is pitch black. You are likely to be eaten by a grue."

- Zork

Some of my fondest video game memories belong to text-based adventure games. Zork was my gateway game into the realm of role-playing games on the computer. RPGs offered excitement and challenges of adventuring into unknown lands ripe with unknown dangers, and helped fuel my imagination. This book is a testament to that imagination, one which refused to be extinguished by age or experience. My hope is that your RPG will keep the burning flames of imagination alive and provide an experience with memories that will last for a lifetime.

The theory, implementation, and lessons taught within these pages should help guide you through the development process of creating your own RPG game. There are many moving parts that add to the complexity of developing a video game, especially RPGs, but the intent of this book is to provide you with a step-by-step guide to the development process. I developed BludBourne, the reference implementation game for this book, at the same time I was writing this book. If there were any issues that I came across during development, or if I found a nice design pattern that solved a problem, I made sure to document the experience in this book so that you would not have to deal with the same pitfalls.

You may have heard about various engines and frameworks, and even tried them, but instead of creating a complete commercial game, you ended up in disappointment, lost in a sea of technologies. Maybe you always wanted to create an RPG, but found the creation process overwhelming. Maybe you would visit forums and post questions, but all you ever got were common replies of derision, such as "Just create your game in RPG Maker." This book simplifies this approach by walking you through the process so that you can extend and customize BludBourne for your own commercial release. The framework that will allow us to bridge the gap from conception of an idea to an actual playable game is LibGDX.

LibGDX is a Java-based framework developed with a heavy emphasis on performance, and it includes cross-platform support out of the box (Windows, OS X, Linux, iOS, Android, and HTML5), and provides all the low-level functionality you need so that you can focus on developing your game instead of battling with the platform. LibGDX also has an engaged and responsive community, active maintenance, and is available for free without a prohibitive license. There are many beginner tutorials using LibGDX, but the aim of this book is to make use of LibGDX libraries for more advanced, complex features used in video games.

By the end of this book, you will have a foundation in game development principles and a set of tools that will help you realize your dreams.

What this book covers

Chapter 1, *As the Prophecy Foretold, a Hero is Born*, introduces you to the fundamentals and specific features of RPG video games, and discusses how this book will help build foundational knowledge for a commercial RPG. This chapter will also walk you through the basics of video game architecture, with a high-level overview of the component layout and application lifecycle in LibGDX. Finally, after learning about setting up your development and build environment, you will run your first demo application.

Chapter 2, *Welcome to the Land of BludBourne*, initially discusses how to create maps for BludBourne with a tile editor and how to load them using asset management classes. You will then implement your main render loop with a camera for displaying your loaded maps. We will then discuss some features specific to maps, including spawn points and a portal system. Finally, you will learn about adding animation to your player sprite and implementing input handling so that your player can move around the game world.

Chapter 3, *It's Pretty Lonely in BludBourne…*, discusses how to implement the Entity Component System design pattern for BludBourne. We will then cover scripting support using JSON to define NPC properties. Finally, we will implement a physics component with collision detection and an input component for the NPCs' movement.

Chapter 4, *Where Do I Put My Stuff?*, covers HUD layouts with skins. We will learn about integrating player stats into the UI. We will then apply this knowledge by implementing a drag and drop inventory system for your player. Finally, we will discuss how to persist player state with save and load game profiles.

Chapter 5, Time to Breathe Some Life into This Town, discusses the theory behind dialog trees and implements an interactive speech system for the NPC characters. Finally, we will develop shop store UIs for the player with item and money transactions.

Chapter 6, So Many Quests, So Little Time..., discusses quest systems, including dependency graph theory and implementation. Finally, we will create a quest log UI, including the steps involved with creating scripts for quests.

Chapter 7, Time to Show These Monsters Who's the Boss, discusses how to implement a battle system with a UI including enemy NPC battle mechanics. We will then look at how we can connect HUD updates to state changes in BludBourne. We will cover a few tricks for implementing the consumption of items from the player's inventory. Finally, we will develop a leveling system for the player.

Chapter 8, Oh, No! Looks Like Drama!, discusses how to integrate sound and music into the world of BludBourne. We will also look at how to create cutscenes and integrate them into the game.

Chapter 9, Time to Set the Mood, covers an assorted list of special effects that can give your RPG some nice polish. We will first learn about creating transitions between screens. We will then learn about the theory behind a shake camera class and implement it. We will then look at how a static lighting model fits into BludBourne, including implementing a day-to-night cycle. Finally, we will cover particle effects that can used to make the spells pop and torches smoke.

Chapter 10, Prophecy Fulfilled, Our Hero Awaits the Next Adventure, covers deployment topics for your game, including discussing digital distribution platforms. We will then look at security measures, including obfuscating save game profiles, executable jars, native launchers, and obfuscating the final packaged JAR. Finally, we will look at a few tips and tricks regarding test coverage for builds and some debugging tips.

What you need for this book

Throughout the book, I have mentioned various technologies and tools that can help at certain stages in the development cycle. I have recommended mostly free software tools and dependencies. However, keep in mind that some may require a separate license for commercial purposes. As a testament to the open source community, I created BludBourne entirely from these free resources.

LibGDX is a cross-platform game development framework that can run on a Windows PC, Linux, Android device, or Mac OS X. The development for this book specifically supports Windows (7/8), so keep this in mind when using the source for BludBourne as there may be some platform-specific considerations outside of Windows.

As a quick summary of tools and libraries used for this book, I have listed them here (may not be an exhaustive list):

- LibGDX (v1.5.5): http://libgdx.badlogicgames.com/download.html
- Java Development Kit (v1.7): http://www.oracle.com/technetwork/java/javase/downloads/index.html
- Git: http://git-scm.com/downloads
- SmartGit (v6.5.9): http://www.syntevo.com/smartgit/download
- IntelliJ IDEA IDE (v14.1.1): http://www.jetbrains.com/idea/download/
- Tiled (v0.11.0): http://www.mapeditor.org/download.html
- libgdx-texturepacker-gui (v3.2.0): http://code.google.com/p/libgdx-texturepacker-gui/
- Android Studio (v1.0): http://developer.android.com/sdk/index.html#Other
- Audacity (2.0.3): http://audacityteam.org/download
- Packr: http://libgdx.badlogicgames.com/packr
- Proguard (5.2.1): http://proguard.sourceforge.net/

The installation and usage instructions for additional tools are provided where necessary.

Who this book is for

If you have always wanted to create an RPG video game but found the creation process overwhelming, either due to lack of tutorials or by getting lost in a sea of game-related technologies, engines or frameworks, then this book is for you.

This book will walk you through the entire development process of creating an RPG title from scratch using the LibGDX framework and it can be used as a reference by everyone from a team developing their first commercial title to the solo hobbyist.

This book does expect that you have software engineering experience, including familiarity with object-oriented programming in the Java language and an understanding of UML.

Conventions

In this book, you will find a number of text styles that distinguish between different kinds of information. Here are some examples of these styles and an explanation of their meaning.

Code words in text, database table names, folder names, filenames, file extensions, pathnames, dummy URLs, user input, and Twitter handles are shown as follows: "The `processInput()` method is the primary business logic that drives this class."

A block of code is set as follows:

```
public class DesktopLauncher {
  public static void main (String[] arg) {
    LwjglApplicationConfiguration config = new
            LwjglApplicationConfiguration();
    new LwjglApplication(new BludBourne(), config);
  }
}
```

When we wish to draw your attention to a particular part of a code block, the relevant lines or items are set in bold:

```
public class DesktopLauncher {
  public static void main (String[] arg) {
    LwjglApplicationConfiguration config = new
            LwjglApplicationConfiguration();
    new LwjglApplication(new BludBourne(), config);
  }
}
```

Any command-line input or output is written as follows:

```
C:\BludBourne>tree /F /A
```

New terms and **important words** are shown in bold. Words that you see on the screen, for example, in menus or dialog boxes, appear in the text like this: "Adding a new tileset is as easy as clicking on the **New** icon in the **Tilesets** area."

Warnings or important notes appear in a box like this.

Tips and tricks appear like this.

Reader feedback

Feedback from our readers is always welcome. Let us know what you think about this book—what you liked or disliked. Reader feedback is important for us as it helps us develop titles that you will really get the most out of.

To send us general feedback, simply e-mail feedback@packtpub.com, and mention the book's title in the subject of your message.

If there is a topic that you have expertise in and you are interested in either writing or contributing to a book, see our author guide at www.packtpub.com/authors.

Customer support

Now that you are the proud owner of a Packt book, we have a number of things to help you to get the most from your purchase.

Downloading the example code

You can download the example code files for all Packt books you have purchased from your account at http://www.packtpub.com. If you purchased this book elsewhere, you can visit http://www.packtpub.com/support and register to have the files e-mailed directly to you. For the most current version, you can grab the latest snapshot from this link: https://github.com/patrickhoey/BludBourne.

Downloading the color images of this book

We also provide you with a PDF file that has color images of the screenshots/ diagrams used in this book. The color images will help you better understand the changes in the output. You can download this file from https://www.packtpub. com/sites/default/files/downloads/MasteringLibGDXGameDevelopment_ ColorImages.pdf.

Errata

Although we have taken every care to ensure the accuracy of our content, mistakes do happen. If you find a mistake in one of our books—maybe a mistake in the text or the code—we would be grateful if you could report this to us. By doing so, you can save other readers from frustration and help us improve subsequent versions of this book. If you find any errata, please report them by visiting http://www.packtpub.com/submit-errata, selecting your book, clicking on the **Errata Submission Form** link, and entering the details of your errata. Once your errata are verified, your submission will be accepted and the errata will be uploaded to our website or added to any list of existing errata under the Errata section of that title.

To view the previously submitted errata, go to https://www.packtpub.com/books/content/support and enter the name of the book in the search field. The required information will appear under the **Errata** section.

Piracy

Piracy of copyrighted material on the Internet is an ongoing problem across all media. At Packt, we take the protection of our copyright and licenses very seriously. If you come across any illegal copies of our works in any form on the Internet, please provide us with the location address or website name immediately so that we can pursue a remedy.

Please contact us at copyright@packtpub.com with a link to the suspected pirated material.

We appreciate your help in protecting our authors and our ability to bring you valuable content.

Questions

If you have a problem with any aspect of this book, you can contact us at questions@packtpub.com, and we will do our best to address the problem.

1

As the Prophecy Foretold, a Hero is Born

Our journey begins with you, our hero, adventuring into the unknown in the hopes of starting and then finishing a role-playing game. We will discuss the history of role-playing games, the game features that we will develop throughout the book, and some considerations when evaluating the tools to help you develop your game. We will learn a brief history of game architecture, and how it relates to and differs from the architecture of LibGDX. Finally, we will look at the LibGDX project structure and run the default application so that we hit the ground running in the next chapter.

We will cover the following topics in this chapter:

- Understanding the fundamentals of role-playing games
- Technologies used when developing a role-playing game
- Understanding the basics of a game architecture
- Understanding the high-level component layout of LibGDX
- Understanding the application lifecycle of LibGDX
- Setting up your development environment
- Understanding the build environment and project structure
- Running the default demo project

Understanding the fundamentals of role-playing games

A treatise on the history of role-playing games is beyond the scope of this book, but a short jaunt through the origins of **role-playing games (RPGs)** that led to the development of **computer-based RPGs (CRPGs)** over the years is necessary to fully explain the type of game that this book covers. This history is covered in much more detail in Neal Hallford's *Swords & Circuitry: A Designer's Guide to Computer Role Playing Games*.

History

In the early twentieth century, two unrelated parallel developments eventually converged into what we call RPGs today.

The first development was a set of simple rules written in 1913 by H.G. Wells in the form of a war game called *Little Wars*. This type of game overhauled complicated game systems at the time making this particular war game approachable by the masses. *Little Wars* included units such as infantry, cavalry, and even artillery that launched wooden projectiles. The rules included simplified mechanics for moving and firing within a set time.

The second development during this time was in the form of a series of novels, starting first with *The Hobbit* (1936) and continuing with *The Lord of the Rings* trilogy (1954) written by J. R. R. Tolkien. The influence of these classic books cannot be overstated as they established the "high fantasy" subgenre in literature, helping to propel fantasy as a distinct and commercial genre. These novels created a world with its own history, cultures, and traditions, at the center of which an epic battle between good and evil waged. Adventures across this world, Middle Earth, included elements of sacrifice and heroism, love and loss, beauty and terror.

Decades later, in the 1960s, Wells' *Little Wars* influence was still felt with ever-increasing complex wargaming experiences, including large-scale board games with hundreds of units. At this time, traditional wargaming revolved around real-world historical scenarios, but people started substituting the more traditional campaigns with recreations of the epic fictional battles from Tolkien's *The Lord of the Rings* novels. These players were without a system that defined rules for integrating magic or explaining the battle mechanics of flying dragons.

Chainmail was published in 1971 by Gary Gygax and Jeff Perren out of this need for a proper rule system for a fantasy-based wargaming experience. *Chainmail* had the first set of wargaming rules for magic spells and fantasy creatures. Years later, Gary Gygax and Dave Arneson collaborated and produced the first role-playing system, *Dungeons & Dragons* (*D&D*), published in 1974. From the late 1970s to early 1980s, the influence of Tolkien fiction and *D&D* seeped into the computer video game arena, and started the evolution of modern day CRPGs that began with the creation of text and graphic-based RPGs.

The first text-based adventure game was *Colossal Cave Adventure* (or *Adventure* for short) created by Will Crowther and Don Woods in 1976 with the first commercial release (renamed to *The Original Adventure*) in 1981. In *Adventure*, the player navigated an interactive story that included Tolkien-inspired monsters, mazes to explore, and puzzles to solve for treasure. The spirit of fantasy adventure in *Adventure* continued with Infocom's release of the *Zork* series as well as the catalyst for Roberta and Ken Williams in forming what would become Sierra Entertainment, and developing graphic adventure titles such as *King's Quest*, *Space Quest*, and *Leisure Suit Larry*.

The first graphic-based role-playing game, *Akalabeth: World of Doom* (*Akalabeth*) was created by Richard Garriott (known as Lord British) and published in 1980 with commercial success. The player assumed the role of the hero, traversing through dungeon labyrinths, collecting gold pieces, slaying monsters, and completing quests. The novel concepts at the time that set the standard for future CRPGs included first-person gameplay in dungeons, required food to survive, had a top-down overhead world view, and boasted procedurally generated dungeons.

Capitalizing on the success of *Akalabeth*, Garriott, after a year of development, published *Ultima I: The First Age of Darkness* (*Ultima*) in 1981. With the commercial success of *Ultima*, this game (and the series as a whole) became the defacto standard that defined graphic CRPGs for decades, with core features and gameplay found even in today's CRPGs. Aside from the features of its predecessor, such as dungeon crawling, turn-based combat, overhead world view, loot collection, and hunger management, *Ultima* also had new features including a character creation screen with point allocation for player statistics, and choice selections for race, class, and gender. Other features included proper leveling with experience points gained through combat, randomly appearing enemies, hit point regeneration, and a magic system managed with consumable one-time use items. *Ultima* even sported a first-person space shooter for part of the game!

Wizardry: Proving Grounds of the Mad Overlord (*Wizardry*) was another influential graphical CRPG published in 1981 and was developed by Andy Greenberg and Robert Woodhead. This dungeon crawler was the first party-oriented CRPG with up to six characters allowed for a party. Each character had three different alignments, four classes to choose from, and also an option for prestige classes that, after meeting certain requirements, would allow the character classes to be upgraded with hybrid abilities. An interesting feature was that upon a total party kill, the new party sent into the same dungeon could recover the bodies and belongings of the wiped party.

While the *Ultima* and *Wizardry* franchises satisfied the hunger of the home computer market in the United States, they also played a large part in the success of home console RPG development in Japan.

In 1986, Japanese company Enix published *Dragon Quest* (later renamed *Dragon Warrior* for the American audiences) as the first console-based RPG that in turn further fueled **Japanese RPG (JRPG)** development. *Dragon Quest* heavily drew on inspiration from *Ultima* and *Wizardry*, while at the same time making the game unique for Japanese audiences. *Dragon Quest* set the standard for the qualities that define a JRPG including greater emphasis on storytelling, emotional involvement of the player, and a streamlined interface. *Dragon Quest* was the game that set the bar for NPC interaction because a significant portion of time was spent gathering information for assorted places and events from the townspeople.

Inspired by Enix's commercially successful *Dragon Quest*, *Final Fantasy* received the green light at Square, and with a team lead by Hironobu Sakaguchi, it was published in 1987. Also heavily inspired by *Ultima* and *Wizardry*, *Final Fantasy*, which is one of the staples of JRPGs, became one of the most commercially successful JRPGs due to its mass appeal. The major features that set *Final Fantasy* apart from the rest include turn-based combat with characters engaged from a two-dimensional side view (up until that time, most combat featured a first-person perspective), and an epic story that spanned three continents.

The next evolutionary jump in the features for RPGS continued with the inclusion of three-dimensional environments, but for the purposes of this book, we will bring our adventure through the halls of computer role-playing history to an end. By understanding the historical precedent for CRPGs, you get a real perspective for the evolution of CRPGS and why certain design choices were made. Instead of working in a vacuum, we can learn from these genre-defining games, and begin to make more informed choices with regard to features instead of bolting on random elements.

RPG features

In general, asking people to define what makes an RPG an *RPG*, will spark an endless debate without ever arriving at a satisfactory answer. For the sake of clarity, a role-playing game, at its core, can be defined as a system with rules where you primarily play a character in some setting with various goals depending on the story.

First, children's make believe, for instance, would be considered role playing, but without rules, it cannot be considered a role-playing game. Once rules are added though, we now have a system in place where people can role play, and this is considered a role-playing game, specifically **live action role-playing** (**LARP**).

The second example of a role-playing game is where players assume the roles of heroes playing out famous battles on a physical miniature battle field. This is considered tabletop role-playing, which is the natural extension of wargaming that began with Wells's *Little Wars*.

The third example of role-playing games would be the pen and paper systems that *D&D* started and set the ground work for Tolkien-inspired fantasy systems with magic and dragons.

Finally, the fourth example of role-playing games would be CRPGs that began their popularity with text-based versions such as *Adventure*, and their graphical counterparts, the *Ultima* and *Wizardry* series, with elements inspired from their pen and paper parents.

With these definitions properly framed, let's lay some ground work for the type of features that will define the core of a graphic CRPG. For the purposes of this book, I will outline the types of qualities and features that *most* people can agree make up an RPG, based on the precedent set from the most influential titles in the graphic CRPG realm. Most likely, there will be some features from your favorite games that will not be outlined in this book. This book is meant to give you a starting place to begin to build out *your* RPG title with a functional model demonstrating most standard features that have come to be expected in most RPGs.

In this book, we will be covering the following features:

- Develop characters with statistical attributes. Since *Ultima*, players have come to expect some measurable ways to gauge their in-game character's progress. As the player overcomes challenges, there should be some mechanism in place for the player to augment their character, demonstrating mastery as they hone their skills. For simplicity, we will only have to select a few attributes, such as the strength attribute for determining weapon usage as well as attack damage bonuses, and intelligence for determining magic usage as well as spell damage bonuses. This attribute system will allow you to easily expand upon later. Other attributes will include hit-points (determines how much physical damage your character can take before dying), magic points (determines how much magic damage your character can inflict before running out), and experience points (at every level, there is a set amount of points your character needs to earn through combat and quests in order to progress to the next level).

- Develop a leveling system where your character grows in power throughout the game, making earlier encounters much easier as the character levels up. This is an important distinction from more modern RPGs such as *Oblivion* (a leveling system where enemies level up and scale relative to your current level). For the purposes of this book, the leveling will be similar to a game such as *Dragon Warrior* where the character at level 10 will have no problem with a level 1 green slime.

- Develop player movement, animation, physics, and collision detection. These are critical to the player's interaction with the game world via their game character. We will delve into the various libraries within LibGDX in order to create the best player experience.

- Create interactive NPC characters with speech windows and immersion via dialog trees. This particular element will draw inspiration from *Dragon Warrior* for its interactions with townspeople, which plays a vital role in gathering information about different locations and quests.

- Create interesting enemies with battle mechanics, spawn points, and AI pathfinding. An RPG experience would not be complete without rescuing a princess from the dark overlord, killing rats, or level grinding on wild pigs.

- Interact with the world through travelling portals and transition between different areas in the map. As the player moves throughout our game world, they should seamlessly be able to travel from shop in the town, to the overworld map, and to a dark and dangerous cave.

- Build inventory management systems for item pickup and equip. Resource management is an important component in any RPG, from collecting animal skins for the local shopkeeper, storing magic potions to replenish magic points, to collecting treasure after vanquishing an evil troll.

- Develop save and load game profiles. Persistent profiles play an important role in allowing the player to experience the game at their convenience over the course of hundreds of potential quests.

- Create scripted cutscenes to add an element of story and drama. This feature takes its inspiration from the *Final Fantasy* playbook in order to give the player an epic story that introduces them to the world of your imagination.

- Develop a quest system to expand out the content of the game. This system will create goals for the player to accomplish for experience and gold, as they go out and explore the world.

- Build inventory and **heads up display** (HUD) layouts with customizable skins and also build logic for updates to health and magic. Constructing this streamlined interface will give the player all the tools they need during gameplay in order to make the best decisions in and out of combat.

- Create a shop store **user interface** (UI) with items and money transactions. The shop will demonstrate how to view, select, purchase, and sell items as part of the resource management part of the game using the in-game currency of gold coins.

- Create special effects to give the game extra "juiciness" and polish, and help build atmosphere. These added effects will cover more advanced topics, but will add a nice polish to your final game.

Based upon the style of the RPG that this book is focused on, the following features will *not* be covered:

- There will be no character creation screens beyond a character name and starting statistical attributes.

- There will be no class selection screens.

- The monster-leveling system in the game will be static in the sense that the monsters will not dynamically level and scale based upon the player's current level, but remain at their predetermined level from the outset.

- There will be no party-based system for dealing with multiple characters or fighting multiple enemies.

- There will be no multilinear game story with multiple endings. The game story will progress (with cutscenes) linearly as the player completes quests.

- There will be no skill trees as we are not dealing with skills at all.

- The combat will be turn-based, so there will be no real-time combat elements.

- The worlds will be built with tile editors and set quests from the beginning, so there will be no procedural-based content generation for this RPG.

- There will be no persistent online world with other players. This RPG will be a single player experience without networking support.

Technologies used when developing a role-playing game

Understanding the different technologies available when creating a game can be frustrating, especially when you feel that committing to one set of tools is locking you into a solution. Sometimes, taking out the various engines or frameworks for a test drive leaves your hard drive littered with unfinished platformer game projects. Other times, when you search for help online, the only responses you get among the forums are the standard smug *look at the source code* answers. These experiences can be exhausting, especially without a plan. First, in order to properly evaluate any solution, we need to properly frame the project goals with certain, pointed questions.

Commercial game versus technology demo

One of the first questions you should ask yourself when evaluating a software solution for your game is one that gets overlooked: Are you interested in the final product (that is, a complete video game for a commercial release), or are you interested more in the implementation details of the game than the final end product?

If you are the latter, then you might consider developing a game engine in your favorite language to learn the core systems yourself, such as graphics, physics, **artificial intelligence (AI)**, and file **input and output (I/O)**. This book will not delve into the details of these different components. There are plenty of great books out there that will guide you through this process, such as *Programming Game AI By Example by Mat Buckland* and *Game Engine Architecture by Jason Gregory*.

If you are the former, then the rest of this section should help you make a better decision given the myriad software solutions available. On the one hand, the sheer amount of solutions for any aspiring indie developer or team opens many doors that were not available years before. On the other hand, it is very easy to get overwhelmed with all the options available.

Target platforms

The second question you should ask yourself is, based on the project scope and requirements, what are your target platforms? This question will drive not only the project schedule, but also have a huge impact on the programming language choice and in turn will determine the software solution for your game.

Years ago, this question used to be easy because there were only a limited amount of available systems with a high barrier of entry for all of them. Today, when creating a commercial game, there should at least be some consideration for all the available channels for distribution. This includes personal computers and laptops running Mac OSX or Windows, mobile devices that have most of the market share running iOS, Android, or Windows Phone, and even home console development including PS4 or Xbox One. Even with game frameworks and engines with cross-platform compilation, you will still need to factor testing for the various platforms into the schedule.

If you plan on adding a series of closed and open beta sessions to the project roadmap (a good idea to gauge the *fun* factor from user feedback as well as a first round of user bugs), there will be differences in how this process works across the various platforms and it needs to be accounted for in your plan. Once the details for target platforms have been ironed out, the choice of programming language should be much clearer. Hopefully, the language is one that you prefer, but if not, there needs to be additional time in the project schedule for training with the programming language.

Game framework versus game engine

The third question you should ask yourself after you have decided that you really want to develop a shippable commercial game, and decided on the target platforms, is whether you would prefer a game engine or a game framework for your solution? The primary motivation deals specifically with control and how this affects your workflow.

A game engine is typically a closed black-box solution (even though sometimes there are options for access to the source code) where you develop your game logic (in a language dictated by the engine) around the scaffolding of the engine, and in turn, the engine calls into your code during the game lifetime as the engine processes the main game loop.

A game framework, on the other hand, is a collection of libraries with exposed **application program interfaces (APIs)** into modules representing higher level abstractions of the core system components, such as graphics and file I/O. Developing with a game framework, in contrast to a game engine, gives control to you, as the owner of the main game loop, to call into the libraries as needed throughout your game lifetime. So, the question boils down to what kind of control you want for developing your game. The answer is not a straightforward one, but one that comes with tradeoffs for either solution.

The following table (*Table 1*) is just a small sampling of the solutions available today for game projects:

Name	Engine/framework	Primary target platforms	Primary programming language
Cocos2d	Framework	Windows, OS X, and Linux	Objective-C
LibGDX	Framework	Windows, OS X, Linux, iOS, Android, and HTML5	Java
Source	Engine	Windows, OS X, Linux, iOS, Android, Xbox 360, and PlayStation 3	C++
Torque2D	Engine	Windows, OS X, Linux, iOS, Android, and HTML5	TorqueScript (proprietary scripting language with a C-like syntax)
Unity	Engine	Windows, OS X, Linux, iOS, Android, Windows Phone, HTML5, Xbox, and PlayStation	C#
Unreal Engine	Engine	Windows, OS X, Linux, iOS, Android, Windows Phone, HTML5, Xbox, and PlayStation	C++

Table 1

Budget

The fourth question you should ask yourself is: What is the actual budget for the development of my title? *Table 1* is just a sampling of the options available for today's game development teams, and most of the options are very reasonably priced even for the indie developer bootstrapping their first commercial release (that is, free). There are much more exhaustive lists out there, but this should give you a feeling for the various programming languages, target platforms, and library support available.

With all the wonderful ideas and features for any commercial product, the *Triple Constraint* will rear its ugly head and quickly ground the project, demanding that you stay bound by time, cost, and quality. Any change to one attribute will affect the other two, constantly maintaining a balance for the project.

For example, if you sourced and received estimates for artwork at $5000, but you only budgeted say $100, this will significantly affect the quality (maybe you can just mash together some programmer stick figures) of the art, as well as time (even with stick figures, you will still need to draw them out, taking time away from development). Commercial titles, even with 2D pixel art, still need to be original and polished to really stand out. Stick figures might work as a gimmick to draw attention, but most audiences have more sophisticated expectations today, even with indie titles.

So, in summary, you really only have three courses when planning the budget:

- Develop a game relatively quickly with great art and music, but at an expensive cost
- Develop a game quickly with stick figures for art and recorded tracks of you singing, but live with the humiliation from friends and family
- Design a fun game with unique and stylistic graphics and a haunting soundtrack with a team working for free, but know that this course of action will take a substantial amount of time

Answering these questions and evaluating the choices available should lead to a more straightforward and educated decision without getting lost in a sea of noise. Originally, I wanted to develop my own game engine from the ground up.

After asking myself the first question, I realized that for me, shipping a commercial game was more important than building a game engine from scratch. There are many mature game frameworks and engines available, and the curiosity of building something from scratch was simply outweighed by more battle-tested solutions supporting multiple target platforms, once I committed to a commercial project.

This leads into the next question about target platforms because I realized, once I started evaluating the different solutions, that the cross-platform ones would significantly reduce my time on the deployment end. The cross-platform solutions are nice because they abstract away platform specifics (and most of them optimize under the covers based on build target), freeing me up to develop my game for one platform without worrying about the scope of work involved in porting to the mobile platforms later.

The third question regarding the preference of a game engine or framework was a little clearer because I wanted control of the game loop. I didn't really want to deal with the training time or cost associated with the various engines, and I didn't want to deal with all the complexities that come with their specific ecosystems (or idiosyncrasies).

Finally, the fourth question regarding budget was straightforward because as an indie developer bootstrapping my way through this process, cost was a significant factor, as I had a specific budget for art, and not much more especially for game engine licensing or tool costs.

These decisions helped frame my choice to go with the LibGDX game framework for my commercial game project. LibGDX is developed with a heavy emphasis on performance, includes cross-platform support out of the box (Windows, OS X, Linux, iOS, Android, and HTML5), provides low-level bookkeeping APIs that free me up so that I focus on developing the gameplay, provides an engaged and responsive community (not one where the forums have tumbleweeds blowing through), has active maintenance (nightly builds instead of one zip from ten years ago), and is available for free without a prohibitive license.

With all the decisions that need to be made when first starting a commercial RPG game, this book aims to help you through the process by minimizing the constraints. First, the time constraint can be reduced with this book by guiding you through the process of creating an RPG from scratch using LibGDX.

By the end of this book, you will have a working base template that you can expand on and add content to in order to make the game uniquely yours with support for multiple target platforms. Also, time will be reduced during the development cycle by developing modular pieces, such as scripting support, which can easily offload the creation of dialogs, items, monsters, levels, and quests so that content can be created in parallel with development without affecting the build process.

Second, recommendations on great free offerings, such as LibGDX, will be made throughout this book keeping the overall project costs low. These recommendations can be used in the toolchain of your development environment to enable you to stay productive and give the biggest *bang for your buck* on the deployment end.

Third, quality can be maximized due to minimizing the time constraint and thereby allowing more time for collecting feedback on usability, beta testing, and overall quality assurance.

Hopefully, the case has been made for adding LibGDX to your commercial endeavor for your RPG game. We will now review some core features of LibGDX as we continue our adventure developing the RPG game.

Understanding the basics of a game architecture

In order to better understand the fundamentals of a typical game architecture at a high level, we can begin with a historical perspective with the first text-based adventure game *Adventure*.

The high-level game loop of Adventure

The following figure (*Figure 1*) describes the high-level game loop of *Adventure* type text-based games where the game would block all updates for its lifetime until it receives user-based text input on the command line:

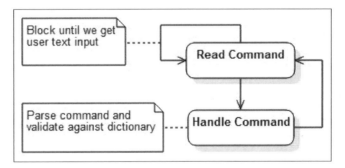

Figure 1

Once the text was read from the command line (carriage returns were typically an indication that the player was finished inputting text), the game would then parse the entire string, breaking up the sentence into its component parts. The most basic system would have a dictionary of actions, or verbs, that the player can do. Each of the words in the sentence would be compared against that player's action list. The same would be for objects, or nouns.

For example, if the player wanted to take the fresh water from a flask and pour it over the dirty floor, they would type in the following command:

```
> pour water
```

The game would process the user input string, break it up into word chunks, and compare against its verb and noun dictionaries (key-value mappings). We would end up with two lists. The action list would contain one valid action, *POUR*. The object list would contain one valid object, *WATER*.

POUR would be the primary action in this sentence with a rule similar to the following:

```
POUR [OBJECT 1] IS SUCCESSFUL
IF PLAYER HAS [OBJECT 1] IN INVENTORY
AND [OBJECT 1] IS POURABLE
```

There would also be some extra data regarding certain properties of objects in the game, such as whether an object is able to be carried in an inventory and whether it is pourable, wearable, or throwable. These could be in the form of a subset list of objects for each of the actions. For example, *POUR* would verify that *WATER* is in the list *POURABLE*, while something such as *FOOD* would not. These edge case checks with object attributes would prevent awkward word combinations as follows:

```
> pour food
```

Checking the words against action and object lists would also have the side-effect of throwing out extraneous words that make English sentences complete. For instance, in some text-based adventure games, the following two commands would work the same way:

```
> go into the building
```
```
> go building
```

This model is the basic concept behind a two-way communication subsystem that deals with NPC interaction, such as asking NPCs questions or viewing shop items. This will be discussed more in-depth when developing a dialog tree system.

The difficulty with a text-driven system is that because the syntax of the parser is so specific, and because of the complexities with equally valid variations of an English sentence, the player can lead down a rabbit hole of frustration, infamously referred to as *guess-the-verb* or *guess-the-noun*, where most of the player's time is spent trying to figure out why certain combinations of words do not work. One example of this problem is best demonstrated with a recent session I had with an online version of *Adventure*:

```
You are standing at the end of a road before a small brick
building. Around you is a forest. A small stream flows out
of the building and down a gully.

> look stream

I don't understand.
stream what?

> look at stream

I don't understand that!

> go into building

I don't understand that!

> go

Where?

> building

You are inside a building, a well house for a large spring.
There are some keys on the ground here.
There is a shiny brass lamp nearby.
There is tasty food here.
There is a bottle of water here.
```

Interestingly enough, when distilled down to its essence, this model is also how event-driven systems such as user interfaces work today.

The high-level event-based loop

The primary target platform for this book is Microsoft Windows, even though compiling for the other target platforms isn't much more effort. There are special considerations to keep in mind when running your game on mobile devices, such as graphic rendering performance, smaller screen real estate to work with for UIs, touch screen controls instead of using a keyboard and mouse, limited access and size constraints to external save game profiles, and smaller overall package size. Mobile device optimizations are topics that deserve their own chapters, but will be beyond the scope of this book.

The following figure (*Figure 2*) refers to an event loop, for instance, in how Windows processes its graphical user interface events. This figure can even be generalized across most platforms, including how Java processes its own event loop within the **Java Virtual Machine (JVM)**:

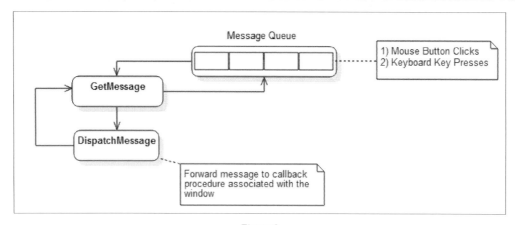

Figure 2

At a high level, a **graphical user interface (GUI)** application processes events from the event loop and only terminates when the application receives a quit message. The **operating system (OS)** will generate an event message based on such events as a mouse button click or keyboard key press and place the message in the message queue. The message queue is processed by the GUI application by processing the first element in the queue, on a first-in-first-out basis, with the newest event message at the end of the queue. The GUI application will then in turn check the message queue for a relevant message, process it if the event message is relevant to the window, and then dispatch the message. The message dispatch will forward the message to the registered callback procedure or message handler associated with that specific event. So, just like the loop for text-based adventure games we saw earlier, the event loop is really just a loop that runs indefinitely, responding to input type events.

The high-level game loop for a graphic-based video game

The following figure (*Figure 3*) demonstrates at a high level how a graphics-based video game loop actually functions at its core:

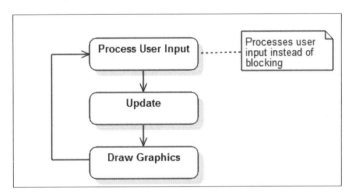

Figure 3

Figure 3 demonstrates at a high level how a graphics-based video game loop actually functions at its core. As previously discussed, a text-based game loop and a GUI event loop share a common methodology of blocking, an interrupt-based approach used for waiting on user input. This model would not work for graphics-based games today because there is always something that needs to be updated every cycle in the loop even if the player is idle, such as AI (NPC movements), physics, or particle effects. Instead of waiting for user input, a game loop polls for events, processing all user input available at that time. Once processed, the loop will then step into the game objects that need to be updated based on the current state of the game world, such as enemies moving and resolving collisions. Once these updates are complete, the loop will then draw the graphics based on the update calculations done previously, rendering them to the screen (or back buffer) when ready to display. This loop then starts again for the next cycle in the game loop.

One cycle of the game loop, represented by *Figure 3*, is generally referred to as a **frame**. The logical question is how fast can we cycle through each frame in the game loop?

The term used to gauge how many cycles we can complete in a fixed amount of time, measured in **frames per second (FPS)**, is called the **frame rate**. The more frames we are able to process per second, the better the perceived experience will be for the player. The game will feel more responsive, there will be better collision detection and enemy movement, and the graphics rendering will be much smoother. This is because we are polling user input, updating, and rendering much more frequently. The lower the frames per second, the more degraded the game experience will be for the player. The player movement will be jerky and not as responsive, there may be collisions that never get detected with objects appearing to go through each other, enemies may appear to teleport across the screen, and the graphics will appear to be very choppy. This is usually caused by polling much less frequently than what is needed. In modern games today, for example, a frame rate of 30 FPS is standard for a good gameplay experience.

There are two primary factors that affect the frame rate of a game:

- The first factor is how fast the underlying target system can process each frame. This factor is influenced by the system's hardware such as the clock speed of the CPU, and whether there is a dedicated **graphics processing unit (GPU)** available to offload rendering. Another factor is the software of the target system, specifically how effective the OS is at parallelizing across multiple cores and how efficient the scheduler is.

- The second factor is determined by how much logic there is to process every frame. Calculations for physics (used in collision detection or velocity updates) and rendering high-fidelity graphics for lots of game objects can affect the amount of work that needs to be accomplished every frame, leading to a frame taking longer to render. Therefore, fewer frames are completed every second.

Given the myriad platforms that the game can run on, these two factors will cause very different experiences based on the platform it's running on. On a mobile phone, the game may not have access to a dedicated GPU, and so the CPU becomes the bottleneck for calculating all the user input, physics, AI, and rendering causing the game to run at a low frame rate. On the flip side, if you have been developing your game on a mid-range system for the last two years, when you release your game, your game may run at a much higher frame rate on newer hardware than what you are accustomed to in your testing. This not only can cause bugs you didn't expect, but also high battery consumption on mobile devices and laptops or hot CPUs and GPUs.

The typical, brute force solution for dealing with these factors that affect the frame rate is to lock the frame rate so that the experience on the various platforms is a consistent one. This is not an optimal solution though, because if the refresh rate of the monitor is not synced with the locked frame rate, then you can get visual artifacts such as screen tearing. Screen tearing usually occurs because multiple frames get updated to the screen during draw calls before the monitor finishes its current refresh cycle.

LibGDX addresses the problem of varying frame rates depending on the device, by passing in a `deltaTime` value during each render call for a frame. This value represents the total time in seconds that the game took to render the last frame. By updating calculations using the `deltaTime` value, the gameplay elements should be synchronized running more consistently across the different devices, using this time-based approach instead of just locking the game to a specific frame rate.

Understanding the high-level component layout of LibGDX

We are now going to review the architecture behind LibGDX. As a quick note, the latest stable release of LibGDX that we are going to use throughout this book is version 1.5.5, which was built on 19 March, 2015.

LibGDX backend modules

The following figure (*Figure 4*) is a diagram illustrating the core interfaces of LibGDX. These are the highest level abstractions available that provide most of the functionality you will need when creating your game (including their associated module libraries):

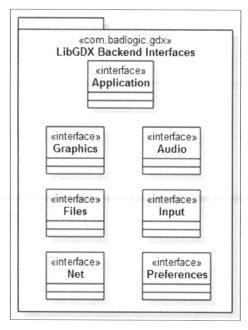

Figure 4

These interfaces are implemented for each of the currently supported target platforms, allowing you to develop your game once, using these APIs and not having to worry about platform-specific issues. An overview of the functionality that each interface contains (once implemented for each supporting platform) is as follows:

- `Application.java`: This interface becomes the entry point that the platform OS uses to load your game. Each implementation will be responsible for setting up a window, handling resize events, rendering to the surfaces, and managing the application during its lifetime. Specifically, `Application.java` will provide the modules for dealing with graphics, audio, input and file I/O handling, as well as logging facilities, memory footprint information, and hooks for extension libraries.

- `Graphics.java`: This interface contains numerous helper methods for communicating with the platform's graphics processor, such as rendering to the screen and querying for available display modes such as graphics resolution and color depth. There are also convenience methods for generating pixmaps and textures. One interesting note is that for cross-platform support, the underlying graphics API (OpenGL ES 2.0 or OpenGL ES 3.0) is emulated for the desktop by mapping OpenGL ES functions to the desktop OpenGL functions.

- `Audio.java`: This interface contains numerous helper methods for creating and managing various audio resources. This interface helps to create sound effects, play music streams, and give direct access to the audio hardware for PCM audio input and output.

- `Files.java`: This interface contains numerous helper methods for accessing the platform's filesystem when managing game assets such as reading and writing files. This abstraction over the different types of file locations includes internal files (located in your game working directory) and external files (external storage such as an SD card).

- `Input.java`: This interface contains numerous helper methods to poll (or process events) for user input from not only standard input such as keyboard key presses and mouse button clicks, but also mobile device input such as touch screens and accelerometer updates. Other helper methods include handling vibrations, compass access, on-screen keyboard input, and cursor capture.

- `Net.java`: This interface contains numerous helper methods for performing certain network-related operations, such as managing HTTP/HTTPS GET and POST requests and creating TCP server/client socket connections.

- `Preferences.java`: This interface contains numerous helper methods for storing and accessing application game setting values as a lightweight setting storage mechanism.

LibGDX core modules

The rest of the functionality that you will use for your game belongs to a host of core modules within the LibGDX framework:

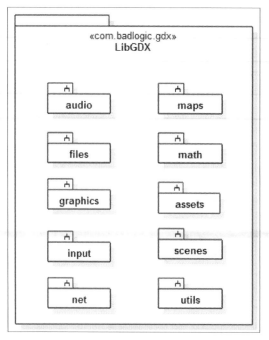

Figure 5

The modules in the left column (audio, files, graphics, input, and net) in *Figure 5* were already discussed previously in *Figure 4*. The other modules are as follows:

- **Maps**: This module contains classes for dealing with different level map implementations, such as maps generated from Tiled (an XML-based format called TMX) and Tide. The convenience methods include handling the loading of the map and referenced assets, rendering the map, accessing properties, and selecting different layers.

- **Math**: This module contains classes with convenient utility methods for dealing with various mathematical calculations such as trigonometry, linear algebra, and probability. These methods are also optimized to be fast. Other classes include geometric classes for dealing with shapes, areas, and volumes, collision detection tests such as intersection and overlap, and interpolation algorithms.

- **Assets**: This module contains classes for managing the loading and storing of assets such as textures, bitmap fonts, particle effects, pixmaps, UI skins, tile maps, sounds, and music. These classes will also deal with different caching strategies to optimize the storage and use of your game assets.

- **Scenes**: This module contains classes for building 2D scene graphs used in creating UIs such as game menus and HUD overlays. This module also provides classes for managing the laying out, drawing, and handling input for the different UIs.

- **Utils**: This module is more of a catchall for various miscellaneous pieces of utility methods that don't quite fit anywhere else. This module supports reading and writing in XML and JSON (with serialization support), custom collections with primitive type support (which helps to avoid performance hits when autoboxing types), timers, and object pools.

There are other libraries that come with LibGDX, but typically maintained by third parties. These will fall under the `extensions` folder. The LibGDX `extensions` folder includes the following:

- `gdx-box2d`: This is a physics engine for 2D rigid bodies

- `gdx-bullet`: This is a real-time physics simulation library

- `gdx-controllers`: This is for gamepad and joystick controller support

- `gdx-freetype`: This generates bitmap fonts on the fly from one **TrueType font (TTF)** file

- `gdx-jnigen`: This allows C/C++ code to be written inline with Java source code

- `gdx-setup`: This is the UI project setup application used to manage LibGDX installs with the Gradle build system

- `gdx-tools`: This is a miscellaneous collection of tools to aid in the development of your game, such as a particle effect editor, a texture packer application, and a bitmap font creator utility

Understanding the application lifecycle of LibGDX

With a better understanding of the core modules included with LibGDX, we can now look at the application lifecycle of a typical game written with LibGDX for the desktop illustrated by the following figure (*Figure 6*):

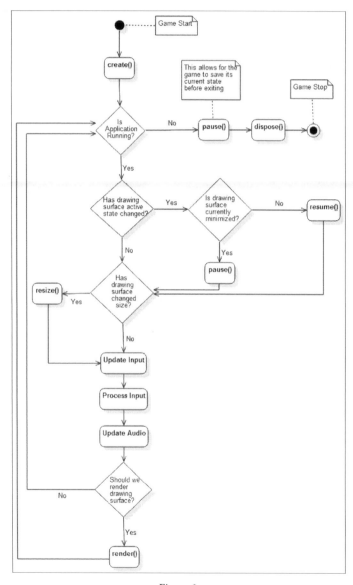

Figure 6

This diagram represents the cycle of your game loop, where one loop through the logic represents a frame. The following steps outline the various paths through the game loop in this figure:

1. The `LwjglApplication` class will bootstrap itself with your starter class instance and the configuration that was passed into its constructor. The `LwjglApplication` constructor will instantiate the various subsystem modules used in LibGDX, populating the `Gdx` (`com.badlogic.gdx`) environment class with static instances of the `Application`, `Graphics`, `Audio`, `Input`, `Files`, and `Net` modules described previously in *Figure 4*. The `LwjglApplication` constructor will then spawn a thread, which we will call the *main loop*, that will run until the game exits. This main loop thread represents the lifecycle of your game and the instantiation is referred to by the **Game Start** note for the **initial node** in the activity diagram. Now, we can move onto step 2.

2. The next node in the diagram after the initial start is an action node designated as `create()`. The `create()` method is an interface method that you must implement when creating your game in order to hook into the lifecycle of LibGDX. During the start of the game loop thread, `create()` will be called only once. This is going to be where the initialization code for your game should be located, including preloading assets, instantiating game screens, and initializing the game subsystems. Now, we can move onto step 3.

3. This step represents our first decision node in the loop that is checked at the beginning of every cycle through the game loop, or once per frame. The test is whether the game is still running or not and allows us to exit if the game state has changed to not running. As a side note, in order to guarantee that you properly exit your game, which allows the execution of cleanup code to happen in the correct order, it is recommended that you follow the LibGDX convention of exiting your game by using the following statement when quitting:

    ```
    Gdx.app.exit();
    ```

    This call into the static instance of the application object will set the running state of the game loop to false and subsequently move to the next step allowing the graceful exit of your game. So, if the game is running, then we can move to step 7. If the game is not running, then we can move to step 4.

4. The action node designated by `pause()` in the activity diagram is one of the interface methods that must be implemented when you create your game. This method guarantees that proper handling of the game will be done, such as saving the current state of the game. After this finishes, we transition to the next step.

5. The action node designated by `dispose()` in the activity diagram is an interface method that guarantees proper cleanup of game resources still in use when the game is in the process of being destroyed and is the proper location to free those resources. For clarification, since this is a Java environment, all objects that implement the `Disposable` interface (`com.badlogic.gdx.utils`) should call their appropriate `dispose()` method here. For example, a `dispose()` method call for an unmanaged `Texture` object, under the covers, will delete the texture from the static OpenGL instance and invalidate its handle. Now, we move onto step 6.

6. After `dispose()` has finished its work, the draw surface is destroyed along with any audio hardware handles still in use and then runs `System.exit()`. This step is referred to in the previous figure by the **Game Stop** note for the **final node** in the activity diagram.

7. The next step in the diagram brings us to a decision node where the game loop figures out whether we are transitioning from a previous change in a draw surface state. When the game loop starts, the previous state of the draw surface is set to active as an initial placeholder and then the current draw surface is checked to see whether we are active. The active state for the draw surface, for the desktop, indicates whether the draw surface is in focus (not behind another window) or maximized. If it is determined that we have transitioned to a new state for the draw surface, then we move to the next decision node on step 8. If there is no transition to a new state, then we can continue onto step 11.

8. After it was determined that some change in the state has occurred since the last frame (the last cycle of the loop), the next step in the diagram of the game loop will determine whether we have transitioned from a previous state of focused to the current state of not focused, or vice versa. If the draw surface was focused in the last frame but now it is not, then we are minimized, so we will transition to the action node designated by `pause()` in step 9. If the draw surface was *not* focused in the last frame, but now *is* focused, then we are maximized, so we will transition to the action node designated by `resume()` in step 10.

9. During a cycle in the game loop, if the drawing surface state has changed from being maximized or in focus to being minimized or not focused, then `pause()` will be called by the game loop. After this completes, we move onto step 11.

10. During a cycle in the game loop, if the drawing surface state has changed from being minimized or not in focus to being maximized or in focus, then `resume()` will be called by the game loop. The action node designated by `resume()` in the activity diagram is another interface method that must be implemented by your game. This method will guarantee proper handling from a previously paused state, such as reloading saved state information from disk. On Android-based devices, this would also be where you would reload unmanaged textures, but this is not a concern for the desktop. After this completes, we move onto step 11.

11. The next node in the diagram represents a decision regarding whether or not the dimensions of the current draw surface have changed since the last frame update. If the dimensions have changed, then we move onto step 12. If the dimensions have not changed, then we move onto step 13.

12. The size of the draw surface has changed since the last frame update, and thus this will trigger a resize event. The action node designated by `resize()` in the activity diagram is an interface method that must be implemented by your game. This method's parameter list represents the new dimensions, width and height in pixels, of the game screen. These dimensions are typically passed through to the screen or draw surface to be updated on the next render call. Once this step completes, we move onto step 13.

13. This action node deals with getting state information from the input devices. This includes updating the `deltaTime` interval for the current frame, updating the mouse cursor location and mouse button press events, and updating the keyboard key press events. After this step completes, we move onto step 14.

14. This action node deals with processing the state information from the input devices. This primarily includes passing the mouse cursor location, mouse button presses, and keyboard key presses up to the input event handler class, `InputProcessor`. Your game will usually instantiate this class and set it in the environment class, `Gdx`, so that you can access the input events every frame. When this step completes, we can move onto step 15.

15. This action node deals with updating the audio resources for the current frame. For the desktop, this is primarily used to update the music since music will be playing across frames. When this step completes, we move onto step 16.

16. This decision node deals specifically with a test for whether we should render the draw surface or not. If we need to render (such as a game object's position has changed this frame, or the mouse cursor has moved), then we move onto step 17. Otherwise, if we do not need to render, then we have completed one cycle of this game loop and we will start back at step 3 for the next frame.

17. The action node designated by `render()` in the activity diagram is an interface method that must be implemented by your game. This method will be the most important one in the lifecycle of your game. Commands to render your game scenes to the screen will live here, along with processing UI components, physics calculation updates, AI routines, and game object updates. Once this step completes and we have finished updating the current frame, we will go back to step 3 to start a new one.

In summary, in the preceding figure, the actions designated as `create()`, `resize()`, `render()`, `pause()`, `resume()`, and `dispose()` are all methods in the `ApplicationListener` interface, as shown in the following figure (*Figure 7*):

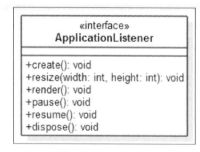

Figure 7

This figure is a class diagram that describes the method names and their corresponding signatures of the `ApplicationListener` interface that your game must implement. These methods represent hooks that the main game loop, in LibGDX, will call into based on certain system events triggered during the lifetime of your game.

A quick recap of the responsibilities that these interface methods represent is as follows:

• `create()`: This is called at the start only once during the lifetime of the game. Typically, this is the proper place for initialization code (in preparation for the start of your game) to live.

• `resize(int width, int height )`: This is called every time the size of the game screen is changed. The parameters both represent the new width and height (in pixels) of the game screen.

- `render()`: This method is called every time the game screen needs to be rendered, such as a resize event or changes in the game screen. The commands to render your game scenes to the screen should live here.

- `pause()`: On the desktop, this method is called when the game screen is minimized, a key is pressed by the user, or when the game is exiting. Typically, this is a good location for saving the game state.

- `resume()`: On the desktop, this method is called when the game screen is maximized, from a previous state of being minimized.

- `dispose()`: This method is called when the game is being destroyed. This would be the appropriate place to clean up and free all resources still in use.

Historically, LibGDX started out as a small library for Android-based devices, which explains why LibGDX is event-driven in nature, since it is modeled after Android's lifecycle. There is no explicit main loop for our game, but for the purposes of defining the main loop, the `render()` method that you implement from the `ApplicationListener` interface will, for all intents and purposes, be the main body of your game.

Now that we have an overview of the packages and lifecycle of LibGDX, we can now generate a starter project that we will develop throughout the remainder of this book.

Setting up your development environment

There are plenty of references available via online blog posts or other books that can walk you through every nuance in the development environment setup and so we will not go into in-depth detail here.

Prerequisite tool installation

We will start by discussing the core dependencies that you will need in order to use LibGDX effectively. For clarity, we will only be concerned about the desktop platform, specifically targeted for Windows. The steps are as follows:

1. First, you will need to install the latest **Java Development Kit (JDK)**, which includes tools for developing, debugging, and monitoring Java applications. At the time of this writing, I am using the minimum supported version of Java that works with LibGDX (version 1.5.5), which is JDK version 1.7. You can get the latest installer from Oracle's website at http://www.oracle.com/ technetwork/java/javase/downloads/index.html.

After installing the JDK, you can make sure that the environment variable, JAVA_HOME, is set by opening a Command Prompt window and typing the following in the command line:

```
java -version
```

If everything is set correctly, you should see something like the following output:

```
java version "1.7.0_45"
Java(TM) SE Runtime Environment (build 1.7.0_45-b18)
Java HotSpot(TM) Client VM (build 24.45-b08, mixed mode, sharing)
```

2. Second, we will need to install and set up an **integrated development environment (IDE)** in order to develop with LibGDX. Out of the box, LibGDX generates the startup projects for the following IDEs:

   ° **IntelliJ IDEA**: The community edition is free and can be found at `http://www.jetbrains.com/idea/download/`. I am using IDEA while writing this book and I am finding that it easily meets my requirements during the development of the BludBourne project.

   ° **Eclipse**: This is a well-known, free, and actively maintained open source IDE. Eclipse can be found at `http://www.eclipse.org/downloads/`.

   ° **NetBeans**: This is another free and actively maintained open source IDE. NetBeans can be found at `http://netbeans.org/downloads/index.html`.

3. Third, we will need to download and run the **gdx-setup** tool, which with a little configuration will generate our project files, platform-specific wrapper class, and our starter classes. You can download the `gdx-setup.jar` file by visiting `http://libgdx.badlogicgames.com/download.html` and then clicking on the **Download Setup App** option. Just as a side note, you may get a warning from your browser that the file is unsafe because this is a JAR file, but this is the correct file that is integrated with the new build system (which will be explained in the next section) for LibGDX.

Running the LibGDX setup tool

Luckily, LibGDX has a relatively straightforward method for generating the startup classes that you will need so that you can get started. For every game that you create, you will use a tool for LibGDX (gdx-setup) that generates boilerplate code for each of the platform targets that you select, which wrap the main entry point for the game. These classes represent the only platform-specific code that will be created for a LibGDX-based game and interface with the backend modules mentioned earlier in the figure illustrating the core interfaces of LibGDX (*Figure 4*). For the purposes of this book, we will be focused primarily on the desktop, so we will only be concerned with generating one project targeted for **Desktop**:

In a Command Prompt window, navigate to where you downloaded the gdx-setup.jar file and run the following command:

```
java -jar gdx-setup.jar
```

You should see following UI (*Figure 8*) when you launch the gdx-setup tool:

Figure 8

The different settings for your LibGDX project setup are labeled for your convenience as follows:

- **Name (1)**: This is typically used for the customer facing name you wish to present for your game. The standard convention is lower case with hyphens representing spaces (for example, `bludbourne-game`). This value is not really used by the build system for a desktop deployment target because the desktop target is a self-executable JAR file (or a runnable JAR file) and not a package. This value is used primarily for the mobile platforms, such as Android (substitutes for the `app_name` variable in the `AndroidManifest.xml` file) and iOS (substitutes for the `app.name` variable in the `Info.plist.xml` file).

- **Package (2)**: This will define the Java-based package name for your game. The naming convention is described in detail at `http://docs.oracle.com/javase/tutorial/java/package/namingpkgs.html`.

  Generally, the package names start with a reversed Internet domain name and are written as all lower case to avoid conflict with class names (for example, `com.packtpub.libgdx.bludbourne`).

- **Game class (3)**: This is the name of your main class that will implement the `ApplicationListener` interface that will hook into the LibGDX game lifecycle. This class name should also follow Java conventions, including being a noun and mixed case with the first letter of each internal word capitalized (for example, `BludBourneGame`).

- **Destination (4)**: This will be the root directory (relative or absolute path) that the gdx-setup tool will output the generated project into (for example, `C:\BludBourne_Project`).

- **Android SDK (5)**: This will be the directory path where the Android SDK lives on your local system (for example, `C:\Program Files (x86)\Android\android-sdk`). If the environment variable `ANDROID_HOME` is set, then its value will be used to populate this field. We should not be concerned with this property at this time. We will not be targeting Android with our project, so when you uncheck the **Android** dependency in the **Sub Projects** option, this box will become greyed out. You can always add this dependency back later though.

- **LibGDX Version (6)**: At the time of writing this book, this is a hardcoded value that represents the version of LibGDX that the gdx-setup tool was built against. So, in general, if you run this gdx-setup tool with the latest `gdx-setup.jar` file, then you will get the latest release snapshot version of LibGDX. I believe this is a placeholder until a more dynamic method is implemented, which will then populate this drop-down list with more versions.

- **Sub Projects (7)**: These represent the current deployment targets that LibGDX actively supports with its backend modules. Currently, LibGDX supports Desktop (Windows, Mac OS X, and Linux), Android, iOS, and HTML 5. For the purposes of this book, we only need to have the **Desktop** option checked.

- **Extensions (8)**: These represent third-party support libraries that fall under the LibGDX umbrella, but in general, are not part of the core libraries. These libraries usually are not part of the core because they are either maintained by third parties or have different release schedules. Currently, these extensions are as follows:

    ° **Bullet**: This is a real-time physics simulation library

    ° **Freetype**: This generates bitmap fonts on the fly from one TrueType font file

    ° **Tools**: This is a miscellaneous collection of tools to aid in the development of your game, such as a particle effect editor, a texture packer application, and a bitmap font creator utility

    ° **Controllers**: This is the gamepad and joystick controller support

    ° **Box2D**: This is the physics engine for 2D rigid bodies

    ° **Box2DLights**: This is a dynamic lighting library for 2D games

    ° **Ashley**: This is a game entity-based framework

  For the purposes of this book, we only need to have the **Tools** option checked as we can always add other support packages later.

- **Show Third Party Extensions (9)**: When selected, a table dialog will pop up with a few more third-party libraries that are not part of the LibGDX core. These selections are parsed from an `extensions.xml` file (found under `com/badlogic/gdx/setup/data`). Currently, these extensions are as follows:

    ° **Overlap2D**: This is a game-level creation tool and UI editor

    ° **VisUI**: This is a UI toolkit library that includes flat skins and widgets such as color pickers and file choosers

- **Advanced (10)**: The following figure (*Figure 9*) represents a dialog box that includes a few miscellaneous options for project setup, such as creating IntelliJ IDEA projects, Eclipse projects, or overriding the default dependency repository. For the purposes of this book, we only need to select the **IDEA** (or **Eclipse**) project generation option here and click on **Save** when done:

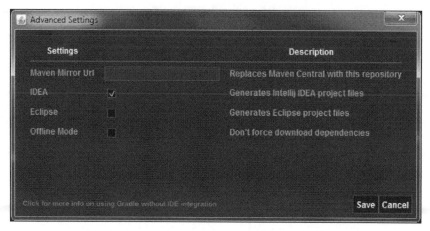

Figure 9

- **Generate (11)**: When all the configuration options are correctly populated, execute the auto-creation process by pressing this button. Your output should look something like the following:

```
Generating app in C:\BludBourne

Executing 'C:\BludBourne/gradlew.bat clean --no-daemon idea'

To honour the JVM settings for this build a new JVM will be
forked. Please consider using the daemon: http://gradle.org/
docs/2.2/userguide/gradle_daemon.html.

Configuration on demand is an incubating feature.

:core:clean UP-TO-DATE

:desktop:clean UP-TO-DATE

:ideaModule

:ideaProject

:ideaWorkspace

:idea

:core:ideaModule

:core:idea

:desktop:ideaModule

:desktop:idea
```

```
BUILD SUCCESSFUL


Total time: 45.313 secs

Done!

To import in Eclipse: File -> Import -> General -> Exisiting
Projects into Workspace

To import to Intellij IDEA: File -> Open -> YourProject.ipr
```

Downloading the example code

You can download the example code files for all Packt books you have purchased from your account at http://www.packtpub.com. If you purchased this book elsewhere, you can visit http://www.packtpub.com/support and register to have the files e-mailed directly to you. For the most current version, you can grab the latest snapshot from https://github.com/patrickhoey/BludBourne.

Understanding the build environment and project structure

Once the gdx-setup tool is finished generating the project files for us, we can look at the general structure to get a better idea of the project layout. In order to understand why certain files are in the project and how third-party dependencies are handled, we will need an overview of **Gradle**, the dependency management and build system that LibGDX currently uses.

Why Gradle?

In the beginning, the only build tool available for Java projects was Make. Projects quickly became unmanageable as the requirements and dependencies exploded along with the popularity of the language. Around the year 2000, Ant came to the rescue with its control of the build process and its low learning curve with much more readable build scripts. As great as Ant's procedural programming methodology was for creating scripts, it proved difficult to maintain in part because the XML-based script files tended to grow in complexity and verbosity. In 2004, Maven came along to address the issues with Ant and improve upon it with its simplicity. Dependency management was Maven's goal with a design that regards all projects as having a specific structure, a set of supported task workflows, and the ability to download dependencies over the network.

Maven didn't come without its own host of problems, including the inability to correctly manage conflicts between different versions of the same library, and the difficulty for someone to create customized build scripts because the scripts didn't exactly fit Maven's rigid structure.

In 2012, Gradle came along and built upon the concepts of both Ant and Maven to get a build tool that represents the best of both systems. First, Gradle uses a **domain specific language** (DSL) based on Groovy instead of the XML-based build scripts. This removes a lot of the verbosity that we had with XML build scripts, leading to shorter and clearer scripts. Also, under the covers, Gradle creates a directed acyclic graph to determine the order in which tasks can run, removing the rigidity of Maven's lifecycle and the complexity of Ant's dependency with partial ordering.

Benefits of Gradle

What is one benefit of using Gradle with LibGDX? Well, before Gradle support was added, all the LibGDX source, release, and native JAR files would live as part of the project hierarchy. This was a problem because LibGDX essentially polluted the source control system, testing the patience of whoever had to update to a later version of LibGDX in order to get one bug fix. Gradle fixes these problems because now LibGDX and all its dependencies live outside your project. If you want to test your game build against a different version of LibGDX (or any of the other dependencies), it is as easy as changing the build version number in the `build.gradle` file in the root directory of your project. When you run the next build, Gradle will pull in the updated libraries that you specified from a central repository and then store them.

What if you missed a dependency when using the gdx-setup tool? All you need to do is add the dependency declarations to your `build.gradle` file in your project's root directory. The dependency declarations adhere to the following convention:

```
compile '<groupId>:<artifactId>:<version>:<classifier>'
```

You can search for third-party extension declarations at `http://github.com/libgdx/libgdx/wiki/Dependency-management-with-Gradle`. After updating your `build.gradle` file and rebuilding, you will now have the dependencies as part of your project.

Project structure

On Windows, if we open up a Command Prompt in the target directory where the gdx-setup tool outputs our project, we can get a better idea of the project structure with the following command:

```
C:\BludBourne>tree /F /A
```

The output will be something similar to the following (numbers were added for an easier reference):

```
C:.
1) |    .gitignore
2) |    BludBourne.iml
3) |    BludBourne.ipr
4) |    BludBourne.iws
5) |    build.gradle
6) |    gradle.properties
7) |    gradlew
8) |    gradlew.bat
9) |    settings.gradle
   |
+---core
10) |   |   build.gradle
11) |   |   core.iml
   |   |
12)     +---assets
   |   |           badlogic.jpg
   |   |
   |   \---src
   |       \---com
   |           \---packtpub
   |               \---libgdx
   |                   \---bludbourne
13) |                           BludBourne.java
   |
+---desktop
```

```
14)|    |    build.gradle
15)|    |    desktop.iml
   |    |
   |    \---src
   |        \---com
   |            \---packtpub
   |                \---libgdx
   |                    \---bludbourne
   |                        \---desktop
16)|                                DesktopLauncher.java
   |
\---gradle
    \---wrapper
17)                 gradle-wrapper.jar
18)                 gradle-wrapper.properties
```

This project structure is the initial project generated with gdx-setup for the reference RPG for this book, called *BludBourne*, and is described as follows:

- .gitignore (**1**): This is a convenience file used by the source control system, Git. Specifically, this file specifies the untracked (not under source control yet) files to ignore. These would include files such as build output and temporary files.

- BludBourne.iml (**2**): This file type is the project configuration information for modules stored as part of the IntelliJ IDEA project. For instance, the initial module will be a Java module that contains all the functionality to build Java projects.

- BludBourne.ipr (**3**): This file type is the core project information and setting for IntelliJ IDEA projects. This would include items such as project paths, compiler options, and Javadoc generation settings. This file is also the launch file type associated with IDEA.

- BludBourne.iws (**4**): This file type stores your personal workspace settings for IntelliJ IDEA projects. It is recommended that this file is not checked into your source control system.

- build.gradle (**5**): This is the primary Gradle build file. It defines all dependencies and plugins to use in your build environment.

- gradle.properties (**6**): These are settings used to configure your Java build environment. This would include items such as JVM memory settings and setting the Java home (path to JDK).

- `gradlew` (**7**): This file is the Gradle startup script for Unix-based systems.
- `gradlew.bat` (**8**): This file is the Gradle startup script for Windows. You can pass command-line operations as well, including the following commands to get information about projects:

```
gradlew -q projects
```

And:

```
gradlew core:tasks
```

- `settings.gradle` (**9**): This file defines all of the submodules for your project. These are the subprojects that you defined in gdx-setup, including `core`.
- `core/build.gradle` (**10**): This is a Gradle build file specific to this submodule. In general, you will not need to update these submodule configuration files.
- `core/core.iml` (**11**): This is a configuration file for modules stored as part of the IntelliJ IDEA project for this subproject. The information will include items such as paths to the LibGDX libraries.
- `core/assets` (**12**): This is the directory where you will store all of your game assets such as bitmaps, sprites, sound, music, and maps for the desktop.
- `BludBourne.java` (**13**): This is the starter class that is autogenerated for the `BludBourne` project with the gdx-setup tool:

```java
package com.packtpub.libgdx.bludbourne;

import com.badlogic.gdx.ApplicationAdapter;
import com.badlogic.gdx.Gdx;
import com.badlogic.gdx.graphics.GL20;
import com.badlogic.gdx.graphics.Texture;
import com.badlogic.gdx.graphics.g2d.SpriteBatch;

public class BludBourne extends ApplicationAdapter {
  SpriteBatch batch;
  Texture img;

  @Override
  public void create () {
    batch = new SpriteBatch();
    img = new Texture("badlogic.jpg");
  }

  @Override
  public void render () {
```

```
        Gdx.gl.glClearColor(1, 0, 0, 1);
        Gdx.gl.glClear(GL20.GL_COLOR_BUFFER_BIT);
        batch.begin();
        batch.draw(img, 0, 0);
        batch.end();
    }
}
```

As we can see, the starter class BludBourne.java (whose instance was passed to the backend constructor LwjglApplication in DesktopLauncher. java) is a concrete implementation of the ApplicationListener interface (or in this case inherits from the abstract base class ApplicationAdapter, which in turn implements the interface with dummy stubs). This is also the location where your source files will live.

- desktop/build.gradle (**14**): This is a Gradle build file specific to this submodule. In general, you will not need to update these submodule configuration files.

- desktop/desktop.iml (**15**): This is a configuration file for modules stored as part of the IntelliJ IDEA project for this subproject. The information will include items such as paths to the LibGDX libraries.

- DesktopLauncher.java (**16**): This is the only platform-specific class for the desktop. Inside this class, we can see how our game fits into the beginning of the LibGDX framework lifecycle:

```
package com.packtpub.libgdx.bludbourne.desktop;

import com.badlogic.gdx.backends.lwjgl.LwjglApplication;
import com.badlogic.gdx.backends.lwjgl.
LwjglApplicationConfiguration;
import com.packtpub.libgdx.bludbourne.BludBourne;

public class DesktopLauncher {
  public static void main (String[] arg) {
    LwjglApplicationConfiguration config = new
      LwjglApplicationConfiguration();
    new LwjglApplication(new BludBourne(), config);
  }
}
```

This autogenerated class implements the main entry point of our game and passes our **starter class** object, `BludBourne`, to the platform's backend implementation of the `Application` interface. The backend implementation of the `Application` interface for the desktop is `LwjglApplication`, which is part of the LibGDX backend package for the desktop called **LWJGL** (`com.badlogic.gdx.backends.lwjgl`).

LWJGL, an abbreviation for **Lightweight Java Game Library**, is a Java-based open source game development library for accessing hardware resources on the desktop. The driving philosophy is to expose underlying technology as a thin wrapper in order to keep the API simple. LWJGL enables cross-platform (Windows, Mac OS X, and Linux) access to popular native APIs such as OpenGL for graphics and OpenAL for audio. As a side note, *Minecraft* was originally developed using LWJGL.

- `gradle-wrapper.jar` (**17**): This is the main binary for Gradle execution on the desktop that is included in the classpath in the `gradlew.bat` file.

- `gradle-wrapper.properties` (**18**): These properties define the version of Gradle to fetch and install.

Version control systems

I highly recommend that you take a look at a **version control system** (**VCS**) and if you have not used one in the past, take some time in ramping up with how to use one. Nothing is worse than to make one small tweak to your game in a late hour before a demo and all of the sudden, you find yourself with some game objects passing through each other and you have no idea what changed. VCS systems also help manage future content updates, such as patch releases and **downloadable content** (**DLC**) for your game. They help you to clearly identify where changes were made and what areas need to be tested, giving you better management over your deadlines by eliminating the guess work.

The role of version control systems is definitely a must in order to have an audit record of all changes made, and a mechanism to look at differences in the file versions to find these subtle bugs. Today, this doesn't even have to affect your budget for your game, as individual indie developers or small teams can usually use these VCS solutions for free.

The following are some VCS solutions available today:

- **Mercurial**: This is a free, distributed source control management tool (http://mercurial.selenic.com/)

- **Perforce**: This is a commercial, proprietary revision control system. Perforce is free for up to 20 users, 20 workspaces, and unlimited files (http://www.perforce.com/)

- **Subversion**: This is a software versioning and revision control system distributed as free software under the Apache License (http://subversion.apache.org/)

- **Git**: This is a free, distributed revision control system (http://git-scm.com/)

I have used many different types of VCS solutions throughout my career, ranging from legacy, bloated, expensive ones, to free ones with limited features. I have found Git to be easy to learn (once you ignore old source code repository models such as a central host server) and very fast. I personally recommend Git, and I will be using it for the *BludBourne* project. There is a host of information available on how to use Git, but I found the book *Pro Git, by Scott Chacon and Ben Straub,* most useful for quickly getting up to speed on Git (it is available for free at http://git-scm.com/book/en/v2).

You can use Git from the command line, but for my purposes, I prefer GUI clients so that I can see the differences between different check-ins and the history of particular files more clearly. There are many different types of GUI clients available; most are listed at http://git-scm.com/download/gui/linux. Some of them are as follows:

- **GitHub for Windows**: This is free and can be found at http://windows.github.com/

- **SmartGit**: This is $79 per user or free for non-commercial use

I have personally found SmartGit easy to use, fast, and actively maintained. For the *BludBourne* project, I will be using SmartGit as my Git client of choice.

I recommend that once you generate your project using the gdx-setup tool, you can create a Git repository at the root project directory and then commit those changes to your local master branch. This will allow you to make changes as you progress through this book, and not worry about breaking your project.

Running the default demo project

Now that we have an overview of the project structure, we can now run the project sample to make sure that your project is configured correctly, is building, and can run.

You can either double-click on the `BludBourne.ipr` file in the project root directory or launch your IDE and import the *BludBourne* project. In order to import with IDEA, execute the following steps:

1. Choose **File | New | Project From Existing Sources**. Choose the root directory of your project in the **Select File or Directory to Import** dialog. Click on **OK**.

2. In the **Import Project** dialog, select **Create project from existing sources** and click on **Next**.

3. On the next page of the wizard, give your project a name on the **Import Project** dialog. Click on **Next**.

4. If source files have been detected, make sure they are selected in the **Import Project** dialog. Click on **Next**.

5. Make sure the **gradle-wrapper** library is found at this stage with the **Import Project** dialog. Click on **Next**.

6. Make sure the module structure includes both the core and desktop modules in the **Import Project** dialog. Click on **Next**. You may get a popup dialog asking whether to overwrite or reuse the files. I would recommend the reuse option.

7. Select the proper Java project SDK in the next **Import Project** dialog. Click on **Next**.

8. On the last page of the wizard, click on **Finish**.

If you are running IDEA, and you committed the initial project to Git, you may see the following Gradle-based balloon notification when you start the IDE for the first time:

```
Unregistered VCS root detected
```

```
The directory C:\BludBourne is under Git, but is not registered in the
Settings.
```

In order to resolve this, with the project open, go to **File | Settings**. Under the **Settings** dialog, select **Version Control**. Your project should be listed under **Directory** on the right panel, under **Unregistered roots**. Select your directory and click on the + button on the right. Select **Apply** and **OK** when finished.

If you are running IDEA, you may also see a Gradle-based balloon notification when you start the IDE for the first time:

```
Unlinked Gradle project?

        Import Gradle project, this will also enable Gradle Tool Window.

        Don't want to see the message for the project again: press here.
```

Click on the **Import Gradle project** link (in the balloon notification at the bottom). In the **Import Project from Gradle** dialog, make sure that your root project `build.gradle` is configured in the **Gradle Project** path. Also, make sure the **Use default gradle wrapper (recommended)** option is enabled. Change the **Project format:** option to **.ipr (file based)**. Click on **OK** when finished.

If you are running IDEA, you may also come across this Gradle-based notification when starting the IDE with a clone of the *BludBourne* project repository:

```
Error:Unable to make the module: <module>, related gradle configuration
was not found.

Please, re-import the Gradle project and try again.
```

In order to resolve this issue, go to **View | Tool Windows | Gradle**. Click on the refresh button in order to synchronize all linked projects.

In IDEA, select **Build | Make Project**. You should now have successfully built the startup project. We will now need to create a run target:

1. Select **Run | Edit Configurations** from the menu in IDEA.

2. Click on the + icon in the upper-left corner and choose **Application**.

3. You will be presented with the **Run/Debug Configurations** dialog.

4. You should give your run target a name, such as `Run`.

5. You will need to update the **Main class:** setting with **DesktopLauncher**.

6. You will also need to set the **Working directory:** path to `<project root>\core\assets`. If you don't set this, you will get the following runtime error:

   ```
   Exception in thread "LWJGL Application" com.badlogic.gdx.utils.
   GdxRuntimeException: Couldn't load file: badlogic.jpg

       at com.badlogic.gdx.graphics.Pixmap.<init>(Pixmap.java:140)

       at com.badlogic.gdx.graphics.TextureData$Factory.
   loadFromFile(TextureData.java:98)
   ```

7. You will need to set the **Use classpath of module** option to **Desktop** since this is where the main entry point of your game lives.

8. Click on **OK** when finished.

Now, everything should be configured to finally run. From the menu, select **Run | Run target**. If all the dependencies are correct, with a proper Gradle build setup and project configuration, you should see the following screen (*Figure 10*):

Figure 10

See also

- http://en.wikipedia.org/wiki/Little_Wars
- http://en.wikipedia.org/wiki/J._R._R._Tolkien
- http://en.wikipedia.org/wiki/Ultima_I:_The_First_Age_of_Darkness
- http://en.wikipedia.org/wiki/Dungeons_%26_Dragons
- http://en.wikipedia.org/wiki/List_of_game_engines
- Hallford N., and Hallford J. *Swords & Circuitry: A Designer's Guide to Computer Role Playing Games*. Roseville, CA: Prima Tech, 2001. Print.
- Nystrom R. *Game Programming Patterns*. Genever Benning. 9780990582908. Web. 04 Apr. 2015.

Summary

This chapter gave some historical context for features that we will be developing throughout this book for your next RPG title. We also covered some business cases that help create a compelling narrative around how LibGDX can help meet your requirements when building your next RPG title. We also reviewed a high-level architecture of LibGDX, as well as how to successfully generate and run our starter project.

In the next chapter, we will develop the infrastructure to load tile maps and move our hero around in the game world.

2
Welcome to the Land of BludBourne

Now that we have a high-level understanding of LibGDX, its modules, and a working starter project, we will now jump into creating the world of BludBourne. We will first learn some concepts and tools related to creating tile-based maps. We will then explore our project source code for this chapter, which will include managing the loading of game assets, including maps, and using player input for character movement around our world.

We will cover the following topics in this chapter:

- Creating and editing tile-based maps
- Implementing the starter classes for *BludBourne*
- Implementing asset management with loading textures and tile-based maps
- Implementing the camera and displaying a map in the render loop
- Implementing map management with spawn points and a portal system
- Implementing your player character with animation
- Implementing input handling for player-character movement

Creating and editing tile-based maps

For the *BludBourne* project map locations, we will be using tilesets, which are terrain and decoration sprites in the shape of squares. These are easy to work with, since LibGDX supports tile-based maps with its core library. The easiest method to create these types of maps is to use a tile-based editor.

There are many different types of tilemap editors, but there are two primary ones that are used with LibGDX because they have built-in support, as follows:

- **Tiled**: This is a free and actively maintained tile-based editor. I used this editor for the *BludBourne* project. Download the latest version from `http://www.mapeditor.org/download.html`.

- **Tide**: This is a free tile-based editor built using Microsoft XNA libraries. The targeted platforms are Windows, Xbox 360, and Windows Phone 7. Download the latest version from `http://tide.codeplex.com/releases`.

For the *BludBourne* project, we will be using Tiled. The following figure (*Figure 1*) is a screenshot from one of the editing sessions when creating the maps for our game:

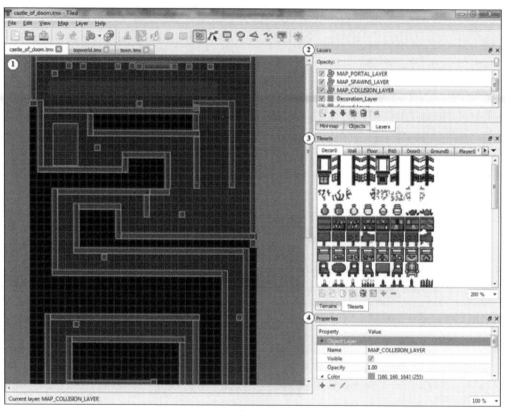

Figure 1

The following is a quick guide for how we can use Tiled for this project:

- **Map View (1)**: The map view is the part of the Tiled editor where you display and edit your individual maps. Numerous maps can be loaded at once, using a tab approach, so that you can switch between them quickly. There is a zoom feature available for this part of Tiled in the lower-right hand corner, and can be easily customized depending on your workflow. The maps are provided in the project directory (under `\core\assets\maps`), but when you wish to create your own maps, you can simply go to **File | New**. In the **New Map** dialog box, set the **Tile size** dimensions first that, for our project, will be a width of 16 pixels and a height of 16 pixels. The other setting is **Map size** that represents the size of your map in unit size, using the tile size dimensions as your unit scale. An example would be creating a map that is 100 units by 100 units, and if our tiles have a dimension of 16 pixels by 16 pixels, then this would give a map size of 1600 pixels by 1600 pixels. Later on, in this chapter, we will be configuring the map renderer with this unit referred to as the unit scale value.

- **Layers (2)**: This represents the different layers of the currently loaded map. You can think of creating a tile map like painting a scene, where you paint the background first and build up the various elements until you get to the foreground. For the maps for this chapter, we will define six different types of layers:

    - **Background_Layer**: This tile layer represents the first layer created for the tilemap. This will be the layer to create the ground elements, such as grass, dirt paths, water, and stone walkways. Nothing else will be shown below this layer.

    - **Ground_Layer**: This tile layer will be the second layer created for the tilemap. This layer will be buildings built on top of the ground, or other structures such as mountains, trees, and villages. The primary reason is to convey a feeling of depth to the map, as well as the fact that structural tiles such as walls have a transparency (alpha channel) so that they look like they belong on the ground where they are being created.

    - **Decoration_Layer**: This third tile layer will contain elements meant to decorate the landscape in order to remove repetition and make more interesting scenes. These elements include rocks, patches of weeds, flowers, and even skulls.

- ° **MAP_COLLISION_LAYER**: This fourth layer is a special layer designated as an object layer. This layer does not contain tiles, but will have objects or shapes. This is the layer that you will configure to create areas in the map that the player character and non-player characters cannot traverse, such as walls of buildings, mountain terrain, ocean areas, and decorations such as fountains.

- ° **MAP_SPAWNS_LAYER**: This fifth layer is another special object layer designated only for player and non-playable character spawns, such as people in the towns. These spawns will represent the various starting locations where these characters will first be rendered on the map.

- ° **MAP_PORTAL_LAYER**: This sixth layer is the last object layer designated to trigger events in order to move from one map into another. These will be locations where the player character walks over, triggering an event that activates the transition to another map. An example of using the portal would be in the village map. When the player walks outside of the village map, they will find themselves on the larger world map.

- **Tilesets (3)**: This area of Tiled represents all of the tilesets you will work with for the current map. Each tileset, or sprite sheet, will get its own tab in this interface, making it easy to move between them. Adding a new tileset is as easy as clicking on the **New** icon in the **Tilesets** area, and loading the tileset image in the **New Tileset** dialog. Tiled will also partition out the tilemap into the individual tiles after you configure the tile dimensions in this dialog.

- **Properties (4)**: This area of Tiled represents the different additional properties that you can set for the currently selected map element, such as a tile or object. An example of where these properties can be helpful is when we create a portal object on the portal layer. We can create a property defining the name of this portal object that represents the map to load. So, when we walk over a small tile that looks like a town in the world overview map, and trigger the portal event, we know that the map to load is TOWN because the name property on this portal object is TOWN.

After reviewing a very brief description of how we can use the Tiled editor for *BludBourne*, the following images show the three maps that we will be using for this project. The first image (*Figure 2*) is of the TOWN map that will be where our hero will discover clues from the villagers, obtain quests, and buy armor and weapons. The town has shops, an inn, as well as a few small homes of local villagers:

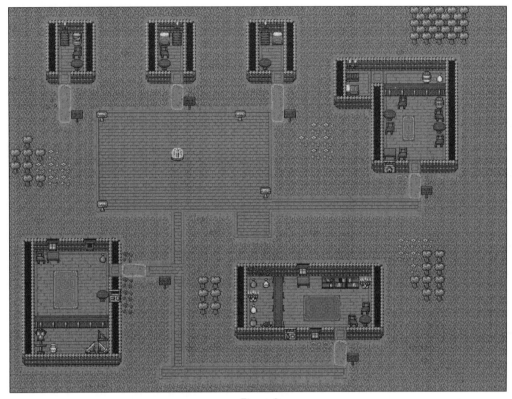

Figure 2

The next image (*Figure 3*) is of the TOP_WORLD map that will be the location where our hero will battle enemies, find clues throughout the land, and eventually make way to the evil antagonist held up in his castle. The hero can see how the pestilence of evil has started to spread across the lands and lay ruin upon the only harvestable fields left:

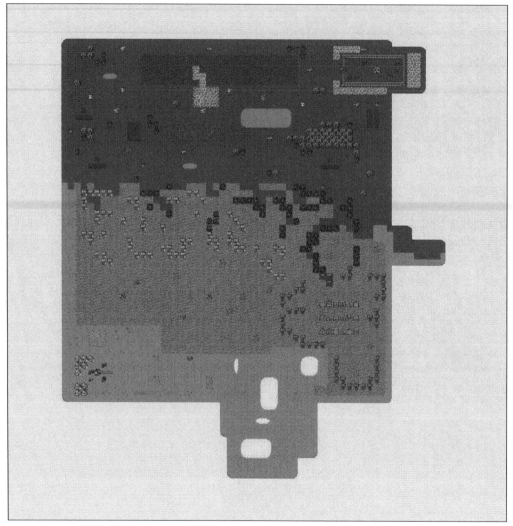

Figure 3

Finally, we make our way to the CASTLE_OF_DOOM map (*Figure 4*) where our hero, once leveled enough, will battle the evil antagonist held up in his throne room of his own castle. Here, the hero will find many high-level enemies, as well as high-valued items for trade:

Figure 4

Implementing the starter classes for BludBourne

Now that we have created the maps for the different locations of *BludBourne*, we can now begin to develop the initial pieces of our source code project in order to load these maps, and move around in our world. The following diagram (*Figure 5*) represents a high-level view of all the relevant classes that we will be creating for this chapter:

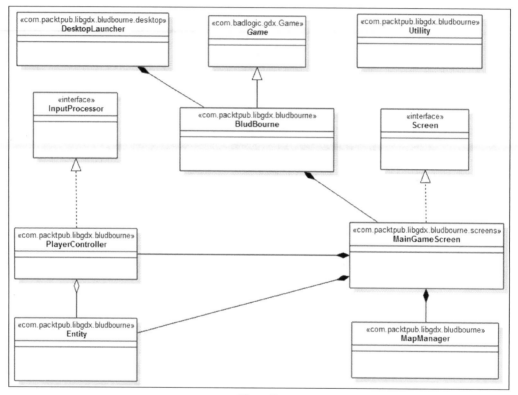

Figure 5

This class diagram is meant to show not only all the classes we will be reviewing in this chapter, but also the relationships that these classes share so that we are not developing them in a vacuum. The main entry point for our game (and the only platform-specific class) is DesktopLauncher, which will instantiate BludBourne and add it along with some configuration information to the LibGDX application lifecycle. BludBourne will derive from Game to minimize the lifecycle implementation needed by the ApplicationListener interface. BludBourne will maintain all the screens for the game. For this chapter, we will only need one class that implements the Screen interface, MainGameScreen. MainGameScreen will be the primary gameplay screen that displays the different maps and player character moving around in them. MainGameScreen will also create MapManager, Entity, and PlayerController. MapManager provides helper methods for managing the different maps and map layers. Entity will represent the primary class for our player character in the game. PlayerController implements InputProcessor and will be the class that controls the player's input and controls on the screen. Finally, we have some asset manager helper methods in the Utility class used throughout the project.

DesktopLauncher

The first class that we will need to modify is DesktopLauncher, which the gdx-setup tool generated. This class can be found at desktop/src/com/packtpub/libgdx/ bludbourne/desktop/DesktopLauncher.java, relative to our project root directory:

```
package com.packtpub.libgdx.bludbourne.desktop;

import com.badlogic.gdx.Application;
import com.badlogic.gdx.Gdx;
import com.badlogic.gdx.backends.lwjgl.LwjglApplication;
import com.badlogic.gdx.backends.lwjgl.LwjglApplicationConfiguration;
import com.packtpub.libgdx.bludbourne.BludBourne;
```

The Application class is responsible for setting up a window, handling resize events, rendering to the surfaces, and managing the application during its lifetime. Specifically, Application will provide the modules for dealing with graphics, audio, input and file I/O handling, logging facilities, memory footprint information, and hooks for extension libraries.

The Gdx class is an environment class that holds static instances of the Application, Graphics, Audio, Input, Files, and Net modules as a convenience for access throughout the game.

The LwjglApplication class is the backend implementation of the Application interface for the desktop. The backend package that LibGDX uses for the desktop is called **LWJGL**. This implementation for the desktop will provide cross-platform access to native APIs for OpenGL. This interface becomes the entry point that the platform OS uses to load your game.

The LwjglApplicationConfiguration class provides a single point of reference for all the properties associated with your game on the desktop:

```java
public class DesktopLauncher {
  public static void main (String[] arg) {
    LwjglApplicationConfiguration config = new
      LwjglApplicationConfiguration();

    config.title = "BludBourne";
    config.useGL30 = false;
    config.width = 800;
    config.height = 600;

    Application app = new LwjglApplication(new BludBourne(),
      config);

    Gdx.app = app;
    //Gdx.app.setLogLevel(Application.LOG_INFO);
    Gdx.app.setLogLevel(Application.LOG_DEBUG);
    //Gdx.app.setLogLevel(Application.LOG_ERROR);
    //Gdx.app.setLogLevel(Application.LOG_NONE);
  }
}
```

The config object is an instance of the LwjglApplicationConfiguration class where we can set top-level game configuration properties, such as the title to display on the display window, as well as display window dimensions. The useGL30 property is set to false so that we use the much more stable and mature implementation of OpenGL ES, version 2.0.

The `LwjglApplicationConfiguration` properties object and our starter class instance, `BludBourne`, are then passed to the backend implementation of the `Application` class. An object reference is then stored in the `Gdx` class. Finally, we will set the logging level for the game. There are four values for the logging levels that represent various degrees of granularity for application level messages output to standard out. `LOG_NONE` is a logging level where no messages are output. `LOG_ERROR` will only display error messages. `LOG_INFO` will display all messages that are not debug-level messages. Finally, `LOG_DEBUG` is a logging level that displays all messages.

BludBourne

The next class to review is `BludBourne`, which can be found at `core/src/com/packtpub/libgdx/bludbourne/BludBourne.java`. The class diagram for `BludBourne` (*Figure 6*) shows the attributes and method signatures for our implementation:

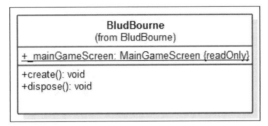

Figure 6

The import packages for `BludBourne` are as follows:

```
package com.packtpub.libgdx.bludbourne;

import com.packtpub.libgdx.bludbourne.screens.MainGameScreen;
import com.badlogic.gdx.Game;
```

The `Game` class is an abstract base class that wraps the `ApplicationListener` interface and delegates the implementation of this interface to the `Screen` class. This provides a convenience for setting the game up with different screens, including ones for a main menu, options, gameplay, and cutscenes.

The `MainGameScreen` is the primary gameplay screen that the player will see as they move their hero around in the game world. We will discuss this class at length later on in this chapter:

```
public class BludBourne extends Game {

public static final MainGameScreen _mainGameScreen = new
MainGameScreen();

    @Override
    public void create(){
      setScreen(_mainGameScreen);
    }

    @Override
    public void dispose(){
      _mainGameScreen.dispose();
    }
}
```

The gdx-setup tool generated our starter class `BludBourne`. This is the first place where we begin to set up our game lifecycle. An instance of `BludBourne` is passed to the backend constructor of `LwjglApplication` in `DesktopLauncher`, which is how we get hooks into the lifecycle of LibGDX.

`BludBourne` will contain all of the screens used throughout the game, but for now we are only concerned with the primary gameplay screen, `MainGameScreen`. We must override the `create()` method so that we can set the initial screen for when `BludBourne` is initialized in the game lifecycle. The `setScreen()` method will check to see whether a screen is already currently active. If the current screen is already active, then it will be hidden, and the screen that was passed into the method will be shown. In the future, we will use this method to start the game with a main menu screen. We should also override `dispose()` since `BludBourne` owns the screen object references. We need to make sure that we dispose of the objects appropriately when we are exiting the game.

Implementing asset management with loading textures and tile-based maps

The next class to review is `Utility`, which can be found at `core/src/com/packtpub/libgdx/bludbourne/Utility.java`. The `Utility` class represents a placeholder for various methods including dealing with the loading and unloading of game assets.

Utility

The class diagram for Utility (*Figure 7*) shows the attributes and method signatures for our implementation:

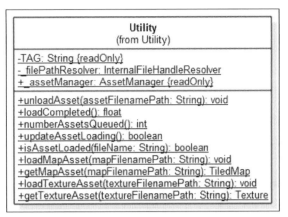

Figure 7

The import packages for Utility are as follows:

```
package com.packtpub.libgdx.bludbourne;

import com.badlogic.gdx.Gdx;
import com.badlogic.gdx.graphics.Texture;
import com.badlogic.gdx.assets.loaders.TextureLoader;
import com.badlogic.gdx.assets.loaders.resolvers.
InternalFileHandleResolver;
import com.badlogic.gdx.maps.tiled.TiledMap;
import com.badlogic.gdx.maps.tiled.TmxMapLoader;
import com.badlogic.gdx.assets.AssetManager;
```

Since LibGDX is built upon OpenGL, we need to understand some nomenclature from OpenGL in order to properly understand how certain classes work in LibGDX.

For our game, our graphics will be raster-based, which means that they will be represented by pixels with specific color values. The alternative is to use vector-based graphics where the graphics are created by executing various draw commands on the fly. Vector graphics will not be used for the simple reason that the rendering bottleneck from generating images on the fly would hinder performance. A raster graphic or image is one large array of color pixel values. Due to the size of these pixel values, especially with a large color space, different image formats were developed to compress or reduce the overall size, such as JPEG, PNG, and BMP.

In order to bridge the gap from an image represented by a 2D array to the 3D space of OpenGL, all image assets must first be transformed into textures. This process involves decoding the image format into raw color data. Then, since OpenGL represents 3D space, we will also need to map this texture to a geometry that the GPU can process and display, such as a 2D quad. Then, you would need to upload this data directly to the platform's GPU for rendering to the display. Luckily, LibGDX wraps all this functionality for us and abstracts away all the complexity with the `Texture` class.

As one would imagine, constantly loading images, decoding, texture mapping, and pushing the data to the GPU would cause significant performance issues due to the limitations of a platform's bus bandwidth and CPU speed. Typically, we would want to load as much as possible at the beginning of our game to decrease the performance hit of loading images during gameplay.

The `Texture` class will be used whenever we are loading image-based assets and will help manage the graphic assets for the game.

The `TextureLoader` class represents the asset loader for textures. One note is that the texture data is loaded by default asynchronously, so make sure before you use an asset with `TextureLoader` that it has been loaded.

The `InternalFileHandleResolver` class is a nice convenience class for managing file handles when resolving paths with assets relative to the current working directory.

The `TiledMap` class inherits from the `Map` class that is a generic map implementation. The `Map` base class only contains map properties that describe general attributes and map layers. The `TiledMap` class extends this functionality with additional fields for tiles and tilesets. These tiles are stored as a 2D array of cells that contain references to the tile as well as rotation and flip attributes.

The `TmxMapLoader` class is a convenience class for loading TMX-based tilemaps and storing them as the `TiledMap` instances.

The `AssetManager` class manages the loading and storing of assets such as textures, bitmap fonts, particle effects, pixmaps, UI skins, tile maps, sounds, and music:

```
public final class Utility {

    public static final AssetManager _assetManager =
      new AssetManager();
```

```
    private static final String TAG =
       Utility.class.getSimpleName();

    private static InternalFileHandleResolver _filePathResolver =
       new InternalFileHandleResolver();

  public static void unloadAsset(String assetFilenamePath){
  // once the asset manager is done loading
  if(_assetManager.isLoaded(assetFilenamePath) ){
    _assetManager.unload(assetFilenamePath);
    } else {
      Gdx.app.debug(TAG, "Asset is not loaded; Nothing to unload:
        " + assetFilenamePath );
    }
  }
```

The unloadAsset() method is a helper method that takes advantage of the fact that there is one static instance of AssetManager for all game assets. This method will check to see whether the asset is loaded, and if it is, then it will unload the asset from memory. The unload() method of AssetManager will check the dependencies with a given asset, and once the reference counter hits zero, call dispose() on the asset and remove it from the manager:

```
public static float loadCompleted(){
   return _assetManager.getProgress();
}

public static int numberAssetsQueued(){
   return _assetManager.getQueuedAssets();
}

public static boolean updateAssetLoading(){
   return _assetManager.update();
}

public static boolean isAssetLoaded(String fileName){
   return _assetManager.isLoaded(fileName);

}
```

The `loadCompleted()` method wraps the progress of `AssetManager` as a percentage of completion. This can be used to update progress meter values when loading asynchronously. The `numberAssetsQueued()` method wraps the number of assets left to load from the `AssetManager` queue. The `updateAssetLoading()` wraps the update call in `AssetManager` and can be called in a `render()` loop, if loading assets asynchronously in order to process the preload queue. The `isAssetLoaded()` method wraps the `AssetManager` method `isLoaded()` and will return a simple `Boolean` value on whether the asset is currently loaded or not:

```
public static void loadMapAsset(String mapFilenamePath){
   if( mapFilenamePath == null || mapFilenamePath.isEmpty() ){
     return;
   }

   //load asset
   if( _filePathResolver.resolve(mapFilenamePath).exists() ){
     _assetManager.setLoader(
        TiledMap.class, new TmxMapLoader(_filePathResolver));

       _assetManager.load(mapFilenamePath, TiledMap.class);

     //Until we add loading screen,
     //just block until we load the map
     _assetManager.finishLoadingAsset(mapFilenamePath);
     Gdx.app.debug(TAG, "Map loaded!: " + mapFilenamePath);
   }
   else{
     Gdx.app.debug(TAG, "Map doesn't exist!: " + mapFilenamePath );
   }
}

public static TiledMap getMapAsset(String mapFilenamePath){
   TiledMap map = null;

   // once the asset manager is done loading
   if(_assetManager.isLoaded(mapFilenamePath) ){
     map =_assetManager.get(mapFilenamePath,TiledMap.class);
   } else {
   Gdx.app.debug(TAG, "Map is not loaded: " + mapFilenamePath );
   }

   return map;
}
```

The `loadMapAsset()` method will take a TMX filename path relative to the working directory and load the TMX file as a `TiledMap` asset, blocking until finished. We can load these assets later asynchronously once we create a screen with a progress bar, instead of blocking on the render thread. The `loadMapAsset()` method is paired with the `getMapAsset()` method because once the `TiledMap` asset is loaded, we can retrieve the asset for use by calling `getMapAsset()`. Separating the loading of an asset from the retrieval gives us the flexibility in the future to load asynchronously when we have a loading screen setup:

```
public static void loadTextureAsset(String textureFilenamePath){
  if( textureFilenamePath == null ||
    textureFilenamePath.isEmpty()){
    return;
  }
  //load asset
  if( _filePathResolver.resolve(textureFilenamePath).exists() ){
    _assetManager.setLoader(Texture.class,
     new TextureLoader(_filePathResolver));

    _assetManager.load(textureFilenamePath, Texture.class);
    //Until we add loading screen,
    //just block until we load the map
    _assetManager.finishLoadingAsset(textureFilenamePath);
  }
  else{
    Gdx.app.debug(TAG, "Texture doesn't exist!: " +
      textureFilenamePath );
  }
}
public static Texture getTextureAsset(String textureFilenamePath){
  Texture texture = null;

  // once the asset manager is done loading
  if(_assetManager.isLoaded(textureFilenamePath) ){
    texture =
      _assetManager.get(textureFilenamePath,Texture.class);
  } else {
  Gdx.app.debug(TAG, "Texture is not loaded: " +
    textureFilenamePath );
  }
return texture;
}
}
```

The `loadTextureAsset()` method will take an image filename path relative to the working directory and load the image file as a `Texture` asset, blocking until finished. The `loadTextureAsset()` method is paired with the `getTextureAsset()` method because once the `Texture` asset is loaded, we can retrieve the asset for use by calling `getTextureAsset()`.

Implementing the camera and displaying a map in the render loop

The next class to review is `MainGameScreen`, which can be found at `core/src/com/packtpub/libgdx/bludbourne/screens/MainGameScreen.java`. The `MainGameScreen` class is the first `Screen` implementation for our game and represents the main gameplay screen used to display the game map, player avatar, and any UI components.

MainGameScreen

The class diagram for `MainGameScreen` (*Figure 8*) shows all the attributes and method signatures for our first pass:

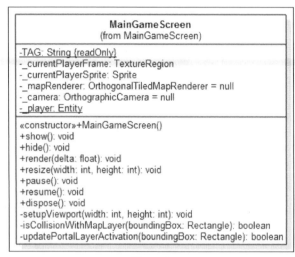

Figure 8

The import packages for `MainGameScreen` are as follows:

```
package com.packtpub.libgdx.bludbourne.screens;

import com.badlogic.gdx.Gdx;
import com.badlogic.gdx.Screen;
import com.badlogic.gdx.graphics.GL20;
import com.badlogic.gdx.graphics.OrthographicCamera;
import com.badlogic.gdx.graphics.g2d.Sprite;
import com.badlogic.gdx.graphics.g2d.TextureRegion;
import com.badlogic.gdx.maps.MapLayer;
import com.badlogic.gdx.maps.MapObject;
import com.badlogic.gdx.maps.objects.RectangleMapObject;
import com.badlogic.gdx.maps.tiled.renderers.
```

```
OrthogonalTiledMapRenderer;
import com.badlogic.gdx.math.Rectangle;
import com.packtpub.libgdx.bludbourne.Entity;
import com.packtpub.libgdx.bludbourne.MapManager;
import com.packtpub.libgdx.bludbourne.PlayerController;
```

The `Camera` class deserves a more detailed discussion with how it works within the LibGDX framework. We will walk through the following diagram (*Figure 9*) and outline the important conceptual pieces that compose the `Camera` class:

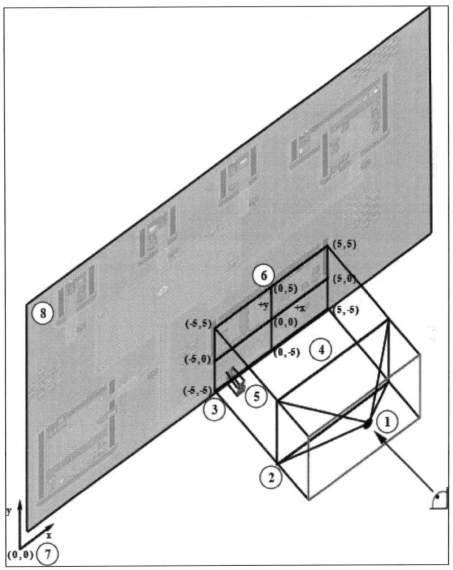

Figure 9

This diagram represents all the pieces that affect how your users will see your game when they are moving around and interacting with your world:

- **Camera (1)**: A virtual camera in the 3D graphics world is more akin to a pinhole camera than the one for photography or movies. Photography and movie cameras focus light through converging lenses and record the image onto some light-sensitive medium. A pinhole camera, on the other hand, is a simple light-proof box without a lens. This camera lets light through a small hole, a single aperture or pinhole, and projects the image onto the other side. The camera represented in the diagram is the OrthographicCamera class that uses orthographic (also referred to as orthogonal or parallel) projection to represent 3D objects in 2D space.

- **Near clipping plane (2)**: This plane is the closest one to the camera. In a perspective camera, objects closer to this plane will appear larger than objects further away. In an orthographic camera, objects will appear the same size regardless of how close they are to this plane as no adjustments are made for distance from the camera with orthographic projections.

- **Far clipping plane (3)**: This plane is the furthest one from the camera. In a perspective camera, objects closer to this plane will appear smaller than objects closer to the near clipping plane. In an orthographic camera, objects will appear the same size regardless how far they are from the camera.

- **View frustum (4)**: This is the cuboid volume whose depth is bounded by the near and far clipping planes. Anything that is inside this volume, including partially intersecting objects, will be rendered to the screen (unless the object is occluded). Everything else outside this volume will not be rendered or will be clipped. This is also referred to as frustum culling. The other item to keep in mind is usually there is a z ordering (depth) of game objects starting at the far clipping plane and moving in a positive direction towards the near clipping plane.

- **Orthographic projection of a sprite (5)**: An example of a Sprite object in the frustum that visually demonstrates an orthographic projection onto the viewport. This shows that no matter where objects are located within the frustum, they will be rendered the same size without any perspective correction. A Sprite class represents a flat 2D image that contains the geometry, color, and texture information for drawing. This allows you rotate and move the Sprite object around the screen.

- **Viewport (6)**: This is a 2D rectangular region of the screen used to project a 3D scene to the position of the camera. In LibGDX, the viewport width and height has its origin located at the center of the screen. The diagram shows a viewport with a width and height of 10 units each and a positive *y* axis pointing up. In this example, we can see how the corresponding position values change depending on what direction we are moving.

- **Coordinate system (7)**: The coordinate system in LibGDX is bottom-left, meaning that the origin coordinate point *(0, 0)* is located at the bottom-left corner with the positive *y* axis pointing up.

- **Map screen (8)**: This is an example of one of the Tiled (TMX format) maps rendered to a `Screen` instance using the `OrthogonalTiledMapRenderer` class in the render thread.

The source for `MainGameScreen` is as follows:

```
public class MainGameScreen implements Screen {
  private static final String TAG =
    MainGameScreen.class.getSimpleName();

  private static class VIEWPORT {
    static float viewportWidth;
    static float viewportHeight;
    static float virtualWidth;
    static float virtualHeight;
    static float physicalWidth;
    static float physicalHeight;
    static float aspectRatio;
  }

  private PlayerController _controller;
  private TextureRegion _currentPlayerFrame;
  private Sprite _currentPlayerSprite;

  private OrthogonalTiledMapRenderer _mapRenderer = null;
  private OrthographicCamera _camera = null;
  private static MapManager _mapMgr;

  public MainGameScreen(){
```

```
    _mapMgr = new MapManager();
}

private static Entity _player;

@Override
public void show() {
  //_camera setup
  setupViewport(10, 10);

  //get the current size
  _camera = new OrthographicCamera();
  _camera.setToOrtho(false, VIEWPORT.viewportWidth,
    VIEWPORT.viewportHeight);

  _mapRenderer = new OrthogonalTiledMapRenderer
    (_mapMgr.getCurrentMap(), MapManager.UNIT_SCALE);
  _mapRenderer.setView(_camera);

  Gdx.app.debug(TAG, "UnitScale value is: " +
    _mapRenderer.getUnitScale());

  _player = new Entity();
  _player.init(_mapMgr.getPlayerStartUnitScaled().x,
    _mapMgr.getPlayerStartUnitScaled().y);

  _currentPlayerSprite = _player.getFrameSprite();

  _controller = new PlayerController(_player);
  Gdx.input.setInputProcessor(_controller);
}

@Override
public void hide() {
}
```

There are two primary methods in the Screen class interface that you will need to override: the show() and hide() methods. Whenever a new screen is set with the setScreen() method in the BludBourne class, the hide() method will be called on the current screen, and a show() method will be called on the new screen. For now, because we have not currently implemented other screens, these member variables can be instantiated in the show() method. In this show() method, we first set up the viewport, which we saw in *Figure 9*, with the dimensions of 10 units for the width and 10 units for the height. The setupViewport() method will be discussed in depth later.

A unit in this context is a `unitScale` attribute that maps the coordinate system on the tiled map from screen pixel coordinates to world unit coordinates. One benefit of using a `unitScale` attribute is that it simplifies collision detection and tile changes on a tile-based map because they are abstracted into whole number indices. In other words, you may have a position on the map that represents the pixel position *(160, 320)* that doesn't easily give us information on which tile we are on relative to the tile map. If all tiles are 16 pixel squares, I can set `unitScale` equal to 1/16, which means that every one unit will represent a square with side lengths of 16 pixels. So, instead of having a position of *(160, 320)* in pixel space, by setting `unitScale` to 1/16, I will have a position of *(10, 20)* in unit space (160/16 for *x*, and 320/16 for *y*), meaning my current position will be the tenth tile to the right (positive *x*) and the twentieth tile up (positive *y*).

We are going to instantiate our `Camera` with a default constructor as an `OrthographicCamera` that was discussed in detail with *Figure 9*. The `setToOrtho()` method takes a Boolean as a first parameter that we should set to `false` so that our coordinate system has the positive *y* facing up. The next two parameters set up our viewport width and height dimensions, respectively. Now that we have defined our orthographic camera to view our world, we now need to render the tile maps.

`OrthogonalTiledMapRenderer`, which was also discussed in *Figure 9*, will take a `TiledMap` and a unit scale value. The `TiledMap` is already loaded from our `MapManager` class, which will be discussed later, and in the future will load the map that was set when saving the game progress. The unit scale is configured for the pixel dimensions of our world, so every tile unit on the map will represent a square with side lengths of 16 pixels. The `setView()` method bridges the rendered map with the viewport of the camera, and so we pass in the `OrthographicCamera` instance that we previously constructed.

`MainGameScreen` will also contain a static instance of `Entity` that represents the player in the game. The lifetime of the player will persist as we load different maps, so for now, it makes sense that the player object lives in this class. The next initializations are specific to setting up our `Entity` object or the player character to move around the map. We will discuss the `Entity` class more in depth later on:

```
@Override
public void render(float delta) {
  Gdx.gl.glClearColor(0, 0, 0, 1);
  Gdx.gl.glClear(GL20.GL_COLOR_BUFFER_BIT);

  //Preferable to lock and center the _camera to the player's
    position
  _camera.position.set(_currentPlayerSprite.getX(),
    _currentPlayerSprite.getY(), 0f);
```

```
    _camera.update();

    _player.update(delta);
    _currentPlayerFrame = _player.getFrame();

    updatePortalLayerActivation(_player.boundingBox);

    if( !isCollisionWithMapLayer(_player.boundingBox) ){
      _player.setNextPositionToCurrent();
    }
    _controller.update(delta);

    _mapRenderer.setView(_camera);
    _mapRenderer.render();

    _mapRenderer.getBatch().begin();
    _mapRenderer.getBatch().draw(_currentPlayerFrame,
      _currentPlayerSprite.getX(), _currentPlayerSprite.getY(),
      1,1);
    _mapRenderer.getBatch().end();
  }
```

You will need to implement your own sorting algorithm in order to make sure certain game objects get rendered in a particular order; otherwise they will be rendered in the order that the draw calls are made. In the future, we will be making draw calls similar to the painter's algorithm where the background layer of the TiledMap map will be drawn first all the way to the character sprites that will be rendered last.

The render() method will be called every frame, and is the primary location for rendering, updating, and checking for collisions in the game lifecycle. First, we will make sure that we lock the viewport (camera position) to the current position of our player character so that the player is always in the middle of the screen. We will then check whether the player has activated a portal, which will be discussed later on in more detail with the MapManager class. We will also check for collisions with the collision layer of the map, and if there are collisions, then we will not update the player's position. We make sure that we update the camera information in the OrthogonalTiledMapRenderer object and then render the TiledMap object first because, as mentioned previously, the order in which you draw your objects matter.

Finally, we will draw the character to the screen, making sure to use the `getBatch()` call for when we have numerous objects to update. By drawing in a batch update, the overhead of updating the textures will be minimal since the GPU will consume the texture updates at one time instead of constantly throttling between updating and rendering separate textures:

```java
@Override
public void resize(int width, int height) {
}

@Override
public void pause() {
}

@Override
public void resume() {
}

@Override
public void dispose() {
  _player.dispose();
  _controller.dispose();
  Gdx.input.setInputProcessor(null);
  _mapRenderer.dispose();
}

private void setupViewport(int width, int height){
  //Make the viewport a percentage of the total display area
  VIEWPORT.virtualWidth = width;
  VIEWPORT.virtualHeight = height;

  //Current viewport dimensions
  VIEWPORT.viewportWidth = VIEWPORT.virtualWidth;
  VIEWPORT.viewportHeight = VIEWPORT.virtualHeight;

  //pixel dimensions of display
  VIEWPORT.physicalWidth = Gdx.graphics.getWidth();
  VIEWPORT.physicalHeight = Gdx.graphics.getHeight();

  //aspect ratio for current viewport
```

```
VIEWPORT.aspectRatio = (VIEWPORT.virtualWidth /
  VIEWPORT.virtualHeight);

//update viewport if there could be skewing
if( VIEWPORT.physicalWidth / VIEWPORT.physicalHeight >=
  VIEWPORT.aspectRatio){
  //Letterbox left and right
  VIEWPORT.viewportWidth = VIEWPORT.viewportHeight *
    (VIEWPORT.physicalWidth/VIEWPORT.physicalHeight);
  VIEWPORT.viewportHeight = VIEWPORT.virtualHeight;
}else{
  //letterbox above and below
  VIEWPORT.viewportWidth = VIEWPORT.virtualWidth;
  VIEWPORT.viewportHeight = VIEWPORT.viewportWidth *
    (VIEWPORT.physicalHeight/VIEWPORT.physicalWidth);
}

Gdx.app.debug(TAG, "WorldRenderer: virtual: (" +
  VIEWPORT.virtualWidth + "," + VIEWPORT.virtualHeight + ")" );
Gdx.app.debug(TAG, "WorldRenderer: viewport: (" +
  VIEWPORT.viewportWidth + "," + VIEWPORT.viewportHeight + ")"
  );
Gdx.app.debug(TAG, "WorldRenderer: physical: (" +
  VIEWPORT.physicalWidth + "," + VIEWPORT.physicalHeight + ")"
  );
}
```

The setupViewport() method helps with the bookkeeping of our inner class VIEWPORT. This is simply a convenience class for maintaining all the parameters that compose our viewport for the camera. This class will also account for the skewing that can occur depending on the width to height ratio and will update the values accordingly:

```
private boolean isCollisionWithMapLayer(Rectangle boundingBox){
  MapLayer mapCollisionLayer = _mapMgr.getCollisionLayer();

  if( mapCollisionLayer == null ){
    return false;
  }

  Rectangle rectangle = null;

  for( MapObject object: mapCollisionLayer.getObjects()){
```

```
      if(object instanceof RectangleMapObject) {
        rectangle = ((RectangleMapObject)object).getRectangle();
        if( boundingBox.overlaps(rectangle) ){
          return true;
        }
      }
    }
  }

  return false;
}
```

The isCollisionWithMapLayer() method is called for every frame in the render() method with the player character's bounding box passed in. This is essentially the rectangle that defines the hitbox of the player. We test the player's hitbox against all rectangle objects on the collision layer of the TiledMap map, and if any of the rectangles overlap, then we know we have a collision and will return true:

```
private boolean updatePortalLayerActivation(Rectangle
  boundingBox){
  MapLayer mapPortalLayer =  _mapMgr.getPortalLayer();

  if( mapPortalLayer == null ){
    return false;
  }

  Rectangle rectangle = null;

  for( MapObject object: mapPortalLayer.getObjects()){
    if(object instanceof RectangleMapObject) {
      rectangle = ((RectangleMapObject)object).getRectangle();
      if( boundingBox.overlaps(rectangle) ){
        String mapName = object.getName();
        if( mapName == null ) {
          return false;
        }
        _mapMgr.setClosestStartPositionFromScaledUnits
          (_player.getCurrentPosition());
        _mapMgr.loadMap(mapName);
        _player.init(_mapMgr.getPlayerStartUnitScaled().x,
          _mapMgr.getPlayerStartUnitScaled().y);
        _mapRenderer.setMap(_mapMgr.getCurrentMap());
```

```
        Gdx.app.debug(TAG, "Portal Activated");
        return true;
      }
    }
  }

  return false;
  }
}
```

The `updatePortalLayerActivation()` method is similar to the `isCollisionWithMapLayer()`, in that we will walk through every rectangle on the portal layer checking for collisions with the player's hitbox. The primary difference is that if a player walks over these special areas on the map, then an event will be triggered letting us know that the player has activated the portal. When portal activation occurs, we will first cache the closest player spawn in the `MapManager` class. This will help when we transition out from the new location, back to the current location. Then, we will load the new map designated by the portal activation name, reset the player position, and set the new map to be rendered in the next frame.

Implementing map management with spawn points and a portal system

The next class represented in our top-level class diagram is `MapManager`, which can be found at `core/src/com/packtpub/libgdx/bludbourne/MapManager.java`. This class has helper methods for loading the `TiledMap` maps, as well as methods for accessing the different `MapLayer`, and `MapObject` objects in the layers.

MapManager

A class diagram that outlines the different attributes and helper methods is represented by the following diagram (*Figure 10*):

```
                    MapManager
                  (from MapManager)
---------------------------------------------------------
-TAG: String {readOnly}
-_mapTable: Hashtable
-_playerStartLocationTable: Hashtable
-TOP_WORLD: String = "TOP_WORLD" {readOnly}
-TOWN: String = "TOWN" {readOnly}
-CASTLE_OF_DOOM: String = "CASTLE_OF_DOOM" {readOnly}
-MAP_COLLISION_LAYER: String = "MAP_COLLISION_LAYER" {readOnly}
-MAP_SPAWNS_LAYER: String = "MAP_SPAWNS_LAYER" {readOnly}
-MAP_PORTAL_LAYER: String = "MAP_PORTAL_LAYER" {readOnly}
-PLAYER_START: String = "PLAYER_START" {readOnly}
-_playerStartPositionRect: Vector2
-_closestPlayerStartPosition: Vector2
-_convertedUnits: Vector2
-_playerStart: Vector2
-_currentMap: TiledMap = null
-_currentMapName: String
-_collisionLayer: MapLayer = null
-_portalLayer: MapLayer = null
-_spawnsLayer: MapLayer = null
+UNIT_SCALE: float {readOnly}
---------------------------------------------------------
«constructor»+MapManager()
+loadMap(mapName: String): void
+getCurrentMap(): TiledMap
+getCollisionLayer(): MapLayer
+getPortalLayer(): MapLayer
+getPlayerStartUnitScaled(): Vector2
-setClosestStartPosition(position: Vector2): void
+setClosestStartPositionFromScaledUnits(position: Vector2): void
```

Figure 10

The import classes are as follows:

```
package com.packtpub.libgdx.bludbourne;

import com.badlogic.gdx.Gdx;
import com.badlogic.gdx.maps.MapLayer;
import com.badlogic.gdx.maps.MapObject;
import com.badlogic.gdx.maps.objects.RectangleMapObject;
import com.badlogic.gdx.maps.tiled.TiledMap;
import com.badlogic.gdx.math.*;


import java.util.Hashtable;
```

We are going to be using `TiledMap` (TMX format) maps that will then be rendered to a `Screen` instance using the `OrthogonalTiledMapRenderer` class in the render thread. Each map contains several `MapLayer` objects that are ordered with a 0-based index. In the future, we will be drawing the `MapLayer` objects by first querying them by name and then drawing them from the background up to the foreground `MapLayer`. We have the other `MapLayer` objects (object layers in Tiled) that will not be rendered, but contain the `MapObject` objects (or more specifically `RectangleMapObjects`) used to test for collisions, portal triggers, and player spawns. We can also see how the viewport only renders a portion of the total map (depending on the units used when setting the width and height dimensions of the viewport).

We are also going to store state information regarding the player start position and the current player position using the `Vector2` class. This class is a convenience class from the LibGDX math library that represents a 2D vector that we can use for position information:

```
public class MapManager {
    private static final String TAG = MapManager.
      class.getSimpleName();

    //All maps for the game
    private Hashtable<String,String> _mapTable;
    private Hashtable<String, Vector2> _playerStartLocationTable;

    //maps
    private final static String TOP_WORLD = "TOP_WORLD";
    private final static String TOWN = "TOWN";
    private final static String CASTLE_OF_DOOM = "CASTLE_OF_DOOM";

    //Map layers
    private final static String MAP_COLLISION_LAYER =
      "MAP_COLLISION_LAYER";
    private final static String MAP_SPAWNS_LAYER =
      "MAP_SPAWNS_LAYER";
    private final static String MAP_PORTAL_LAYER =
      "MAP_PORTAL_LAYER";

    private final static String PLAYER_START = "PLAYER_START";

    private Vector2 _playerStartPositionRect;
```

```
    private Vector2 _closestPlayerStartPosition;
    private Vector2 _convertedUnits;

    private Vector2 _playerStart;
    private TiledMap _currentMap = null;
    private String _currentMapName;
    private MapLayer _collisionLayer = null;
    private MapLayer _portalLayer = null;
    private MapLayer _spawnsLayer = null;

    public final static float UNIT_SCALE  = 1/16f;

    public MapManager(){
        _playerStart = new Vector2(0,0);
        _mapTable = new Hashtable();

        _mapTable.put(TOP_WORLD, "maps/topworld.tmx");
        _mapTable.put(TOWN, "maps/town.tmx");
        _mapTable.put(CASTLE_OF_DOOM, "maps/castle_of_doom.tmx");

        _playerStartLocationTable = new Hashtable();
        _playerStartLocationTable.put(TOP_WORLD,
          _playerStart.cpy());
        _playerStartLocationTable.put(TOWN, _playerStart.cpy());
        _playerStartLocationTable.put(CASTLE_OF_DOOM,
          _playerStart.cpy());

        _playerStartPositionRect = new Vector2(0,0);
        _closestPlayerStartPosition = new Vector2(0,0);
        _convertedUnits = new Vector2(0,0);
    }
}
```

For this iteration of the `MapManager` class, we are going to have two primary containers for managing the maps. The first container is a `Hashtable` for storing the relative paths to the actual TMX files located under the assets directory. The keys used for the hashing will be static strings defined by `MapManager`. These strings will also be used in the name properties of the TMX maps, so we need to make sure that the strings match. The second container is also a `Hashtable` that will be used for caching the closest player spawn point in the current loaded map. The keys used for the hashing will be the same static strings defined by `MapManager`.

The reason why we need these cached values will be explained further down:

```
public void loadMap(String mapName){
    _playerStart.set(0,0);

    String mapFullPath = _mapTable.get(mapName);

    if( mapFullPath == null || mapFullPath.isEmpty() ) {
        Gdx.app.debug(TAG, "Map is invalid");
        return;
    }

    if( _currentMap != null ){
        _currentMap.dispose();
    }

    Utility.loadMapAsset(mapFullPath);
    if( Utility.isAssetLoaded(mapFullPath) ) {
        _currentMap = Utility.getMapAsset(mapFullPath);
        _currentMapName = mapName;
    }else{
        Gdx.app.debug(TAG, "Map not loaded");
        return;
    }

    _collisionLayer = _currentMap.getLayers().
      get(MAP_COLLISION_LAYER);
    if( _collisionLayer == null ){
        Gdx.app.debug(TAG, "No collision layer!");
    }

    _portalLayer = _currentMap.getLayers().
      get(MAP_PORTAL_LAYER);
    if( _portalLayer == null ){
        Gdx.app.debug(TAG, "No portal layer!");
    }

    _spawnsLayer = _currentMap.getLayers().
      get(MAP_SPAWNS_LAYER);
```

```
        if( _spawnsLayer == null ){
            Gdx.app.debug(TAG, "No spawn layer!");
        }else{
            Vector2 start = _playerStartLocationTable.
              get(_currentMapName);
            if( start.isZero() ){
                setClosestStartPosition(_playerStart);
                start = _playerStartLocationTable.
                  get(_currentMapName);
            }
            _playerStart.set(start.x, start.y);
        }

        Gdx.app.debug(TAG, "Player Start: (" + _playerStart.x +
          "," + _playerStart.y + ")");
    }
```

The loadMap() method is a straightforward helper method that verifies that the
string passed in is a valid path and checks to see whether the asset exists; if it does,
it loads it. At this point, we copy the object references of the different layers for fast
access later, such as the collision layer, portal layer, and spawn layer. One item of
note is near the end, we check to see whether the starting location is set to *(0, 0)*. If it
is, we know that we have not cached a player location yet, meaning that this is the
first time we have loaded this map. At this point, we will cache a location closest to
this starting position:

```
    public TiledMap getCurrentMap(){
        if( _currentMap == null ) {
            _currentMapName = TOWN;
            loadMap(_currentMapName);
        }
        return _currentMap;
    }

    public MapLayer getCollisionLayer(){
        return _collisionLayer;
    }

    public MapLayer getPortalLayer(){
```

```
        return _portalLayer;
    }


    public Vector2 getPlayerStartUnitScaled(){
        Vector2 playerStart = _playerStart.cpy();
        playerStart.set(_playerStart.x * UNIT_SCALE,
          _playerStart.y * UNIT_SCALE);
        return playerStart;
    }
```

One item to keep note of in the getPlayerStartUnitScaled() method is that
when we set a player start location from the MapObject, the location will be in pixel
coordinates. We need to convert these coordinates to unit coordinates so that when this
method is called, the character will start in the correct location using the map units:

```
private void setClosestStartPosition(final Vector2 position){
    //Get last known position on this map
    _playerStartPositionRect.set(0,0);
    _closestPlayerStartPosition.set(0,0);
    float shortestDistance = 0f;

    //Go through all player start positions and choose closest to
    //last known position
    for( MapObject object: _spawnsLayer.getObjects()){
        if( object.getName().equalsIgnoreCase(PLAYER_START) ){
                ((RectangleMapObject)object).getRectangle().
                    getPosition(_playerStartPositionRect);
            float distance = position.dst2(_playerStartPositionRect);

            if( distance < shortestDistance ||
                shortestDistance == 0 ){
                        _closestPlayerStartPosition.set(
                        _playerStartPositionRect);
                    shortestDistance = distance;
            }
        }
    }
}
```

```
        _playerStartLocationTable.put(
        _currentMapName, _closestPlayerStartPosition.cpy());
}
```

The `setClosestStartPosition()` method will cache the closest spawn location to the player on the current map. This is used when the portal activation occurs in order to start the player in the correct location when transitioning out of the new location, back to the previous location. For instance, there are two player start locations on the TOP_WORLD map. One player's start spawn is near the village represented by the TOWN map, and the other one is outside the enemy's castle, represented by the CASTLE_OF_DOOM map. In order to resolve the ambiguity of which *player start* location we should choose, we call this method when we are transitioning to another location. So, if you enter the enemy castle and then leave, you will start at the player start spawn outside the castle because when you first entered the castle, this player start spawn was the closest to your location at that time.

Also, note that we used the `dst2()` method from the `Vector2` class because, in general, when checking distances between objects, we only care about the relative distance, not the absolute distance. In order to get the absolute distance, we would need to take the square root of the value, and in general, this is an expensive operation. Small performance choices like this can add up to a large benefit throughout your game:

```
public void setClosestStartPositionFromScaledUnits(
  Vector2 position){
        if( UNIT_SCALE <= 0 )
            return;

        _convertedUnits.set(position.x/UNIT_SCALE,
          position.y/UNIT_SCALE);
        setClosestStartPosition(_convertedUnits);
    }
}
```

The `setClosestStartPositionFromScaledUnits()` method is a helper method that wraps `setClosestStartPosition()` so that we can map the unit coordinate location back into pixel coordinate space used in the map.

Implementing your player character with animation

The next class that we will look at in our class diagram hierarchy is the `Entity` class that can be found at `core/src/com/packtpub/libgdx/bludbourne/Entity.java`. The `Entity` class represents the primary game object, including the player character and **non-playable characters** (**NPCs**), which can move around in the world and interact with their environment.

Entity

The following class diagram demonstrates the relevant attributes and methods that we are going to use for this chapter (*Figure 11*):

Figure 11

We will discuss some of the imports from the source code of `Entity`:

```
package com.packtpub.libgdx.bludbourne;

import java.util.UUID;

import com.badlogic.gdx.Gdx;
import com.badlogic.gdx.graphics.Texture;
import com.badlogic.gdx.graphics.g2d.Animation;
import com.badlogic.gdx.graphics.g2d.Sprite;
import com.badlogic.gdx.graphics.g2d.TextureRegion;
import com.badlogic.gdx.math.Rectangle;
import com.badlogic.gdx.math.Vector2;
import com.badlogic.gdx.utils.Array;
```

First, `TextureRegion` will be used throughout the creation of the game and will be the primary container for using image assets. The `TextureRegion` class is analogous to using a sprite (`TextureRegion`) from a sprite sheet (`Texture`). The following screenshot (*Figure 12*) visually outlines how the `TextureRegion` class can be used:

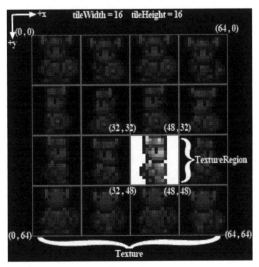

Figure 12

When we load an image asset, we will be storing the image asset as a `Texture` object in the `AssetManager` class by using the `loadTextureAsset()` and `getTextureAsset()` helper methods from our `Utility` class. The `Texture` object will include the entire image consisting of 16 different sprites. In order to reference a specific sprite (for rendering), `TextureRegion` can be used to get access to a subregion of the `Texture` object.

Second, the `Animation` class is another one that deserves a little more detailed explanation. The `Animation` class is described visually in the following screenshot (*Figure 13*):

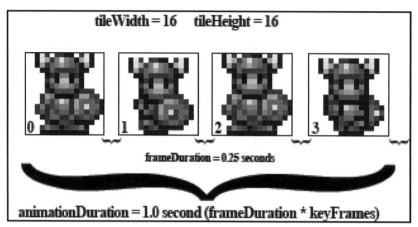

Figure 13

Whenever we construct an `Animation` object, we will be passing in the frame duration, the `TextureRegion` references, and the type of loop used in animating these `TextureRegion`. Each `TextureRegion` is an indexed keyframe that represents one frame in the animation cycle. An animation is composed of cycling over the keyframes for the full animation duration. Depending on your individual needs, there are various types of play loops that can be configured, such as playing the keyframes once in order, backwards, continuously, or in a random order. The frame duration is going to be the time between frames representing how long each frame will be displayed for, in seconds. In our figure, each frame duration lasts a quarter of one second or 0.25. A full play loop through all four keyframes will give us a total animation cycle of one second. Figuring out the exact frame duration is a little more art than science, depending on how you want the character to feel when moving around in a game:

```
public class Entity {

    private static final String TAG = Entity.class.getSimpleName();
    private static final String _defaultSpritePath =
        "sprites/characters/Warrior.png";

    private Vector2 _velocity;
    private String _entityID;

    private Direction _currentDirection = Direction.LEFT;
    private Direction _previousDirection = Direction.UP;

    private Animation _walkLeftAnimation;
    private Animation _walkRightAnimation;
```

```
private Animation _walkUpAnimation;
private Animation _walkDownAnimation;

private Array<TextureRegion> _walkLeftFrames;
private Array<TextureRegion> _walkRightFrames;
private Array<TextureRegion> _walkUpFrames;
private Array<TextureRegion> _walkDownFrames;

protected Vector2 _nextPlayerPosition;
protected Vector2 _currentPlayerPosition;
protected State _state = State.IDLE;
protected float _frameTime = 0f;
protected Sprite _frameSprite = null;
protected TextureRegion _currentFrame = null;

public final int FRAME_WIDTH = 16;
public final int FRAME_HEIGHT = 16;
public static Rectangle boundingBox;

public enum State {
  IDLE, WALKING
}

public enum Direction {
  UP,RIGHT,DOWN,LEFT;
}

public Entity(){
  initEntity();
}

public void initEntity(){
  this._entityID = UUID.randomUUID().toString();
  this._nextPlayerPosition = new Vector2();
  this._currentPlayerPosition = new Vector2();
  this.boundingBox = new Rectangle();
  this._velocity = new Vector2(2f,2f);

  Utility.loadTextureAsset(_defaultSpritePath);
  loadDefaultSprite();
  loadAllAnimations();
}

public void update(float delta){
```

```
    _frameTime = (_frameTime + delta)%5; //Want to avoid overflow

    //We want the hitbox to be at the feet for a better feel
    setBoundingBoxSize(0f, 0.5f);
}
```

This `update()` method will be called on any game object entity before it is rendered. One of the states we need to maintain for smooth animation cycles is `frameTime`, which is simply the accumulation of the deltas between frame updates. This allows the animation to account for changes in the frame rate of the game. One quick note is that depending on how long the game is playing, we don't want to have a value increasing for the entire lifetime of the game since there is the potential for an overflow. One simple solution is to mod the value to 5, essentially resetting the value every five seconds:

```
public void init(float startX, float startY){
    this._currentPlayerPosition.x = startX;
    this._currentPlayerPosition.y = startY;

    this._nextPlayerPosition.x = startX;
    this._nextPlayerPosition.y = startY;
}
public void setBoundingBoxSize(float percentageWidthReduced,
    float percentageHeightReduced){
    //Update the current bounding box
    float width;
    float height;

    float widthReductionAmount = 1.0f - percentageWidthReduced;
        //.8f for 20% (1 - .20)
    float heightReductionAmount = 1.0f - percentageHeightReduced;
        //.8f for 20% (1 - .20)

    if( widthReductionAmount > 0 && widthReductionAmount < 1){
        width = FRAME_WIDTH * widthReductionAmount;
    } else{
        width = FRAME_WIDTH;
    }

    if( heightReductionAmount > 0 && heightReductionAmount < 1){
        height = FRAME_HEIGHT * heightReductionAmount;
    } else{
```

```
      height = FRAME_HEIGHT;
    }

    if( width == 0 || height == 0){
      Gdx.app.debug(TAG, "Width and Height are 0!! " + width +
        ":" + height);
    }

    //Need to account for the unitscale, since the map coordinates
      will be in pixels
    float minX;
    float minY;
    if( MapManager.UNIT_SCALE > 0 ) {
      minX = _nextPlayerPosition.x / MapManager.UNIT_SCALE;
      minY = _nextPlayerPosition.y / MapManager.UNIT_SCALE;
    } else{
      minX = _nextPlayerPosition.x;
      minY = _nextPlayerPosition.y;
    }

    boundingBox.set(minX, minY, width, height);
  }
```

The `setBoundingBoxSize()` method allows us to customize the hitbox for the different entities. In our case, we currently only use this for our player character in the game. Based on the tileset graphics, the default area of the hitbox for the player is the width and height of the sprite. This could cause issues when trying to traverse through forested areas with collision rectangles spread about, as well as when blocking the player from moving along the bottom of mountain ranges or on the top of lakes in the game. One solution is to reduce the height of the hitbox to half, which gives us a hitbox of a rectangle from the waist to the bottom of the character. This allows a better feeling movement of the player and also looks much better when moving through obstacles:

```
private void loadDefaultSprite()
{
  Texture texture = Utility.getTextureAsset(_defaultSpritePath);
  TextureRegion[][] textureFrames = TextureRegion.split(texture,
    FRAME_WIDTH, FRAME_HEIGHT);
  _frameSprite = new Sprite(textureFrames[0][0].getTexture(),
    0,0,FRAME_WIDTH, FRAME_HEIGHT);
```

```
      _currentFrame = textureFrames[0][0];
  }

 private void loadAllAnimations(){
    //Walking animation
    Texture texture = Utility.getTextureAsset
      (_defaultSpritePath);
    TextureRegion[][] textureFrames = TextureRegion.split
      (texture, FRAME_WIDTH, FRAME_HEIGHT);
    _walkDownFrames = new Array<TextureRegion>(4);
    _walkLeftFrames = new Array<TextureRegion>(4);
    _walkRightFrames = new Array<TextureRegion>(4);
    _walkUpFrames = new Array<TextureRegion>(4);

    for (int i = 0; i < 4; i++) {
      for (int j = 0; j < 4; j++) {
        TextureRegion region = textureFrames[i][j];
        if( region == null ){
          Gdx.app.debug(TAG, "Got null animation frame " + i +
            "," + j);
        }
        switch(i)
        {
          case 0:
            _walkDownFrames.insert(j, region);
            break;
          case 1:
            _walkLeftFrames.insert(j, region);
            break;
          case 2:
            _walkRightFrames.insert(j, region);
            break;
          case 3:
            _walkUpFrames.insert(j, region);
            break;
        }
      }
    }

    _walkDownAnimation = new Animation(0.25f, _walkDownFrames,
      Animation.PlayMode.LOOP);
    _walkLeftAnimation = new Animation(0.25f, _walkLeftFrames,
      Animation.PlayMode.LOOP);
```

```
   _walkRightAnimation = new Animation(0.25f, _walkRightFrames,
     Animation.PlayMode.LOOP);
   _walkUpAnimation = new Animation(0.25f, _walkUpFrames,
     Animation.PlayMode.LOOP);
}
```

The loadAnimation() method should only be called when first instantiating the
entity objects. For this iteration of our game, we can assume that the sprite sheets
for the player character animation will look like *Figure 12*. The Texture will include
the entire image consisting of 16 different sprites, each row representing a different
direction animation of four frames, including walking down, walking to the left,
walking to the right, and walking up. When we want to use the individual sprites,
we can call the split() static method in the TextureRegion class by passing in the
Texture and the width and height dimensions representing one sprite. We will then
get back an array of TextureRegion objects that represent the individual keyframes
for the animation. We can render these objects since each TextureRegion references
a specific subregion of the Texture. We can then take these arrays of TextureRegion
objects and create four Animation objects, for each of the four cardinal directions:

```
public void dispose(){
   Utility.unloadAsset(_defaultSpritePath);
}

public void setState(State state){
   this._state = state;
}

public Sprite getFrameSprite(){
   return _frameSprite;
}

public TextureRegion getFrame(){
   return _currentFrame;
}

public Vector2 getCurrentPosition(){
   return _currentPlayerPosition;
}

public void setCurrentPosition(float currentPositionX, float
   currentPositionY){
   _frameSprite.setX(currentPositionX);
   _frameSprite.setY(currentPositionY);
```

```
    this._currentPlayerPosition.x = currentPositionX;
    this._currentPlayerPosition.y = currentPositionY;
}

public void setDirection(Direction direction,  float
  deltaTime){
  this._previousDirection = this._currentDirection;
  this._currentDirection = direction;

  //Look into the appropriate variable when changing position

  switch (_currentDirection) {
  case DOWN :
    _currentFrame = _walkDownAnimation.getKeyFrame(_frameTime);
    break;
  case LEFT :
    _currentFrame = _walkLeftAnimation.getKeyFrame(_frameTime);
    break;
  case UP :
    _currentFrame = _walkUpAnimation.getKeyFrame(_frameTime);
    break;
  case RIGHT :
    _currentFrame = _walkRightAnimation.
      getKeyFrame(_frameTime);
    break;
  default:
    break;
  }
}
```

The setDirection() method deals with updating the animation keyframes based on our current cardinal direction. This method will be called every time we process input from the event queue. During every frame of the render loop, the current TextureRegion frame that represents the player character will be retrieved and rendered. Based on the current facing direction, this method will guarantee that the proper frame is set at that time:

```
public void setNextPositionToCurrent(){
  setCurrentPosition(_nextPlayerPosition.x,
    _nextPlayerPosition.y);
}

public void calculateNextPosition(Direction currentDirection,
  float deltaTime){
```

```
        float testX = _currentPlayerPosition.x;
        float testY = _currentPlayerPosition.y;

        _velocity.scl(deltaTime);

        switch (currentDirection) {
        case LEFT :
          testX -= _velocity.x;
          break;
        case RIGHT :
          testX += _velocity.x;
          break;
        case UP :
          testY += _velocity.y;
          break;
        case DOWN :
          testY -= _velocity.y;
          break;
        default:
          break;
    }


      _nextPlayerPosition.x = testX;
      _nextPlayerPosition.y = testY;

      //velocity
      _velocity.scl(1 / deltaTime);
    }
  }
```

The `calculateNextPosition()` method is called every time that player input is detected. Sometimes, collisions are not detected during a frame update because the velocity value is too fast to be calculated in the current frame. By the time the next frame checks the collision, the game objects have already passed through each other. Basically, this method represents one technique to deal with collisions between two moving objects in the game world. We are going to "look ahead" and predict what the next position value will be by using our current velocity and the time to render the last frame. By multiplying the current velocity vector, `_velocity`, and by the `deltaTime` scalar quantity using the `scl()` method, we get a value that represents the distance we would travel (displacement). We add or subtract this distance to our next position based upon our direction. If this new position collides with an object, then it is not set to our current position. Otherwise, we will use that value as our current position.

Implementing input handling for player character movement

Our final class that we need to implement for this chapter is `PlayerController`. `PlayerController` is responsible for handling all of the input events and providing mechanisms to process these events in the queue. This class can be found at `core/src/com/packtpub/libgdx/bludbourne/PlayerController.java`.

PlayerController

A class diagram of this class is shown in the following screenshot (*Figure 14*):

Figure 14

The source for `PlayerController` is listed here:

```
package com.packtpub.libgdx.bludbourne;

import java.util.HashMap;
import java.util.Map;

import com.badlogic.gdx.Gdx;
import com.badlogic.gdx.Input;
import com.badlogic.gdx.InputProcessor;
import com.badlogic.gdx.math.Vector3;
```

`InputProcessor` is an interface that you should implement in order to process input events such as mouse cursor location changes, mouse button presses, and keyboard key presses from the input event handler. Your game will usually instantiate this class and set it in the environment class, `Gdx`, so that you can process the input events every frame:

```
public class PlayerController implements InputProcessor {

    private final static String TAG = PlayerController.
      class.getSimpleName();

    enum Keys {
      LEFT, RIGHT, UP, DOWN, QUIT
    }

    enum Mouse {
      SELECT, DOACTION
    }

    private static Map<Keys, Boolean> keys = new HashMap
      <PlayerController.Keys, Boolean>();
    private static Map<Mouse, Boolean> mouseButtons = new HashMap
      <PlayerController.Mouse, Boolean>();
    private Vector3 lastMouseCoordinates;

    //initialize the hashmap for inputs
    static {
      keys.put(Keys.LEFT, false);
      keys.put(Keys.RIGHT, false);
      keys.put(Keys.UP, false);
      keys.put(Keys.DOWN, false);
```

```
        keys.put(Keys.QUIT, false);
    };

    static {
      mouseButtons.put(Mouse.SELECT, false);
      mouseButtons.put(Mouse.DOACTION, false);
    };

    private Entity _player;

    public PlayerController(Entity player){
        this.lastMouseCoordinates = new Vector3();
        this._player = player;
    }

    @Override
    public boolean keyDown(int keycode) {
      if( keycode == Input.Keys.LEFT || keycode == Input.Keys.A){
        this.leftPressed();
      }
      if( keycode == Input.Keys.RIGHT || keycode == Input.Keys.D){
        this.rightPressed();
      }
      if( keycode == Input.Keys.UP || keycode == Input.Keys.W){
        this.upPressed();
      }
      if( keycode == Input.Keys.DOWN || keycode == Input.Keys.S){
        this.downPressed();
      }
      if( keycode == Input.Keys.Q){
        this.quitPressed();
      }

      return true;
    }

    @Override
    public boolean keyUp(int keycode) {
      if( keycode == Input.Keys.LEFT || keycode == Input.Keys.A){
        this.leftReleased();
      }
      if( keycode == Input.Keys.RIGHT || keycode == Input.Keys.D){
        this.rightReleased();
      }
```

```
    if( keycode == Input.Keys.UP || keycode == Input.Keys.W ){
      this.upReleased();
    }
    if( keycode == Input.Keys.DOWN || keycode == Input.Keys.S){
      this.downReleased();
    }
    if( keycode == Input.Keys.Q){
      this.quitReleased();
    }
    return true;
}
```

The keyDown() and keyUp() pair of methods will process specific key presses and releases, respectively, by caching them in a Hashtable object. This allows us to process the input later, without losing keyboard key press or release events and appropriately removing redundant key events from the queue:

```
@Override
public boolean keyTyped(char character) {
  return false;
}

@Override
public boolean touchDown(int screenX, int screenY, int pointer,
  int button) {

  if( button == Input.Buttons.LEFT || button ==
    Input.Buttons.RIGHT ){
    this.setClickedMouseCoordinates(screenX, screenY);
  }

  //left is selection, right is context menu
  if( button == Input.Buttons.LEFT){
    this.selectMouseButtonPressed(screenX, screenY);
  }
  if( button == Input.Buttons.RIGHT){
    this.doActionMouseButtonPressed(screenX, screenY);
  }
  return true;
}

@Override
public boolean touchUp(int screenX, int screenY, int pointer,
  int button) {
  //left is selection, right is context menu
```

```
    if( button == Input.Buttons.LEFT){
      this.selectMouseButtonReleased(screenX, screenY);
    }
    if( button == Input.Buttons.RIGHT){
      this.doActionMouseButtonReleased(screenX, screenY);
    }
    return true;
}
```

The `touchDown()` and `touchUp()` pair of methods will process specific mouse button presses and releases, respectively, by caching the position in a `Hashtable` object. This allows us to process the input later, without losing mouse button press or release events and appropriately removing redundant mouse press events from the queue:

```
@Override
public boolean touchDragged(int screenX, int screenY, int
  pointer) {
  return false;
}

@Override
public boolean mouseMoved(int screenX, int screenY) {
  return false;
}

@Override
public boolean scrolled(int amount) {
  return false;
}

public void dispose(){

}

//Key presses
public void leftPressed(){
  keys.put(Keys.LEFT, true);
}

public void rightPressed(){
  keys.put(Keys.RIGHT, true);
}

public void upPressed(){
  keys.put(Keys.UP, true);
```

```
    }

    public void downPressed(){
      keys.put(Keys.DOWN, true);
    }
    public void quitPressed(){
      keys.put(Keys.QUIT, true);
    }

    public void setClickedMouseCoordinates(int x, int y){
      lastMouseCoordinates.set(x, y, 0);
    }

    public void selectMouseButtonPressed(int x, int y){
      mouseButtons.put(Mouse.SELECT, true);
    }

    public void doActionMouseButtonPressed(int x, int y){
      mouseButtons.put(Mouse.DOACTION, true);
    }

    //Releases

    public void leftReleased(){
      keys.put(Keys.LEFT, false);
    }

    public void rightReleased(){
      keys.put(Keys.RIGHT, false);
    }

    public void upReleased(){
      keys.put(Keys.UP, false);
    }

    public void downReleased(){
      keys.put(Keys.DOWN, false);
    }

    public void quitReleased(){
      keys.put(Keys.QUIT, false);
    }

    public void selectMouseButtonReleased(int x, int y){
```

```
      mouseButtons.put(Mouse.SELECT, false);
   }

   public void doActionMouseButtonReleased(int x, int y){
      mouseButtons.put(Mouse.DOACTION, false);
   }


   public void update(float delta){
      processInput(delta);
   }

   public static void hide(){
      keys.put(Keys.LEFT, false);
      keys.put(Keys.RIGHT, false);
      keys.put(Keys.UP, false);
      keys.put(Keys.DOWN, false);
      keys.put(Keys.QUIT, false);
   }

   private void processInput(float delta){

      //Keyboard input
      if( keys.get(Keys.LEFT)){
        _player.calculateNextPosition(Entity.Direction.LEFT,
          delta);
        _player.setState(Entity.State.WALKING);
        _player.setDirection(Entity.Direction.LEFT, delta);
      } else if( keys.get(Keys.RIGHT)){
        _player.calculateNextPosition(Entity.Direction.RIGHT,
          delta);
        _player.setState(Entity.State.WALKING);
        _player.setDirection(Entity.Direction.RIGHT, delta);
      } else if( keys.get(Keys.UP)){
        _player.calculateNextPosition(Entity.Direction.UP, delta);
        _player.setState(Entity.State.WALKING);
        _player.setDirection(Entity.Direction.UP, delta);
      } else if(keys.get(Keys.DOWN)){
        _player.calculateNextPosition(Entity.Direction.DOWN,
          delta);
        _player.setState(Entity.State.WALKING);
        _player.setDirection(Entity.Direction.DOWN, delta);
      } else if(keys.get(Keys.QUIT)){
        Gdx.app.exit();
```

```
    } else{
      _player.setState(Entity.State.IDLE);
    }

    //Mouse input
    if( mouseButtons.get(Mouse.SELECT)) {
      mouseButtons.put(Mouse.SELECT, false);
    }
  }
}
```

The `processInput()` method is the primary business logic that drives this class. During the beginning of every frame in the render loop, `processInput()` will be called before rendering any graphics. This will be where the cached values of the keyboard and mouse input will be processed. We will first calculate the next position, as explained in the previous section, in order to avoid issues with two fast-moving game objects colliding and missing a collision check. Then, we set the state and direction of the player character during this time.

Summary

In this chapter, we were able to start creating the foundation for our game and actually see some real progress with moving around the world of *BludBourne*. We first learned about tile-based maps and how to create them with the Tiled editor. We then learned about the high-level architecture of the classes we would create for this chapter and implemented starter classes that allowed us to hook into the LibGDX application lifecycle. After that, we learned about textures, TMX formatted tile maps, and how to manage them with the asset manager. We then learned how the orthographic camera works within our game and how to display the map within the render loop. We implemented a map manager that dealt with collision layers, spawn points, and a portal system that allowed us to transition between different locations seamlessly. Finally, we implemented a player character with animation cycles and input handling for moving around the game map.

In the next chapter, we will begin to populate our world with NPCs, including implementing their movements, handling collisions between game objects, and adding player NPC selection capabilities.

3
It's Pretty Lonely in BludBourne…

Now that we have begun to create some map locations and started to navigate through our world using our player character, we can start to plan out how we are going to populate this world with NPCs.

We will cover the following topics in this chapter:

- The **Entity Component System (ECS)** design pattern
- Using JSON scripts for defining NPC properties
- Physics component with entity collision handling
- Selecting NPCs for an interaction with the input component
- Overall map design

Following the standard **object oriented design (OOD)** methodologies, we could just use the Entity class that we created as the base class for all in-game characters, including NPCs and enemies. The reality with this standard approach is that we will usually end up with a massive base class that tries to do everything, including wide and deep hierarchies that become difficult to manage. One disastrous side-effect is that when one tries to change one small property in the base class, the effects can ripple out, touching every game object without knowing the total ramifications of the change until play testing.

One possible solution to this problem is that instead of using inheritance to model the game objects in our world, we can use composition that gives us much more flexibility and adaptability for future changes. This decoupling approach requires a refactoring of the original Entity class, including parceling out core logic into its component parts. Hopefully, using the original Entity class as a starting place and following the modifications in this chapter will give better insight into why these changes are useful.

The following screenshot (*Figure 1*) demonstrates the final result of this chapter with populating the town map with varying NPCs:

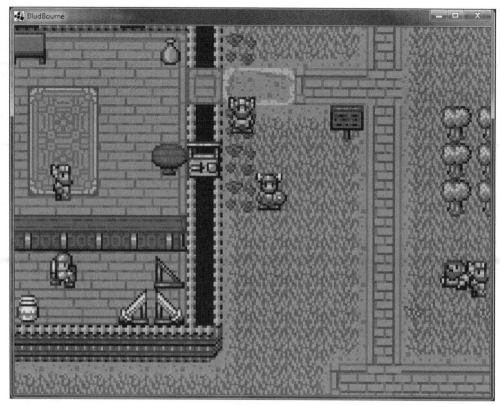

Figure 1

The Entity Component System design pattern

The model that we are going to implement for our game objects is typically referred to as the Entity Component System, which is a pattern that uses composition over inheritance to manage the game objects. The entity defined in ECS is a general purpose object that contains some unique ID and is a container for all the components. The component defined in ECS determines how the entity interacts with the world and owns its own domain, such as physics, graphic updates, or input handling. Finally, the system defined in ECS determines how the entity and its constituent components get updated throughout the lifetime of the game. As a quick note, this pattern is discussed in much more detail in *Game Programming Patterns by Robert Nystrom* under the *Component* chapter.

Like most design decisions in software development, the ECS model doesn't come without its own host of tradeoffs. One issue is since these entities are now composed of different components without any common base class, how do these different components communicate with each other? In this chapter, we will discuss one solution that includes creating a messaging system across all components. Another issue is the cost of iterating through all entities for updates. For a video game, we would need to consider the cost of iterating through all entities that interact with the game world anyways. One solution discussed in this chapter is to only load those entities specific to the map (from a cache if previously loaded) currently loaded in order to minimize the amount of entities to update.

The following class diagram (*Figure 2*) describes our refactored architecture that uses the ECS pattern for our game:

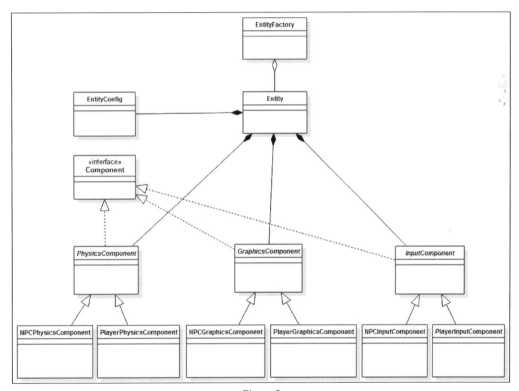

Figure 2

The first class at the top of our hierarchy is the `EntityFactory` class that instantiates and returns the `Entity` objects specified by the `EntityType` enum passed into the static factory method `getEntity()`. The source for `EntityFactory`, which can be found at `core/src/com/packtpub/libgdx/bludbourne/EntityFactory.java`, relative to the current project directory for this chapter, is as follows:

```java
package com.packtpub.libgdx.bludbourne;

import com.badlogic.gdx.utils.Json;

public class EntityFactory {

    private static Json _json = new Json();

    public static enum EntityType{
        PLAYER,
        DEMO_PLAYER,
        NPC
    }

    public static String PLAYER_CONFIG = "scripts/player.json";

    static public Entity getEntity(EntityType entityType){
        Entity entity = null;
        switch(entityType){
            case PLAYER:
                entity = new Entity(
                    new PlayerInputComponent(),
                    new PlayerPhysicsComponent(),
                    new PlayerGraphicsComponent());
                entity.setEntityConfig(
                    Entity.getEntityConfig(
                        EntityFactory.PLAYER_CONFIG));
                entity.sendMessage(
                    Component.MESSAGE.LOAD_ANIMATIONS,
                        _json.toJson(entity.getEntityConfig()));
                return entity;
            case DEMO_PLAYER:
                entity = new Entity(
                    new NPCInputComponent(),
                    new PlayerPhysicsComponent(),
                    new PlayerGraphicsComponent());
                return entity;
            case NPC:
                entity = new Entity(
                    new NPCInputComponent(),
```

```
                    new NPCPhysicsComponent(),
                    new NPCGraphicsComponent());
                return entity;
            default:
                return null;
        }
    }
}
```

`EntityFactory` provides a convenience for creating the different `Entity` objects defined by their components. One example of the usefulness for this class is that, if we were demonstrating the game at a kiosk, we could simply have a timer go off at the main menu screen, and instead of loading the PLAYER type, we could get an `Entity` type DEMO_PLAYER. The only difference between the PLAYER type and the DEMO_PLAYER type is that the DEMO_PLAYER type contains `NPCInputComponent` for input instead of the `PlayerInputComponent`. This means that the AI logic that controls the movement of NPCs would be used to move our player around the screen in a "demo" mode instead of waiting for user input. The flexibility with swapping out components and recombining them in order to yield different behaviors is just one of the many benefits using this model.

Using JSON scripts for NPC properties

The only piece of `EntityFactory` left to discuss is the inclusion of the `Json` class. **JavaScript Object Notation (JSON)** is a standard human-readable data format for transmitting data objects as attribute-value pairs. Despite its name, the JSON format is language-independent and is supported natively in LibGDX. For our game, we will be using scripts to load property information, instead of hardcoding specific values in the source code. The primary reason for using scripts is that we avoid recompiling the entire project every time one simple change is made. Rebuilding a project in order to test and evaluate properties is not an efficient use of time nor is it very flexible when testing features at runtime.

There are technologies available for scripting support. Our first option is to use Lua, a fast, lightweight, embeddable scripting language commonly used in video games. For the purposes of our game, we want to stick with a solution that has native support in LibGDX and is cross-platform without requiring third-party libraries. A second option would be to create a proprietary binary format that reads and writes the properties and loads them into objects, but this would be reinventing the wheel as well, using up resources to support this new format. Our third option would be to use XML, defining the tags and attributes of the properties, but we would end up with bloated property files given enough time. Finally, our fourth and best option is to use JSON since it is simpler to use than XML, especially for data exchange including object serialization and deserialization.

The following is an excerpt from `core/assets/scripts/player.json`, which demonstrates how a JSON-based file is structured:

```
{
entityID : PLAYER
state : IDLE
direction : DOWN
animationConfig: [
   {
      frameDuration: 0.25
      animationType: WALK_DOWN
      texturePaths: [
        sprites/characters/Warrior.png
      ]
      gridPoints: [
        {
          x: 0
          y: 0
        }

        {
          x: 0
          y: 1
        }
        {
            x: 0
          y: 2
        }
        {
            x: 0
          y: 3
        }
      ]
   }
 ]
}
```

The `player.json` configuration script is very readable with simple mappings between attributes and their corresponding values, including support for arrays that will come in handy later when referencing multiple objects in one file.

LibGDX handles all the complexities of JSON parsing and is set up to automatically serialize and deserialize objects without having to create customized readers and writers for JSON (a nice benefit of having Java Reflection). The only real requirement for using these convenience features in LibGDX is to create a very basic property bag class. This pattern is typically referred to as a **plain old Java object** (**POJO**), which is sometimes referred to in the Java ecosystem as a **JavaBean**. POJOs typically have a no argument constructor and allow access to the properties with getter and setter methods. This allows an object to easily be serialized to JSON and deserialized from JSON without any additional work.

An example of a POJO used when deserializing from JSON is the `EntityConfig` class that can be found at `core/src/com/packtpub/libgdx/bludbourne/EntityConfig.java`. The following class diagram (*Figure 3*) neatly outlines how the `EntityConfig` class will load the data from the `player.json` file with the basic setters and getters and using the member object names to map from the JSON file:

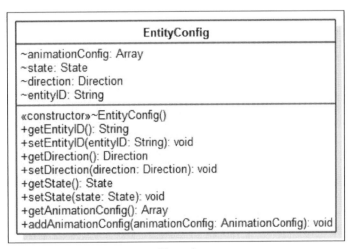

Figure 3

Entity

The next class in our hierarchy is `Entity`, which is the core shell class that binds the different components together and acts as the top-level container class that passes messages to all the components. The `Entity` class can be found at `core/src/com/packtpub/libgdx/bludbourne/Entity.java` and the source code is as follows:

```
package com.packtpub.libgdx.bludbourne;

import com.badlogic.gdx.Gdx;
import com.badlogic.gdx.graphics.g2d.Batch;
```

```java
import com.badlogic.gdx.math.MathUtils;
import com.badlogic.gdx.math.Rectangle;
import com.badlogic.gdx.math.Vector2;
import com.badlogic.gdx.utils.Json;
import com.badlogic.gdx.utils.Array;
import com.badlogic.gdx.utils.JsonValue;
import java.util.ArrayList;

public class Entity {
    private static final String TAG = Entity.class.getSimpleName();
    private Json _json;
    private EntityConfig _entityConfig;

    public static enum Direction {
        UP,
        RIGHT,
        DOWN,
        LEFT;

        static public Direction getRandomNext() {
            return Direction.values()[
                        MathUtils.random(Direction.values().length - 1)];
        }

        public Direction getOpposite() {
            if( this == LEFT){
                return RIGHT;
            }else if( this == RIGHT){
                return LEFT;
            }else if( this == UP){
                return DOWN;
            }else{
                return UP;
            }
        }
    }

    public static enum State {
        IDLE,
        WALKING,

        IMMOBILE;//This should always be last

        static public State getRandomNext() {
```

```
        //Ignore IMMOBILE which should be last state
        return State.values()[
                    MathUtils.random(State.values().length - 2)];
    }
}

public static enum AnimationType {
    WALK_LEFT,
    WALK_RIGHT,
    WALK_UP,
    WALK_DOWN,
    IDLE,
    IMMOBILE
}

public static final int FRAME_WIDTH = 16;
public static final int FRAME_HEIGHT = 16;

private static final int MAX_COMPONENTS = 5;
private Array<Component> _components;

private InputComponent _inputComponent;
private GraphicsComponent _graphicsComponent;
private PhysicsComponent _physicsComponent;
```

`Entity` contains not only the components that define the different aspects of its behavior, but also an `EntityConfig` object that is populated from its corresponding JSON properties file. There are a few state enums defined in `Entity` that are consistent across all the `Entity` objects, such as `Direction`, `State`, and `AnimationType`:

```
public Entity(InputComponent inputComponent, PhysicsComponent
    physicsComponent, GraphicsComponent graphicsComponent){
    _entityConfig = new EntityConfig();
    _json = new Json();

    _components = new Array<Component>(MAX_COMPONENTS);

    _inputComponent = inputComponent;
    _physicsComponent = physicsComponent;
    _graphicsComponent = graphicsComponent;

    _components.add(_inputComponent);
    _components.add(_physicsComponent);
```

```
        _components.add(_graphicsComponent);
    }

    public EntityConfig getEntityConfig() {
        return _entityConfig;
    }
```

Since `EntityFactory` defines the collection of components based on `EntityType`, we will pass in the assorted components to the `Entity` constructor, allocate and assign the object references, and finally store them in an `Array` container:

```
    public void sendMessage(Component.MESSAGE messageType, String ...
    args){
        String fullMessage = messageType.toString();

        for (String string : args) {
            fullMessage += Component.MESSAGE_TOKEN + string;
        }

        for(Component component: _components){
            component.receiveMessage(fullMessage);
        }
    }
```

The `sendMessage()` method will collect the `MessageType` to be used as a header for the message and then build the message string from the variable argument list passed in. This gives us flexibility when a message needs to get sent to the components without restricting us to one type of format. Each individual component can then decide which messages it cares about in the abstract method `receiveMessage()`, which each component needs to implement:

```
    public void update(MapManager mapMgr, Batch batch, float delta){
        _inputComponent.update(this, delta);
        _physicsComponent.update(this, mapMgr, delta);
        _graphicsComponent.update(this, mapMgr, batch, delta);
    }
```

The `update()` method simply passes the specific parameters to the relevant components on every frame update. This delegates all the responsibility for the most recent updates to the individual components:

```
    public void dispose(){
        for(Component component: _components){
```

```
        component.dispose();
    }
}
```

```
    public Rectangle getCurrentBoundingBox(){
        return _physicsComponent._boundingBox;
    }
```

This `getCurrentBoundingBox()` method returns the bounding box of the current entity used in collision detection. This is one of those situations where we don't want to cache the information in another component as it may be out of date by the time we access it, so instead we will provide this convenience method and access the bounding box directly. These are the type of tradeoffs we make in any design because usually there is no black and white separation between parts:

```
    public void setEntityConfig(EntityConfig entityConfig){
        this._entityConfig = entityConfig;
    }
```

```
    static public EntityConfig getEntityConfig(String
        configFilePath){
        Json json = new Json();
        return json.fromJson(EntityConfig.class,
                    Gdx.files.internal(configFilePath));
    }
```

The `getEntityConfig()` method will load the JSON script from disk and return the object reference to the `EntityConfig` object, if it exists:

```
    static public Array<EntityConfig> getEntityConfigs(String
        configFilePath){
        Json json = new Json();
        Array<EntityConfig> configs = new Array<EntityConfig>();

        ArrayList<JsonValue> list = json.fromJson(ArrayList.class,
                                Gdx.files.internal(configFilePath));

        for (JsonValue jsonVal : list) {
            configs.add(json.readValue(EntityConfig.class,
                    jsonVal));
        }

        return configs;
    }
}
```

The getEntityConfigs() method is a convenience method for returning a collection of EntityConfig objects from one JSON properties file. This proved convenient when defining the properties of a number of town-folk NPCs that walk around the TOWN map. We don't want to get lost dealing with scores of JSON files where every NPC is defined in a separate JSON file, especially if they don't have many differences between them. This method allows us to define any number of similar NPCs in one file. In our example, we define 15 town folk entities in one town_folk.json file.

Component interface

The next class in our hierarchy in *Figure 2* is the Component class, which provides the interface for all subsequent component classes. This class can be found at core/src/com/packtpub/libgdx/bludbourne/Component.java, and its source is defined as follows:

```java
package com.packtpub.libgdx.bludbourne;

public interface Component {

    public static final String MESSAGE_TOKEN = ":::::";

    public static enum MESSAGE{
        CURRENT_POSITION,
        INIT_START_POSITION,
        CURRENT_DIRECTION,
        CURRENT_STATE,
        COLLISION_WITH_MAP,
        COLLISION_WITH_ENTITY,
        LOAD_ANIMATIONS,
        INIT_DIRECTION,
        INIT_STATE,
        INIT_SELECT_ENTITY,
        ENTITY_SELECTED,
        ENTITY_DESELECTED
    }

    void dispose();
    void receiveMessage(String message);
}
```

In `Component`, we define the structure of the messages with the MESSAGE_TOKEN string, which acts as a parser token to separate out the message header from the rest of the message string and defines all the different types of messages that can be sent to the different components. Finally, we define two methods that each component needs to override. The `dispose()` method will deal with cleaning up any objects that need to be deallocated (or at least flagged for garbage collection) and the `receiveMessage()` method will implement the logic necessary for parsing out the message parameters for each component.

For this chapter, we have defined three core components that define the behavior for the `Entity` objects: `PhysicsComponent`, `GraphicsComponent`, and `InputComponent`. Each class implements the `Component` interface and handles common logic between the player-based components and the NPC-based components as an abstract base class. We can think of these classes as making up a `Component` layer in *Figure 2*.

PhysicsComponent

The first class that we will review from this layer is `PhysicsComponent`, which can be found at `core/src/com/packtpub/libgdx/bludbourne/PhysicsComponent.java`. Much of the source is refactored from the `Entity` class and it is already explained in the last chapter. We will be looking at only a few excerpts (with ... designating the areas where the code is hidden) with the following source:

```
public abstract class PhysicsComponent implements Component{

    . . .

    public abstract void update(Entity entity, MapManager mapMgr,
        float delta);
```

The `update()` interface method is simply delegated to the concrete derived class:

```
    . . .

    public Rectangle _boundingBox;
    protected BoundingBoxLocation _boundingBoxLocation;

    public static enum BoundingBoxLocation{
        BOTTOM_LEFT,
        BOTTOM_CENTER,
        CENTER,
```

```
    }

    PhysicsComponent(){
    ...
    }

    protected boolean isCollisionWithMapEntities(Entity entity,
        MapManager mapMgr){
        Array<Entity> entities = mapMgr.getCurrentMapEntities();
        boolean isCollisionWithMapEntities = false;

        for(Entity mapEntity: entities){
            //Check for testing against self
            if( mapEntity.equals(entity) ){
                continue;
            }

            Rectangle targetRect =
                        mapEntity.getCurrentBoundingBox();
            if (_boundingBox.overlaps(targetRect) ){
                //Collision
                entity.sendMessage(MESSAGE.COLLISION_WITH_ENTITY);
                isCollisionWithMapEntities = true;
                break;
            }
        }
        return isCollisionWithMapEntities;
    }
```

The `isCollisionWithMapEntities()` method is a method used to test whether the current `Entity` object has collided with any other entities on the currently loaded map location. We will iterate over all entities that are on the current map by first checking to make sure we aren't testing for a collision with ourselves and then checking all other entities. If there is an overlap between bounding boxes, we then send a message to the components that we have a collision with an entity:

```
    protected boolean isCollision(Entity entitySource, Entity
        entityTarget){
        boolean isCollisionWithMapEntities = false;

        if( entitySource.equals(entityTarget) ){
            return false;
        }

        if (entitySource.getCurrentBoundingBox().overlaps(
```

```
            entityTarget.getCurrentBoundingBox()) ){
              //Collision
              entitySource.sendMessage(
                  MESSAGE.COLLISION_WITH_ENTITY);
              isCollisionWithMapEntities = true;
        }

        return isCollisionWithMapEntities;
    }
```

The isCollision() method is similar to the previous
isCollisionWithMapEntities(), but is meant more of a convenience to test against
two specific entities instead of an entire collection. This method is primarily used to
test whether an NPC entity has collided with the player-character entity. The player-
character entity is not included in the currently loaded container of map entities
since its lifetime persists outside the current map:

```
        protected boolean isCollisionWithMapLayer(Entity entity,
          MapManager mapMgr){
            ...
        }

        protected void setNextPositionToCurrent(Entity entity){
            ...
        }

        protected void calculateNextPosition(float deltaTime){
            ...
        }

        protected void initBoundingBox(float percentageWidthReduced,
          float percentageHeightReduced){
            //Update the current bounding box
            float width;
            float height;

            float origWidth =  Entity.FRAME_WIDTH;
            float origHeight = Entity.FRAME_HEIGHT;

            //.8f for 20% (1 - .20)
            float widthReductionAmount = 1.0f -
                  percentageWidthReduced;

            //.8f for 20% (1 - .20)
            float heightReductionAmount = 1.0f -
```

```
                    percentageHeightReduced;

    if( widthReductionAmount > 0 && widthReductionAmount < 1){
        width = Entity.FRAME_WIDTH * widthReductionAmount;
    }else{
        width = Entity.FRAME_WIDTH;
    }

    if( heightReductionAmount > 0 &&
        heightReductionAmount < 1){
        height = Entity.FRAME_HEIGHT * heightReductionAmount;
    }else{
        height = Entity.FRAME_HEIGHT;
    }

    if( width == 0 || height == 0){
        Gdx.app.debug(TAG, "Width and Height are 0!! " +
            width + ":" + height);
    }

    //Need to account for the unitscale, since the map
    //coordinates will be in pixels
    float minX;
    float minY;

    if( Map.UNIT_SCALE > 0 ) {
        minX = _nextEntityPosition.x / Map.UNIT_SCALE;
        minY = _nextEntityPosition.y / Map.UNIT_SCALE;
    }else{
        minX = _nextEntityPosition.x;
        minY = _nextEntityPosition.y;
    }

    _boundingBox.setWidth(width);
    _boundingBox.setHeight(height);

    switch(_boundingBoxLocation){
        case BOTTOM_LEFT:
            _boundingBox.set(minX, minY, width, height);
            break;
        case BOTTOM_CENTER:
            _boundingBox.setCenter(minX + origWidth/2,
                                   minY + origHeight/4);
            break;
```

```
            case CENTER:
                _boundingBox.setCenter(minX + origWidth/2,
                                        minY + origHeight/2);
                break;
        }
    }
```

The methods for handling the bounding box have been refactored and split into two separate methods. The first method, `initBoundingBox()`, is to be called from the specific entities constructor to set up and initialize the initial position and size of the bounding box. One of the new features here is that we can specify the position of the bounding box, such as centering in the middle of the sprite or on the bottom using the `BoundingBoxLocation` parameter:

```
protected void updateBoundingBoxPosition(Vector2 position){
    //Need to account for the unitscale, since the map
    //coordinates will be in pixels
    float minX;
    float minY;

    if( Map.UNIT_SCALE > 0 ) {
        minX = position.x / Map.UNIT_SCALE;
        minY = position.y / Map.UNIT_SCALE;
    }else{
        minX = position.x;
        minY = position.y;
    }

    switch(_boundingBoxLocation){
        case BOTTOM_LEFT:
            _boundingBox.set(minX, minY,
                _boundingBox.getWidth(),
                _boundingBox.getHeight());
            break;
        case BOTTOM_CENTER:
            _boundingBox.setCenter(
                minX + Entity.FRAME_WIDTH/2,
                minY + Entity.FRAME_HEIGHT/4);
            break;
        case CENTER:
            _boundingBox.setCenter(
                minX + Entity.FRAME_WIDTH/2,
                minY + Entity.FRAME_HEIGHT/2);
            break;
    }
```

```
            }
    }
```

Finally, the `updateBoundingBoxPosition()` method will be used from the `update()` call of the component to update the bounding box position on every frame update.

GraphicsComponent

The graphic-specific updates were refactored from the `Entity` class from the last chapter and moved to the `GraphicsComponent` class, which can be found at `core/src/com/packtpub/libgdx/bludbourne/GraphicsComponent.java`. The excerpted code is as follows:

```java
public abstract class GraphicsComponent implements Component {
    ...
    protected Hashtable<Entity.AnimationType, Animation>
        _animations;
    protected ShapeRenderer _shapeRenderer;

    protected GraphicsComponent(){
    ...
    }

    public abstract void update(Entity entity, MapManager
        mapManager, Batch batch, float delta);

    protected void updateAnimations(float delta){
        //Want to avoid overflow
        _frameTime = (_frameTime + delta)%5;

        //Look into the appropriate variable
        //when changing position
        switch (_currentDirection) {
            case DOWN:
                if (_currentState == Entity.State.WALKING) {
                    Animation animation = _animations.get(
                                Entity.AnimationType.WALK_DOWN);
                    if( animation == null ) return;
                    _currentFrame = animation.getKeyFrame(
                        _frameTime);
                }else if(_currentState == Entity.State.IDLE) {
                    Animation animation = _animations.get(
```

```
                        Entity.AnimationType.WALK_DOWN);
            if( animation == null ) return;
            _currentFrame = animation.getKeyFrames()[0];
        }else if(_currentState == Entity.State.IMMOBILE) {
            Animation animation = _animations.get(
                        Entity.AnimationType.IMMOBILE);
            if( animation == null ) return;
            _currentFrame = animation.getKeyFrame(
                _frameTime);
        }
        break;
    case LEFT:
    ...
        break;
    case UP:
    ...
        break;
    case RIGHT:
    ...
        break;
    default:
        break;
    }
}
```

One of the changes to the GraphicsComponent class is that instead of defining every single animation as a separate variable, we simply keep a Hashtable hashed by AnimationType as the key. This allows us to load the AnimationType information from the JSON property file and simply place it in this Hashtable to be accessed later, depending on the Entities configuration information. For instance, if we have an NPC in town that just stands in one location, then we can just get the AnimationType of the NPC for when it's not moving, which in our case is defined as IMMOBILE, and grab the relevant keyframe for that particular animation frame update from the animation Hashtable:

```
//Specific to two frame animations where each frame is stored
//in a separate texture
protected Animation loadAnimation(String firstTexture, String
    secondTexture, Array<GridPoint2> points, float
    frameDuration){
    Utility.loadTextureAsset(firstTexture);
    Texture texture1 = Utility.getTextureAsset(firstTexture);

    Utility.loadTextureAsset(secondTexture);
```

```
      Texture texture2 = Utility.getTextureAsset(secondTexture);

      TextureRegion[][] texture1Frames = TextureRegion.split(
                  texture1,
                  Entity.FRAME_WIDTH,
                  Entity.FRAME_HEIGHT);
      TextureRegion[][] texture2Frames = TextureRegion.split(
                  texture2,
                  Entity.FRAME_WIDTH,
                  Entity.FRAME_HEIGHT);

      Array<TextureRegion> animationKeyFrames = new
                  Array<TextureRegion>(2);

      GridPoint2 point = points.first();

      animationKeyFrames.add(texture1Frames[point.x][point.y]);
      animationKeyFrames.add(texture2Frames[point.x][point.y]);

      return new Animation(frameDuration, animationKeyFrames,
            Animation.PlayMode.LOOP);
   }

   protected Animation loadAnimation(String textureName, Array
      <GridPoint2> points, float frameDuration){
      Utility.loadTextureAsset(textureName);
      Texture texture = Utility.getTextureAsset(textureName);

      TextureRegion[][] textureFrames = TextureRegion.split(
                  texture,
                  Entity.FRAME_WIDTH,
                  Entity.FRAME_HEIGHT);

      Array<TextureRegion> animationKeyFrames = new
                  Array<TextureRegion>(points.size);

      for( GridPoint2 point : points){
         animationKeyFrames.add(
            textureFrames[point.x][point.y]);
      }

      return new Animation(frameDuration, animationKeyFrames,
            Animation.PlayMode.LOOP);
   }
}
```

Both `loadAnimation()` methods are convenience methods for loading the two distinct kinds of animations that we have with our sprite sheets. Specifically, there are some characters, such as our player hero and guard NPCs, that walk around the town. For these scenarios, we need sprites that support all directions, depending on the current direction the `Entity` is facing. For this scenario, we have four keyframes for each of the directions, so a total of 16 sprites, or `TextureRegion` where we define each `TextureRegion` with a whole number index defined with the `GridPoint2` class. The latter `loadAnimation()` method will correctly read from this configuration and load the animations into the `Animation` container. The former `loadAnimation()` method will load animations that are separated out into two sprite sheets, where the first sprite sheet represents one keyframe and the second sprite sheet represents the second keyframe, for a total of two keyframes of animation. These are intended for more static characters in the game, such as an innkeeper or local blacksmith.

InputComponent

The final class in the component layer in *Figure 2* is `InputComponent`, which can be found at `core/src/com/packtpub/libgdx/bludbourne/InputComponent.java`. The source is as follows:

```java
package com.packtpub.libgdx.bludbourne;

import com.badlogic.gdx.utils.Json;

import java.util.HashMap;
import java.util.Map;

public abstract class InputComponent implements Component {

    protected Entity.Direction _currentDirection = null;
    protected Entity.State _currentState = null;
    protected Json _json;

    protected enum Keys {
        LEFT, RIGHT, UP, DOWN, QUIT
    }

    protected enum Mouse {
        SELECT, DOACTION
    }

    protected static Map<Keys, Boolean> keys = new
                                HashMap<Keys, Boolean>();
    protected static Map<Mouse, Boolean> mouseButtons = new
```

```
                                        HashMap<Mouse, Boolean>();

    //initialize the hashmap for inputs
    static {
        keys.put(Keys.LEFT, false);
        keys.put(Keys.RIGHT, false);
        keys.put(Keys.UP, false);
        keys.put(Keys.DOWN, false);
        keys.put(Keys.QUIT, false);
    };

    static {
        mouseButtons.put(Mouse.SELECT, false);
        mouseButtons.put(Mouse.DOACTION, false);
    };

    InputComponent(){
        _json = new Json();
    }


    public abstract void update(Entity entity, float delta);


}
```

This component handles all input from the keyboard and mouse and also handles the AI movement for the NPCs in the `NPCInputComponent` class.

We are now at the bottom of our ECS hierarchy in *Figure 2*. We won't get into the specifics of the implementation of the NPC components (defined by `NPCPhysicsComponent`, `NPCGraphicsComponent`, and `NPCInputComponent`) as their source is available, but we will instead take a look at the player-based component implementations. The first concrete implementation of the `PhysicsComponent` class is the `PlayerPhysicsComponent`, which can be found at `core/src/com/packtpub/libgdx/bludbourne/PlayerPhysicsComponent.java`. The excerpts of the source are as follows:

```
package com.packtpub.libgdx.bludbourne;

...

import com.badlogic.gdx.math.collision.Ray;

public class PlayerPhysicsComponent extends PhysicsComponent {
...
    private Vector3 _mouseSelectCoordinates;
    private boolean _isMouseSelectEnabled = false;
```

```java
private Ray _selectionRay;
private float _selectRayMaximumDistance = 32.0f;

public PlayerPhysicsComponent(){
    _mouseSelectCoordinates = new Vector3(0,0,0);
    _selectionRay = new Ray(new Vector3(), new Vector3());
}


@Override
public void dispose(){
}

@Override
public void receiveMessage(String message) {
    String[] string = message.split(Component.MESSAGE_TOKEN);

    if( string.length == 0 ) return;

    //Specifically for messages with 1 object payload
    if( string.length == 2 ) {
        if (string[0].equalsIgnoreCase(
                MESSAGE.INIT_START_POSITION.toString())) {
            _currentEntityPosition =
                _json.fromJson(Vector2.class, string[1]);
            _nextEntityPosition.set(_currentEntityPosition.x,
                _currentEntityPosition.y);
        } else if (string[0].equalsIgnoreCase(
                    MESSAGE.CURRENT_STATE.toString())) {
            _state =
                _json.fromJson(Entity.State.class, string[1]);
        } else if (string[0].equalsIgnoreCase(
                    MESSAGE.CURRENT_DIRECTION.toString())) {
            _currentDirection =
                _json.fromJson(Entity.Direction.class,
                  string[1]);
        } else if (string[0].equalsIgnoreCase(
                    MESSAGE.INIT_SELECT_ENTITY.toString())) {
            _mouseSelectCoordinates =
                _json.fromJson(Vector3.class, string[1]);
            _isMouseSelectEnabled = true;
        }
    }
}
```

In the `receiveMessage()` method, we can see all the messages that `PlayerPhysicsComponent` cares about, such as the initial starting position, the current entity state, the current direction, and when we receive input from the mouse. All this state information will be used when determining collision detections and rays used in distance calculations. The `PlayerPhysicsComponent` is the primary class that handles the selection of objects in our game:

```
private void selectMapEntityCandidate(MapManager mapMgr){
    Array<Entity> currentEntities =
                    mapMgr.getCurrentMapEntities();

    //Convert screen coordinates to world coordinates,
    //then to unit scale coordinates
    mapMgr.getCamera().unproject(_mouseSelectCoordinates);
    _mouseSelectCoordinates.x /= Map.UNIT_SCALE;
    _mouseSelectCoordinates.y /= Map.UNIT_SCALE;

    for( Entity mapEntity : currentEntities ) {
        //Don't break, reset all entities
        mapEntity.sendMessage(MESSAGE.ENTITY_DESELECTED);
        Rectangle mapEntityBoundingBox =
                    mapEntity.getCurrentBoundingBox();

        if (mapEntity.getCurrentBoundingBox().contains(
          _mouseSelectCoordinates.x,
          _mouseSelectCoordinates.y)) {
          //Check distance
          _selectionRay.set(_boundingBox.x, _boundingBox.y,
              0.0f, mapEntityBoundingBox.x,
              mapEntityBoundingBox.y, 0.0f);
          float distance = _selectionRay.origin.dst(
                    _selectionRay.direction);

          if( distance <= _selectRayMaximumDistance ){
              //We have a valid entity selection
              //Picked/Selected
              Gdx.app.debug(TAG, "Selected Entity! " +
                  mapEntity.getEntityConfig().getEntityID());
              mapEntity.sendMessage(MESSAGE.ENTITY_SELECTED);
          }
        }
    }
}
```

Entity selection

The Ray class in LibGDX represents an object that has a starting position and a unit length direction. This Ray object is used when implementing ray casting, a technique that checks the coordinates along a line for any intersection with other objects. This ray casting process is started with a left mouse button click. The selectMapEntityCandidate() method is called if the mouse button has been clicked and tests the intersection of the ray with the map entities. A part of this intersection check includes testing for distance as well, since we only want to be able to select entities close to the player.

The following sequence diagram (*Figure 4*) shows the typical flow of messages when testing for ray cast intersections:

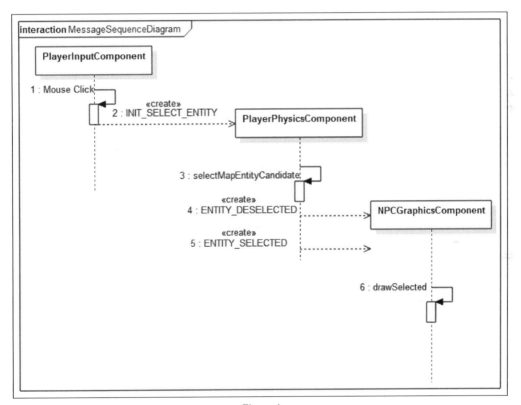

Figure 4

The `PlayerInputComponent` receives a mouse button click event and then sends an `INIT_SELECT_ENTITY` message to the components. The `PlayerPhysicsComponent` sees the message and parses out the mouse coordinates (serialized as JSON) from the message. The `PlayerPhysicsComponent` then checks the mouse coordinates against all entities to see if a ray intersects with any of the objects. If there is an intersection, then we send a message to all the components of the NPC that the `Entity` has been selected. Finally, the `NPCGraphicsComponent` will handle the `ENTITY_SELECTED` message and draw the selection graphics for `Entity`:

```
@Override
public void update(Entity entity, MapManager mapMgr, float
   delta) {
    //We want the hitbox to be at the feet for a better feel
    updateBoundingBoxPosition(_nextEntityPosition);
    updatePortalLayerActivation(mapMgr);

    if( _isMouseSelectEnabled ){
        selectMapEntityCandidate(mapMgr);
        _isMouseSelectEnabled = false;
    }

    if (    !isCollisionWithMapLayer(entity, mapMgr) &&
            !isCollisionWithMapEntities(entity, mapMgr) &&
            _state == Entity.State.WALKING){
        setNextPositionToCurrent(entity);

        Camera camera = mapMgr.getCamera();
        camera.position.set(_currentEntityPosition.x,
           _currentEntityPosition.y, 0f);
        camera.update();
    }else{
        updateBoundingBoxPosition(_currentEntityPosition);
    }

    calculateNextPosition(delta);
}

private boolean updatePortalLayerActivation(MapManager
   mapMgr){
```

```
        . . .
    }
}
```

In the `update()` method, we check every frame if the mouse input was set for a selection and also check for all collisions, including map entities and the collision map layer.

The next concrete class is `PlayerGraphicsComponent`, which is an implementation for the `GraphicsComponent` abstract base class that can be found at `core/src/com/packtpub/libgdx/bludbourne/PlayerGraphicsComponent.java`. An excerpt from `PlayerGraphicsComponent` is as follows:

```java
public class PlayerGraphicsComponent extends GraphicsComponent {
    . . .
    public PlayerGraphicsComponent(){
    }

    @Override
    public void receiveMessage(String message) {
        String[] string = message.split(MESSAGE_TOKEN);

        if( string.length == 0 ) return;

        //Specifically for messages with 1 object payload
        if( string.length == 2 ) {
            if (string[0].equalsIgnoreCase(
                MESSAGE.CURRENT_POSITION.toString())) {
                _currentPosition = _json.fromJson(Vector2.class,
                    string[1]);
            } else if (string[0].equalsIgnoreCase(
                MESSAGE.INIT_START_POSITION.toString())) {
                _currentPosition = _json.fromJson(Vector2.class,
                    string[1]);
            } else if (string[0].equalsIgnoreCase(
                MESSAGE.CURRENT_STATE.toString())) {
                _currentState = _json.fromJson(Entity.State.class,
                    string[1]);
            } else if (string[0].equalsIgnoreCase(
                MESSAGE.CURRENT_DIRECTION.toString())) {
                _currentDirection = _json.fromJson(
                    Entity.Direction.class, string[1]);
```

```
        } else if (string[0].equalsIgnoreCase(
            MESSAGE.LOAD_ANIMATIONS.toString()))) {
        EntityConfig entityConfig = _json.fromJson(
                    EntityConfig.class, string[1]);
        Array<AnimationConfig> animationConfigs =
                    entityConfig.getAnimationConfig();

        for( AnimationConfig animationConfig :
           animationConfigs ){
           Array<String> textureNames =
                    animationConfig.getTexturePaths();
           Array<GridPoint2> points =
                    animationConfig.getGridPoints();
           Entity.AnimationType animationType =
                    animationConfig.
                       getAnimationType();
           float frameDuration =
                    animationConfig.
                       getFrameDuration();
           Animation animation = null;

           if( textureNames.size == 1) {
               animation = loadAnimation(
                 textureNames.get(0), points,
                   frameDuration);
           }else if( textureNames.size == 2){
               animation =
                 loadAnimation(textureNames.get(0),
                 textureNames.get(1), points,
                   frameDuration);
           }

           _animations.put(animationType, animation);
        }
      }
     }
    }
```

In the `receiveMessage()` method, other than caching some state information, `PlayerGraphicsComponent` is also responsible for loading and displaying the animations. A `LOAD_ANIMATIONS` message is typically sent on the creation of `Entity`, including loading the JSON property files from disk, deserializing the file into `EntityConfig` objects, and then sending this message to the `Entity` components. Here, the animation-specific properties are packaged with the message, such as the texture filenames, the type of animation, frame duration, and the specific `TextureRegion` objects. Depending on the number of texture filenames, the corresponding `loadAnimation()` method from the base class is then called to load the animations:

```
@Override
public void update(Entity entity, MapManager mapMgr, Batch
  batch, float delta){
    updateAnimations(delta);

    Camera camera = mapMgr.getCamera();
    camera.position.set(_currentPosition.x,
                    _currentPosition.y, 0f);
    camera.update();

    batch.begin();
    batch.draw(_currentFrame, _currentPosition.x,
            _currentPosition.y, 1, 1);
    batch.end();

    ...
}

@Override
public void dispose(){
}
}
```

Finally, the `update()` method will update the correct keyframes by passing in the delta time; it will also update the center of the camera position and draw the entity.

The final concrete class, PlayerInputComponent, implements InputComponent and can be found at core/src/com/packtpub/libgdx/bludbourne/ PlayerInputComponent.java. A snippet of the source code is as follows:

```
public class PlayerInputComponent extends InputComponent
   implements InputProcessor {

   private final static String TAG = PlayerInputComponent.
      class.getSimpleName();
   private Vector3 _lastMouseCoordinates;

   public PlayerInputComponent(){
      this._lastMouseCoordinates = new Vector3();
      Gdx.input.setInputProcessor(this);
   }
```

Here, we instantiate a Vector3 object in order to store the latest mouse coordinates captured from the input processor, which we set in the same constructor:

```
@Override
public void receiveMessage(String message) {
   String[] string = message.split(MESSAGE_TOKEN);

   if( string.length == 0 ) return;

   //Specifically for messages with 1 object payload
   if( string.length == 2 ) {
      if (string[0].equalsIgnoreCase(
            MESSAGE.CURRENT_DIRECTION.toString())) {
         _currentDirection =
               _json.fromJson(Entity.Direction.class, string[1]);
      }
   }
}
@Override
public void dispose(){
   Gdx.input.setInputProcessor(null);
}

@Override
public void update(Entity entity, float delta){
   //Keyboard input
   if( keys.get(Keys.LEFT)){
      entity.sendMessage(MESSAGE.CURRENT_STATE,
```

```
                    _json.toJson(Entity.State.WALKING));
            entity.sendMessage(MESSAGE.CURRENT_DIRECTION,
                    _json.toJson(Entity.Direction.LEFT));
    } else if( keys.get(Keys.RIGHT)){
        entity.sendMessage(MESSAGE.CURRENT_STATE,
                _json.toJson(Entity.State.WALKING));
        entity.sendMessage(MESSAGE.CURRENT_DIRECTION,
                _json.toJson(Entity.Direction.RIGHT));
    } else if( keys.get(Keys.UP)){
        entity.sendMessage(MESSAGE.CURRENT_STATE,
                _json.toJson(Entity.State.WALKING));
        entity.sendMessage(MESSAGE.CURRENT_DIRECTION,
                _json.toJson(Entity.Direction.UP));
    } else if(keys.get(Keys.DOWN)){
        entity.sendMessage(MESSAGE.CURRENT_STATE,
                _json.toJson(Entity.State.WALKING));
        entity.sendMessage(MESSAGE.CURRENT_DIRECTION,
                _json.toJson(Entity.Direction.DOWN));
    } else if(keys.get(Keys.QUIT)){
        Gdx.app.exit();
    } else{
        entity.sendMessage(MESSAGE.CURRENT_STATE,
                _json.toJson(Entity.State.IDLE));
        if( _currentDirection == null ){
            entity.sendMessage(MESSAGE.CURRENT_DIRECTION,
                    _json.toJson(Entity.Direction.DOWN));
        }
    }


    //Mouse input
    if( mouseButtons.get(Mouse.SELECT)) {
        entity.sendMessage(MESSAGE.INIT_SELECT_ENTITY,
                _json.toJson(_lastMouseCoordinates));
        mouseButtons.put(Mouse.SELECT, false);
    }
}
...
}
```

In the input() method, we can see where before, in the last chapter, we were setting the member variables for the change in state directly. However, with our new model, whenever the input changes, we send messages so that the pertinent components process or save that state information for processing their logic.

Map design

The following class diagram (*Figure 5*) shows the top-level architecture for handling the loading of multiple maps and their corresponding entities:

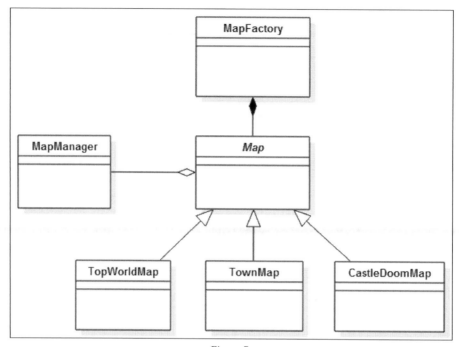

Figure 5

Here, we first start with the `MapFactory` class, which can be found at `core/src/com/packtpub/libgdx/bludbourne/MapFactory.java`, with the source code as follows:

```
package com.packtpub.libgdx.bludbourne;

import java.util.Hashtable;

public class MapFactory {
    //All maps for the game
    private static Hashtable<MapType,Map> _mapTable = new
Hashtable<MapType, Map>();

    public static enum MapType{
        TOP_WORLD,
```

```
            TOWN,
            CASTLE_OF_DOOM
    }

    static public Map getMap(MapType mapType){
        Map map = null;
        switch(mapType){
            case TOP_WORLD:
                map = _mapTable.get(MapType.TOP_WORLD);
                if( map == null ){
                    map = new TopWorldMap();
                    _mapTable.put(MapType.TOP_WORLD, map);
                }
                break;
            case TOWN:
                map = _mapTable.get(MapType.TOWN);
                if( map == null ){
                    map = new TownMap();
                    _mapTable.put(MapType.TOWN, map);
                }
                break;
            case CASTLE_OF_DOOM:
                map = _mapTable.get(MapType.CASTLE_OF_DOOM);
                if( map == null ){
                    map = new CastleDoomMap();
                    _mapTable.put(MapType.CASTLE_OF_DOOM, map);
                }
                break;
            default:
                break;
        }
        return map;
    }
}
```

MapFactory not only instantiates map objects, but also caches them in a local
Hashtable. This prevents us from having to reload maps from scratch once the player
has entered a previously visited location. Depending on requirements, we could limit
the amount of maps that are cached by flushing the cache once a certain limit threshold
is reached. Having a collection of loaded maps also makes persisting of the map state
much easier, especially when we implement the save and restore feature.

The original `MapManager` from the last chapter has also been refactored. The common properties of the different maps have been localized to the abstract `Map` class, which is primarily a container for properties with simple getters and setters. Most of the methods have already been explained in the previous chapter, and so the following is a class diagram (*Figure 6*) outlining how `Map` (found at `core/src/com/packtpub/libgdx/bludbourne/Map.java`) is currently structured:

```
                        Map
--------------------------------------------------------
-TAG: String {readOnly}
+UNIT_SCALE: float {readOnly}
#COLLISION_LAYER: String = "MAP_COLLISION_LAYER" {readOnly}
#SPAWNS_LAYER: String = "MAP_SPAWNS_LAYER" {readOnly}
#PORTAL_LAYER: String = "MAP_PORTAL_LAYER" {readOnly}
#PLAYER_START: String = "PLAYER_START" {readOnly}
#NPC_START: String = "NPC_START" {readOnly}
#_json: Json
#_playerStartPositionRect: Vector2
#_closestPlayerStartPosition: Vector2
#_convertedUnits: Vector2
#_currentMap: TiledMap = null
#_playerStart: Vector2
#_npcStartPositions: Array
#_specialNPCStartPositions: Hashtable
#_collisionLayer: MapLayer = null
#_portalLayer: MapLayer = null
#_spawnsLayer: MapLayer = null
#_currentMapType: MapType
#_mapEntities: Array
--------------------------------------------------------
«constructor»~Map(mapType: MapType, fullMapPath: String)
+getMapEntities(): Array
+getPlayerStart(): Vector2
+updateMapEntities(mapMgr: MapManager, batch: Batch, delta: float): void
+getCollisionLayer(): MapLayer
+getPortalLayer(): MapLayer
+getCurrentTiledMap(): TiledMap
+getPlayerStartUnitScaled(): Vector2
-getNPCStartPositions(): Array
-getSpecialNPCStartPositions(): Hashtable
-setClosestStartPosition(position: Vector2): void
+setClosestStartPositionFromScaledUnits(position: Vector2): void
```

Figure 6

The `MapManager` class still exists, but is used mostly as a pass through for access to the currently loaded map, with some convenience methods for things such as access to the camera.

Finally, we look at one of the concrete implementations of the `Map` class, `TownMap`. With the current model, we can see how we will load and configure map-specific items, demonstrated with the following source:

```
package com.packtpub.libgdx.bludbourne;

import com.badlogic.gdx.graphics.g2d.Batch;
import com.badlogic.gdx.math.Vector2;
import com.badlogic.gdx.utils.Array;

public class TownMap extends Map{
    private static final String TAG = PlayerPhysicsComponent.
      class.getSimpleName();

    private static String _mapPath = "maps/town.tmx";
    private static String _townGuardWalking =
                           "scripts/town_guard_walking.json";
    private static String _townBlacksmith =
                           "scripts/town_blacksmith.json";
    private static String _townMage = "scripts/town_mage.json";
    private static String _townInnKeeper =
                           "scripts/town_innkeeper.json";
    private static String _townFolk = "scripts/town_folk.json";
```

We can define the map-specific JSON property files, including the NPCs that inhabit the map:

```
    TownMap(){
        super(MapFactory.MapType.TOWN, _mapPath);

        for( Vector2 position: _npcStartPositions){
            _mapEntities.add(initEntity(Entity.getEntityConfig(
                           _townGuardWalking), position));
        }

        //Special cases
        _mapEntities.add(initSpecialEntity(Entity.getEntityConfig(
                       _townBlacksmith)));
        _mapEntities.add(initSpecialEntity(Entity.getEntityConfig(
                       _townMage)));
        _mapEntities.add(initSpecialEntity(Entity.getEntityConfig(
                       _townInnKeeper)));

        //When we have multiple configs in one file
```

```
        Array<EntityConfig> configs =
                        Entity.getEntityConfigs(_townFolk);
        for(EntityConfig config: configs){
            _mapEntities.add(initSpecialEntity(config));
        }
    }
}
```

In the `TownMap` constructor, we first pass the map information to the `Map` base class in order to load the TMX map file and store the information for the various layers including start positions, portals, and the collision map. Then, we will initialize all the entities for the map, including the walking guards, and special entities including the blacksmith, mage, and innkeeper. Finally, we will load all the town folks that populate the town:

```
@Override
public void updateMapEntities(MapManager mapMgr, Batch batch,
    float delta){
        for( int i=0; i < _mapEntities.size; i++){
            _mapEntities.get(i).update(mapMgr, batch, delta);
        }
    }
```

In the `updateMapEntities()` method, we iterate over the container of map entities every frame:

```
private Entity initEntity(EntityConfig entityConfig, Vector2
    position){
        Entity entity = EntityFactory.getEntity
            (EntityFactory.EntityType.NPC);
        entity.setEntityConfig(entityConfig);

        entity.sendMessage(Component.MESSAGE.LOAD_ANIMATIONS,
            _json.toJson(entity.getEntityConfig()));
        entity.sendMessage(Component.MESSAGE.INIT_START_POSITION,
            _json.toJson(position));
        entity.sendMessage(Component.MESSAGE.INIT_STATE,
            _json.toJson(entity.getEntityConfig().getState()));
        entity.sendMessage(Component.MESSAGE.INIT_DIRECTION,
            _json.toJson(entity.getEntityConfig().getDirection()));

        return entity;
    }
```

The `initEntity()` method is a convenience method that gets a fresh `Entity` object from `EntityFactory` and will then initialize the entities with their specific `EntityConfig` values:

```
private Entity initSpecialEntity(EntityConfig entityConfig){
    Vector2 position = new Vector2(0,0);

    if( _specialNPCStartPositions.containsKey(
        entityConfig.getEntityID()) ) {
        position = _specialNPCStartPositions.get(
            entityConfig.getEntityID());
    }
    return initEntity(entityConfig, position);
  }
}
```

The `initSpecialEntity()` method is a special purpose method that will use the `Entity` object's ID to access the special NPC starting positions, and set that position as the starting position if found.

Summary

In this chapter, we learned the Entity Component System model for managing the entities in order to populate our world with NPCs. We learned how to implement collision detection with these entities and also how to implement logic to make the NPCs selectable by the player via mouse picking. We also learned how these NPC characters can spawn from certain points on the map (spawn points) specified in their JSON property file and move around on the map on their own (basic AI). As part of this chapter, we also refactored the `MapManager` class in order to give us the flexibility to generate map-specific entities and events.

In the next chapter, we will begin to look at GUI development including inventory and HUD layouts with skins. We will also start looking into developing an inventory management UI with character stats and saving and loading game profiles.

4

Where Do I Put My Stuff?

The next milestone in the development of our game will be to create some GUIs that will help convey certain information on status and inventory items, presented to the user in a **heads-up display** (**HUD**). This chapter will also discuss how to create screens that help guide the user through the creation process for their initial game profile and how to implement the logic to save and restore their game profiles.

We will cover the following topics in this chapter:

- Inventory and HUD layouts with skins
- Character design with stats
- Item equip with inventory management
- Save and load game profiles

Inventory and HUD layouts with skins

By the end of this chapter, you will have a functional UI that will display the player's current status and an interactive inventory where the player can drag and drop their items around the inventory slots, stack like items to conserve space, and equip certain items such as armor and weapons.

The following screenshot demonstrates that end result (*Figure 1*):

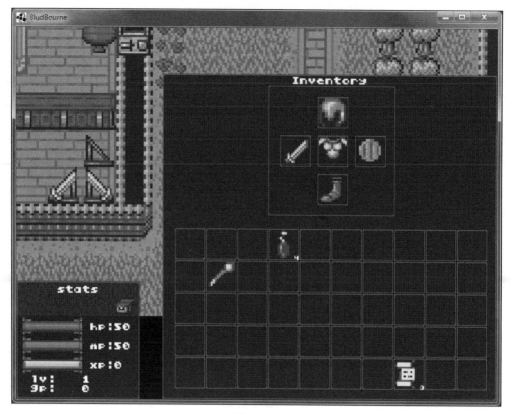

Figure 1

PlayerHUD with Scene2D

We need to set the ground work in order to develop a UI with LibGDX. The first
item that we need to tackle in this chapter is the UI toolkit that comes with LibGDX,
Scene2D, and how we can use the tools provided to start creating the in-game
UI. The Scene2D library in LibGDX conceptually is a scene graph that can contain
hierarchies of widgets. This library contains classes for building game menus, HUD
overlays, tools, and other UIs. Scene2D also includes helper classes for laying out
and drawing widgets and also handling input.

In our game, the player will need a means of interacting with their in-game character's status and items. These UI elements start with a HUD that is typically displayed at all times. The primary class from our project that implements this functionality is `PlayerHUD`, and it is composed of two UI classes, `StatusUI` and `InventoryUI`. `PlayerHUD` is our top-level class for receiving user input and displaying our different UI windows.

Just as `MainGameScreen` is our primary screen for displaying game objects rendered in the game loop, we need a similar mechanism for displaying the `PlayerHUD` class. We need to consider that `PlayerHUD` needs to be viewed with consistent size constraints on the viewing window and needs to sit on top of the viewing screen (or `MainGameScreen` in our case). The best method for achieving this effect is to configure `PlayerHUD` with its own separate camera. We initialize `PlayerHUD` with the following code snippet from the `MainGameScreen` class:

```
public class MainGameScreen implements Screen {
    ...
    private OrthographicCamera _hudCamera = null;
    private InputMultiplexer _multiplexer;
    private static PlayerHUD _playerHUD;

    public MainGameScreen(BludBourne game){
        ...
      _hudCamera = new OrthographicCamera();
    _hudCamera.setToOrtho(
          false, VIEWPORT.physicalWidth, VIEWPORT.physicalHeight);
    _playerHUD = new PlayerHUD(_hudCamera, _player);

    _multiplexer = new InputMultiplexer();
    _multiplexer.addProcessor(_playerHUD.getStage());
    _multiplexer.addProcessor(_player.getInputProcessor());
    Gdx.input.setInputProcessor(_multiplexer);
        ...
    }
```

Also, note that we need to set the input processor to use the `InputMultiplexer` class. This allows us to process input based upon priorities, which are set in the order they are added. This chaining of the `InputProcessor` objects gives top priority to the first `InputProcessor` added, second priority to the second `InputProcessor` added, and so on. In our case, the `PlayerHUD` class will receive the input first so we can process the UI interactions, and then the player input will be processed next.

The implementation of the `PlayerHUD` class itself is minimal, described in the following class diagram (*Figure 2*):

```
┌─────────────────────────────────────────────────────────────────┐
│                          PlayerHUD                                │
├─────────────────────────────────────────────────────────────────┤
│ -_stage: Stage                                                    │
│ -_viewport: Viewport                                              │
│ -_camera: Camera                                                  │
├─────────────────────────────────────────────────────────────────┤
│ «constructor»+PlayerHUD(camera: Camera, player: Entity)           │
│ +getStage(): Stage                                                │
│ +onNotify(profileManager: ProfileManager, event: ProfileEvent): void │
│ +show(): void                                                     │
│ +render(delta: float): void                                       │
│ +resize(width: int, height: int): void                            │
│ +pause(): void                                                    │
│ +resume(): void                                                   │
│ +hide(): void                                                     │
│ +dispose(): void                                                  │
└─────────────────────────────────────────────────────────────────┘
```

Figure 2

The item of note specific to `PlayerHUD` is the `Stage` class that manages all the different aspects of a widget's lifecycle, such as drawing the widget and distributing the relevant input events. The individual nodes that compose the Scene2D scene graph are referred to as **Actors** (synonymous with widgets in our case) that contain their own position, size, origin, scale, rotation, and color. The following is a snippet from the `PlayerHUD` class demonstrating how the `Stage` class is configured and used:

```
public class PlayerHUD implements Screen, ProfileObserver {
    ...
  private Stage _stage;
   private Viewport _viewport;

   public PlayerHUD(Camera camera, Entity player) {
      _viewport = new ScreenViewport(_camera);
      _stage = new Stage(_viewport);

    _statusUI = new StatusUI();
    _inventoryUI = new InventoryUI();
```

```
    _stage.addActor(_statusUI);
      _stage.addActor(_inventoryUI);
    ...
  }
```

The `ProfileObserver` class will be explained later on in the *Observer pattern* section of this chapter.

The `StatusUI` and `InventoryUI` classes derive from `Window` (a type of Actor) and so we add them to the `Stage` class object so that they can be managed:

```
@Override
public void render(float delta) {
    _stage.act(delta);
    _stage.draw();
}
```

The `render()` method is part of the `Screen` interface that needs to be implemented in `PlayerHUD`. Here, we let the `Stage` class object handle the work for rendering our widgets to the screen:

```
@Override
public void resize(int width, int height) {
    _stage.getViewport().update(width, height, true);
}
```

In the case of a `resize()` event, we need to make sure that we pass the new width and height parameters to the viewport of `Stage` so that the display changes get propagated correctly:

```
@Override
public void dispose() {
    _stage.dispose();
  }
}
```

Finally, we need to make sure we call dispose on the `Stage` class object so that it can manage its own cleanup.

Developing UIs with LibGDX

Previously, we have seen how `PlayerHUD` is a container class for the different UI components for our game. This section will begin to discuss some preliminary steps needed in order to take full advantage of the UI toolkit in LibGDX, including recommendations for some free tools as part of our workflow.

Widget styles

When creating a UI with the widgets in LibGDX, we first need to consider the overall look and feel of the widgets, such as the texture to apply, overall shape, color, and other drawable attributes. These characteristics that define the look and feel of widgets are called styles. Each widget in LibGDX, under the **Scene2D.ui** library, defines a static nested class for all the configurable attributes of that widget. For instance, one of the widgets we will use for our `StatusUI` is an `ImageButton` that defines all of its attributes in its static nested class `ImageButtonStyle`, such as what the `ImageButton` will present during a mouse pointer hover, when pressed down or even when disabled.

The first part of creating styles is defining the attributes of the look and feel properties. We are going to define the styles for the widgets used in `StatusUI` in a JSON configuration file named `statusui.json` under the `assets/skin` directory. We are going to define the colors of the displayed text, `Bitmapfont` type, `Label` style, `Window` style, `Imagebutton` style, `TextButton` style, `List` style, and `TextField` style. These properties are simple name/value pairs, where the name of the property represents the name of the member variable in the widget's nested style class. The value represents the key that will act as an index that references a texture or some other property in the JSON file.

An example of the defined styles for an `ImageButton` from the `statusui.json` file is described here:

```
{
...
"com.badlogic.gdx.scenes.scene2d.ui.ImageButton$ImageButtonStyle": {
"inventory-button":
{
    "imageUp": "inventory_button_closed",
    "imageChecked": "inventory_button_open" }
},
...
}
```

Texture atlas

The second part of creating styles is to generate a texture atlas that contains the string-based keys for the values these style properties reference. For instance, for our `ImageButtonStyle` style, we define values of `imageUp` and `imageChecked`, with the index values `inventory_button_closed` and `inventory_button_open`, respectively. These indices represent the named keys that reference the texture names for the images.

A texture atlas is an efficient way for managing textures because a sprite sheet packed with images can be loaded as one texture and pushed to the GPU. The alternative is constantly loading and unloading single image files as separate textures, which can negatively impact performance. Using a texture atlas is the better approach as it keeps the thrashing of the GPU pipeline to a minimum and is a nice performance gain for your game. The texture atlas is composed of two pieces, an image file (or sprite sheet) with all the images packed together and a text-based description (typically designated with an .atlas file extension) of the properties for each of these textures in the image, such as position, size, and offset values. For example, the following image (*Figure 3*) represents the sprite sheet portion of the texture atlas for the StatusUI (statusui.png):

Figure 3

The images referenced by the inventory_button_closed and inventory_button_ open values are clearly identified in red for illustration purposes in the preceding screenshot. In the statusui.atlas file configuration, information for these two textures are listed as follows:

```
statusui.png
format: RGBA8888
filter: Nearest,Nearest
repeat: none
...
inventory_button_closed
  rotate: false
  xy: 197, 9
  size: 16, 16
  orig: 16, 16
  offset: 0, 0
  index: -1
inventory_button_open
  rotate: false
  xy: 215, 9
  size: 16, 16
```

```
orig: 16, 16
offset: 0, 0
index: -1
```

Creating a texture atlas by hand would be a tedious experience to say the least. Luckily, there are a few ways to generate these texture atlas files, such as running from the command line, from a GUI, or as a build target. I used a GUI tool called **libgdx-texturepacker-gui** (version 3.2.0) for the purposes of this book. This project includes an executable JAR (gdx-texturepacker.jar) for launching the GUI, which can be found at http://code.google.com/p/libgdx-texturepacker-gui/. The following screenshot (*Figure 4*) shows a sample session with the libgdx-texturepacker-gui launched:

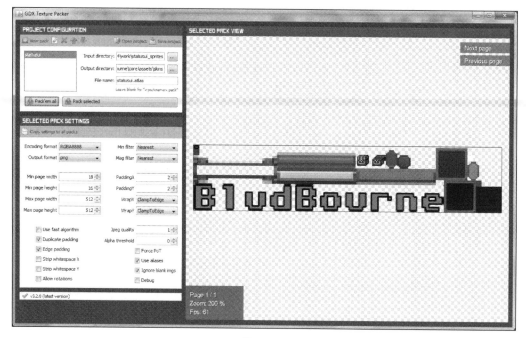

Figure 4

The default settings were fine for my purposes, but the wiki (http://github.com/libgdx/libgdx/wiki/Texture-packer#settings) clearly identifies what each setting means so that you can configure your project accordingly.

First, I set the **Input directory** option to point to where all of my images (that I wanted to be included for this specific texture atlas) were stored. One quick note is that the filenames of the images will be used as the index (alias) names in the texture atlas. Second, I set the **Output directory** option to point to my assets/skin directory where both the texture atlas sprite sheet and configuration file (specified in the **File name** field as statusui.atlas) will be stored once generated. Then, I just clicked on **Pack'em all** and the process was done.

9-patch

When designing the UI for our game, creating and managing a fixed size image texture for each of the different use cases, such as dialog boxes, buttons, inventory windows, and status windows, can become cumbersome. These images can quickly fill up your sprite sheet with a separate image for each use case, when in actuality they are really just duplicates of a base image differentiated only by the different sizes. We really want to reduce the overall bookkeeping of these types of images, and 9-patch images help because they can be resized to accommodate the contents of the view and the size of the screen. 9-patch images are natively supported within LibGDX and so they are a natural fit to solve this image redundancy issue.

9-patch images are broken up into 9 separate pieces, defining the areas that are static and those that are able to be repeated or stretched. The four corner pieces are the static pieces of the overall image that will not be repeated. There are four additional pieces that define the top, bottom, left, and right side of the image that can be repeated or stretched on their respective sides. Finally, the middle of the image defines the area that can be repeated in order to fill the inside of the image. These 9 pieces or patches define a 9-patch image. We could programmatically create these 9-patch images, but there is a **What you see is what you get (WYSIWYG)** tool available that will generate the 9-patch image files for us with a little manual configuration on our part.

The name of the tool that will generate the 9-patch images for us is **Draw 9-patch** and it is bundled with the standalone Android SDK Tools, which is available at http://developer.android.com/sdk/index.html#Other. Once installed, the tool (launched by running the batch file draw9patch.bat) can be found in the SDK installation directory under tools.

When you launch the tool, it should look similar to the following screenshot (*Figure 5*):

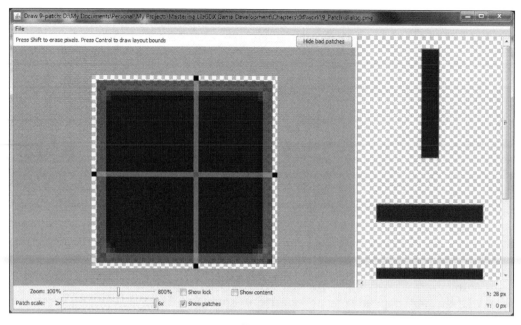

Figure 5

There is a much more thorough tutorial of this tool available at `http://developer.android.com/tools/help/draw9patch.html`. First, you drag and drop your image that you want to convert to a 9-patch image into the main display screen. A preview of what the buttons or dialog boxes will look like with the 9-patch will be displayed on the right panel of the main display screen. Second, click within the 1-pixel perimeter to draw the lines that define the stretchable patches and content area. These selected parts of the image are scaled horizontally and vertically with green-colored indicators drawn within the image. Third, when you are finished defining the 9-patch areas, you can save with **File | Save 9-patch** and your image should be saved with the `.9.png` filename.

As a quick note, we need to include this image in a texture atlas in order to use this as a 9-patch image. The libgdx-texturepacker-gui tool will detect whether we have a raw 9-patch file and correctly process the stretchable patches, adding this information to the `.atlas` configuration file under the `split` property. Otherwise, without this metadata, the LibGDX `NinePatch` class will not properly load the image as a 9-patch.

Skins

Every time you create a widget, you will need to set the style, or look and feel, of that particular widget. We do this in LibGDX by passing a `Skin` object to the constructor of the widget. The `Skin` class simply stores resources for later use. For example, for the `StatusUI`, we define two paths. One for the texture atlas of all the images associated with the `StatusUI` window and widgets (`statusui.atlas`) and one path for the style information of the widgets (`statusui.json`):

```
public final class Utility {
    …
    private final static String STATUSUI_TEXTURE_ATLAS_PATH =
                            "skins/statusui.atlas";
    private final static String STATUSUI_SKIN_PATH =
                            "skins/statusui.json";
```

We then create both a `TextureAtlas` and a `Skin` object from the files that we have created at this point:

```
    public static TextureAtlas STATUSUI_TEXTUREATLAS = new
                    TextureAtlas(STATUSUI_TEXTURE_ATLAS_PATH);
    public static Skin STATUSUI_SKIN = new
                    Skin(Gdx.files.internal(STATUSUI_SKIN_PATH),
                        STATUSUI_TEXTUREATLAS);
}
```

Developing UI summary

Previously, we have defined the look and feel of our widgets with styles, referencing images in a texture atlas . We also created and used 9-patch images for the buttons and dialog boxes. All of these steps lay the ground work for creating widgets and placing them in a layout.

When designing the placement of UI widgets, such as buttons and labels, we have to position them within the window based on either fixed or relative positioning. Due to the fact that screen resolutions can change, windows and widgets can be resized, and other factors can change the position of UI elements, as a rule, we should be using a relative position layout for the UI widgets. This relative positioning of UI widgets in a toolkit is generally handled with a widget layout manager. Fortunately, for us, LibGDX does include a class, `Table`, which can be used as a layout manager.

One item to keep note of is, when developing a UI, structure is important for better readability that in turn helps to fix layout issues. So, the convention is to first construct all of the widgets, then lay them all out, and finally implement any listeners needed for the widgets, in that order.

StatusUI

The StatusUI class will allow the player to view their character's health status, magic points, current experience, current level, and gold coins. The following image (*Figure 6*) is a debug view of the StatusUI window with labels identifying the important pieces of the window as we walk through the construction, layout, and finally the button listeners:

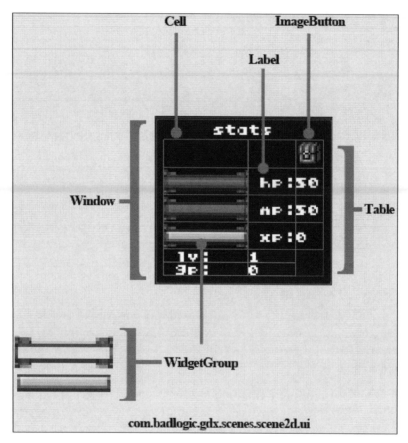

Figure 6

The code that *Figure 6* represents is as follows:

```
package com.packtpub.libgdx.bludbourne.UI;

import com.badlogic.gdx.scenes.scene2d.ui.ImageButton;
import com.badlogic.gdx.scenes.scene2d.ui.Window;
import com.badlogic.gdx.scenes.scene2d.ui.Image;
import com.badlogic.gdx.scenes.scene2d.ui.WidgetGroup;
import com.badlogic.gdx.scenes.scene2d.ui.Label;
import com.badlogic.gdx.scenes.scene2d.utils.Align;
import com.packtpub.libgdx.bludbourne.Utility;
```

Let's go through the various widgets that are used in `StatusUI`. First, the `ImageButton` widget is a button that contains an `Image` object to display an image. Here, the `ImageButton` is represented by a chest that, when clicked on or checked, will open up the `InventoryUI` screen. Second, the `WidgetGroup` widget can contain other widgets; it is able to be used in a layout and has a z-order equal to the order in which they were inserted into the group. Third, the `Label` widget is used to display text:

```
public class StatusUI extends Window {
```

The `StatusUI` class derives from `Window`, which is a table that can be dragged around the screen or act as a modal dialog with the top padding reserved for the title label. This gives flexibility to the player if they wish to reposition the UI when playing the game:

```
private Image _hpBar;
private Image _mpBar;
private Image _xpBar;
private ImageButton _inventoryButton;

//Attributes
private int _levelVal = 1;
private int _goldVal = 0;
private int _hpVal = 50;
private int _mpVal = 50;
private int _xpVal = 0;
```

These values represent UI text that will be updated when the values change. For instance, when the player receives gold from a quest, a notification will be sent to the StatusUI so that the gold value increases in relation to the value that was added:

```
public StatusUI(){
    super("stats", Utility.STATUSUI_SKIN);
```

Here, we set the title of the StatusUI with the first parameter and then the overall look and feel with our static Skin object for the second parameter:

```
//groups
WidgetGroup group = new WidgetGroup();
WidgetGroup group2 = new WidgetGroup();
WidgetGroup group3 = new WidgetGroup();
```

We construct our three WidgetGroup groups (representing health, magic, and experience), which will be composed of two images as seen in *Figure 6*:

```
//images
_hpBar = new Image(
    Utility.STATUSUI_TEXTUREATLAS.findRegion("HP_Bar"));
Image bar = new Image(
    Utility.STATUSUI_TEXTUREATLAS.findRegion("Bar"));
_mpBar = new Image(
    Utility.STATUSUI_TEXTUREATLAS.findRegion("MP_Bar"));
Image bar2 = new Image(
    Utility.STATUSUI_TEXTUREATLAS.findRegion("Bar"));
_xpBar = new Image(
    Utility.STATUSUI_TEXTUREATLAS.findRegion("XP_Bar"));
Image bar3 = new Image(
    Utility.STATUSUI_TEXTUREATLAS.findRegion("Bar"));
```

We get the assorted images from the TextureAtlas based on their string value in preparation for adding them to their corresponding WidgetGroup:

```
//labels
Label hpLabel = new Label(" hp:", Utility.STATUSUI_SKIN);
Label hp = new Label(
        String.valueOf(_hpVal), Utility.STATUSUI_SKIN);
Label mpLabel = new Label(" mp:", Utility.STATUSUI_SKIN);
Label mp = new Label(
        String.valueOf(_mpVal), Utility.STATUSUI_SKIN);
Label xpLabel = new Label(" xp:", Utility.STATUSUI_SKIN);
```

```
Label xp = new Label(
        String.valueOf(_xpVal), Utility.STATUSUI_SKIN);
Label levelLabel = new Label(
        " lv:", Utility.STATUSUI_SKIN);
Label levelVal = new Label(
        String.valueOf(_levelVal), Utility.STATUSUI_SKIN);
Label goldLabel = new Label(
        " gp:", Utility.STATUSUI_SKIN);
Label goldVal = new Label(
        String.valueOf(_goldVal), Utility.STATUSUI_SKIN);
```

Here, we construct all the `Label` widgets used for displaying text in the `StatusUI`, passing in a static `Skin` object for the label style:

```
//buttons
_inventoryButton= new ImageButton(
    Utility.STATUSUI_SKIN, "inventory-button");
_inventoryButton.getImageCell().size(32, 32);
```

For the `ImageButton`, we defined the style in the `statusui.json` file for the opening and checked the operations of the `ImageButton` with the name `inventory-button`. The next step is to pass in that string in order to configure the widget with those properties:

```
//Align images
_hpBar.setPosition(3, 6);
_mpBar.setPosition(3, 6);
_xpBar.setPosition(3, 6);

//add to widget groups
group.addActor(bar);
group.addActor(_hpBar);
group2.addActor(bar2);
group2.addActor(_mpBar);
group3.addActor(bar3);
group3.addActor(_xpBar);
```

Once we finish adding the images to the `WidgetGroup` container, they are ready to be added to the layout:

```
//Add to layout
defaults().expand().fill();
```

The `defaults()` method returns a cell that is comprised of default properties for all cells in the table. The `expand()` method allows the cell to contain extra space in both the *x* and *y* directions and distribute the space evenly. The `fill()` method allows a widget to be sized to the cell in both the *x* and *y* directions:

```
//account for the title padding
this.pad(this.getPadTop() + 10, 10, 10, 10);

this.add();
this.add();
this.add(_inventoryButton).align(Align.right);
this.row();
```

Here, we add two cells so that we can add `ImageButton` to the third column, as seen in *Figure 6*. We call `row()` so that we start the next part of the layout on the next row:

```
this.add(group).size(bar.getWidth(), bar.getHeight());
this.add(hpLabel);
this.add(hp).align(Align.left);
this.row();

this.add(group2).size(bar2.getWidth(), bar2.getHeight());
this.add(mpLabel);
this.add(mp).align(Align.left);
this.row();

this.add(group3).size(bar3.getWidth(), bar3.getHeight());
this.add(xpLabel);
this.add(xp).align(Align.left);
this.row();
```

We are adding the `WidgetGroup` container to the table, making sure we set the size to the bar image, otherwise the preferred height and width may be zero. We then add the corresponding `Label` to the next two columns for each `WidgetGroup` row:

```
this.add(levelLabel).align(Align.left);
this.add(levelVal).align(Align.left);
this.row();
this.add(goldLabel);
this.add(goldVal).align(Align.left);
```

We put the final `Label` on the `StatusUI` representing the current player level and current amount of gold coins:

```
this.pack();
```

Finally, we call the `pack()` method to make sure this table sizes itself to its preferred width and height:

```
    }

    public ImageButton getInventoryButton() {
        return _inventoryButton;
    }
}
```

Drag and drop

The `InventoryUI` class will allow the user to interact with their inventory, move items around, stack items, look at attributes of their items via tooltips, and equip their new, shiny weapons and armor. The following screenshot (*Figure 7*) identifies the important pieces that make up the drag and drop feature of the inventory and the tooltip feature for the inventory items placed in the slots:

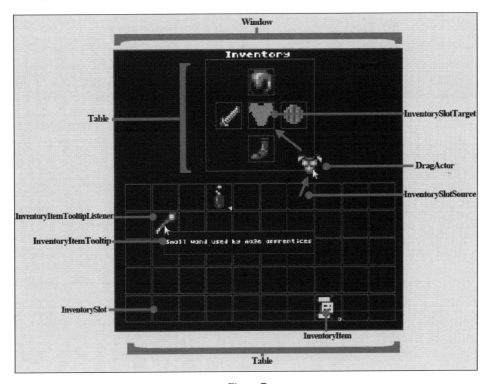

Figure 7

In order to get a high-level understanding of the structure, the following class diagram (*Figure 8*) outlines the relationships across the different classes that compose `InventoryUI`:

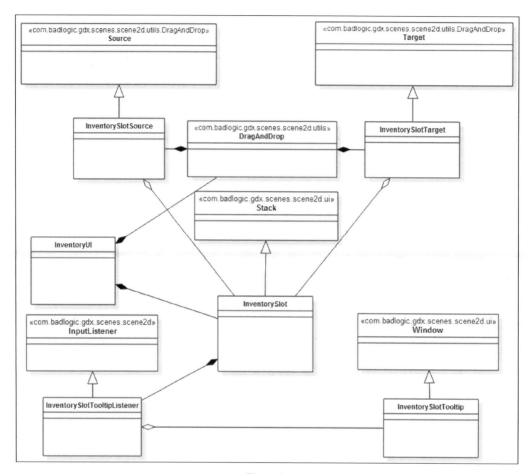

Figure 8

InventorySlot

The `InventoryUI` class contains the `InventorySlot` objects that are derived from the `Stack` class. The `Stack` class manages multiple child widgets by stacking them one on top of the other with the last child widget added as the topmost widget visible. The class diagram of `InventorySlot` is described in the following class diagram (*Figure 9*):

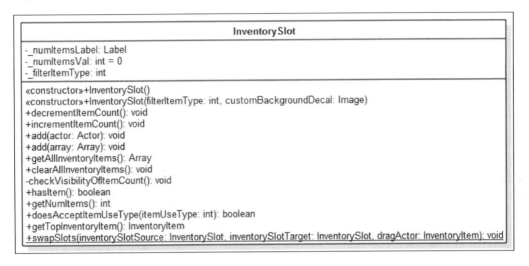

Figure 9

`InventorySlot` keeps track of how many `InventoryItem` objects are stacked and contains methods for adding and removing the `InventoryItem` objects. The `InventorySlot` class even has a filter method, `doesAcceptItemUseType()`, in order to only allow specific types of items to be added to the slot. In the `InventoryUI` class, we also register the `InventorySlotTooltipListener` objects with the `InventorySlot` objects so that when a mouse hovers over `InventorySlot`, a notification can be routed to the `InventorySlotTooltipListener` and an `InventorySlotTooltip` can be presented based on this event.

InventoryItem

The `InventoryItem` objects are images (loaded from the texture atlas files `items.atlas` and `items.png` under the `assets/skins` directory) that contain some metadata specific to the items. The class diagram (*Figure 10*) is as follows:

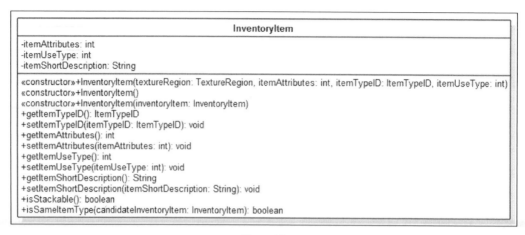

InventoryItem
-itemAttributes: int -itemUseType: int -itemShortDescription: String
«constructor»+InventoryItem(textureRegion: TextureRegion, itemAttributes: int, itemTypeID: ItemTypeID, itemUseType: int) «constructor»+InventoryItem() «constructor»+InventoryItem(inventoryItem: InventoryItem) +getItemTypeID(): ItemTypeID +setItemTypeID(itemTypeID: ItemTypeID): void +getItemAttributes(): int +setItemAttributes(itemAttributes: int): void +getItemUseType(): int +setItemUseType(itemUseType: int): void +getItemShortDescription(): String +setItemShortDescription(itemShortDescription: String): void +isStackable(): boolean +isSameItemType(candidateInventoryItem: InventoryItem): boolean

Figure 10

The `InventoryItem` objects are defined by the following:

- `itemAttributes`: This `int` type defines the item as consumable (used once and gone), equippable (can be used in the equip slots in the inventory), or stackable (can place more than one of the same type of item on top of each other). Because these values represent an integer datatype, we can OR (|) these values together so that an item can have multiple attributes and mask out the values we want to check later on.

- `itemUseType`: This `int` type defines whether the item restores health or magic and whether the item is an armor item or a weapon.

- `itemTypeID`: This defines a unique identifier for each of the items.

- `itemShortDescription`: This string defines a short description of the item, usually used for the tooltip functionality.

The `InventoryItem` objects are created by the `InventoryItemFactory` class, loading the specified items from the `inventory_items.json` configuration file under the `assets/scripts` directory. An example of an item specified in the `inventory_items.json` file is as follows:

```
[
{

  itemAttributes: 2
  itemUseType: 128
  itemTypeID: SHIELD01
  itemShortDescription: Medium tier shield forged from copper

},
]
```

The `InventoryUI` class also contains a `DragAndDrop` object that manages the drag and drop functionality for `InventoryItem` objects placed in an `InventorySlot` location. The `DragAndDrop` class manages drag and drop operations through registered drag sources and drop targets.

InventorySlotSource

The `InventorySlotSource` derives from `Source` and is the drag source for our `DragAndDrop` implementation. The `InventorySlotSource` is described in the following class diagram (*Figure 11*):

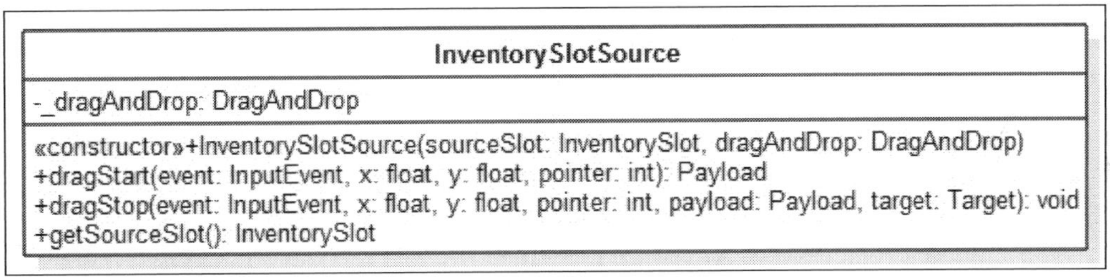

Inventory SlotSource
- _dragAndDrop: DragAndDrop
«constructor»+InventorySlotSource(sourceSlot: InventorySlot, dragAndDrop: DragAndDrop) +dragStart(event: InputEvent, x: float, y: float, pointer: int): Payload +dragStop(event: InputEvent, x: float, y: float, pointer: int, payload: Payload, target: Target): void +getSourceSlot(): InventorySlot

Figure 11

`InventorySlotSource` implements a few methods that warrant further detail in the following code snippet:

```
public class InventorySlotSource extends Source {
@Override
    public Payload dragStart(InputEvent event, float x, float y,
        int pointer) {
        Payload payload = new Payload();

        _sourceSlot = (InventorySlot)getActor().getParent();
        _sourceSlot.decrementItemCount();

        payload.setDragActor(getActor());
        _dragAndDrop.setDragActorPosition(
            -x, -y + getActor().getHeight());

        return payload;
    }
```

The `dragStart()` method will be called once the mouse clicks on a registered source (`InventorySlotSource`) on an `InventorySlot` and starts to drag the `InventoryItem` across the UI. We make sure that the source slot updates its item count to reflect the item being removed. We then set the payload (which is `InventoryItem` in our case) to be handed off to the drop target and then we make sure to set the `InventoryItem` position so that `InventoryItem` follows the mouse cursor:

```
    @Override
    public void dragStop (InputEvent event, float x, float y, int
        pointer, Payload payload, Target target) {
        if( target == null ){
            _sourceSlot.add(payload.getDragActor());
        }
    }
}
```

The `dragStop()` method will be called once the drag operation has stopped and the `InventoryItem` is released. We want to make sure that if there are no viable drop targets, that we put the `InventoryItem` back at its original location.

InventorySlotTarget

The `InventorySlotTarget` derives from `Target` and is the drop target for our `DragAndDrop` implementation. The `InventorySlotTarget` is described in the following class diagram (*Figure 12*):

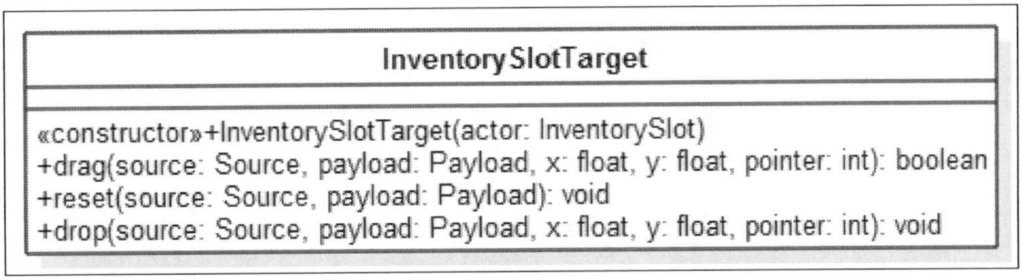

Inventory SlotTarget
«constructor»+InventorySlotTarget(actor: InventorySlot) +drag(source: Source, payload: Payload, x: float, y: float, pointer: int): boolean +reset(source: Source, payload: Payload): void +drop(source: Source, payload: Payload, x: float, y: float, pointer: int): void

Figure 12

`InventorySlotTarget` implements a method described in further detail in the following code snippet:

```
public class InventorySlotTarget extends Target {
    ...
    @Override
    public void drop(Source source, Payload payload, float x,
        float y, int pointer) {
        InventoryItem sourceActor = (InventoryItem)
                    payload.getDragActor();
        InventoryItem targetActor =
                    _targetSlot.getTopInventoryItem();
        InventorySlot sourceSlot =
                    ((InventorySlotSource)source).getSourceSlot();

        if( sourceActor == null ) {
            return;
        }

        //First, does the slot accept the source item type?
        if( !_targetSlot.doesAcceptItemUseType(
            sourceActor.getItemUseType())) {
            //Put item back where it came from,
            //slot doesn't accept item
            sourceSlot.add(sourceActor);
            return;
        }
```

```
        if( !_targetSlot.hasItem() ){
            _targetSlot.add(sourceActor);
        }else{
            //If the same item and stackable, add
            if( sourceActor.isSameItemType(targetActor) &&
                sourceActor.isStackable()){
                _targetSlot.add(sourceActor);
            }else{
                //If they aren't the same items or
                //the items aren't stackable, then swap
                InventorySlot.swapSlots(
                    sourceSlot, _targetSlot, sourceActor);
            }
        }
    }
}
```

In the `drop()` method of `InventorySlotTarget`, we go through a list of checks to see whether the drag source `InventoryItem` is acceptable. As previously mentioned, the `InventorySlot` class can filter itself to only accept certain item types. First, we check to see whether the drop target accepts the `InventoryItem`. If the drop target does not accept the item, then we place the `InventoryItem` object back at its source. If the drop target does accept the `InventoryItem` object type, and it's empty, then we just add the `InventoryItem` object to the `InventorySlot` location. If there are currently `InventoryItem` objects in the `InventorySlot` location, then we check to see whether they are the same type of items, and if they are, check to see whether they are stackable. If neither of these conditions hold true, then we swap the items.

The design of `InventoryUI` can be partitioned into three segments: the `InventorySlot` objects and how they are managed in the `Table` layout, the `DragAndDrop` functionality for the inventory, and finally the `InventorySlotTooltip` for inventory items.

InventoryUI

The following code snippet for `InventoryUI` outlines the widget creation and layout for the UI:

```
public class InventoryUI extends Window {
...
private int _numSlots = 50;
private int _lengthSlotRow = 10;
```

```java
private Table _inventorySlotTable;
private Table _playerSlotsTable;
private Table _equipSlots;
private final int _slotWidth = 52;
private final int _slotHeight = 52;

public InventoryUI(){
        super("Inventory", Utility.STATUSUI_SKIN,
          "solidbackground");

        //create
        _inventorySlotTable = new Table();
        _inventorySlotTable.setName("Inventory_Slot_Table");

        _playerSlotsTable = new Table();
        _equipSlots = new Table();
        _equipSlots.setName("Equipment_Slot_Table");

        _equipSlots.defaults().space(10);

        InventorySlot headSlot = new InventorySlot(
                ItemUseType.ARMOR_HELMET.getValue(),
                new Image(Utility.ITEMS_TEXTUREATLAS.findRegion(
                    "inv_helmet")));

        InventorySlot leftArmSlot = new InventorySlot(
                ItemUseType.WEAPON_ONEHAND.getValue() |
                ItemUseType.WEAPON_TWOHAND.getValue() |
                ItemUseType.ARMOR_SHIELD.getValue() |
                ItemUseType.WAND_ONEHAND.getValue() |
                ItemUseType.WAND_TWOHAND.getValue(),
                new Image(Utility.ITEMS_TEXTUREATLAS.findRegion(
                    "inv_weapon"))
        );

        InventorySlot rightArmSlot = new InventorySlot(
                ItemUseType.WEAPON_ONEHAND.getValue() |
                ItemUseType.WEAPON_TWOHAND.getValue() |
                ItemUseType.ARMOR_SHIELD.getValue() |
                ItemUseType.WAND_ONEHAND.getValue() |
                ItemUseType.WAND_TWOHAND.getValue(),
```

```
                    new Image(Utility.ITEMS_TEXTUREATLAS.findRegion(
                        "inv_shield"))
            );

            InventorySlot chestSlot = new InventorySlot(
                    ItemUseType.ARMOR_CHEST.getValue(),
                    new Image(Utility.ITEMS_TEXTUREATLAS.findRegion(
                        "inv_chest")));

            InventorySlot legsSlot = new InventorySlot(
                    ItemUseType.ARMOR_FEET.getValue(),
                    new Image(Utility.ITEMS_TEXTUREATLAS.findRegion(
                        "inv_boot")));
```

Here, we are setting up the equip `InventorySlot` objects at the top of the `InventoryUI` passing in `ItemUseType` values into the constructor, which act as filters for acceptable item types. We can see the definition of `ItemUseType` (defined in the `InventoryItem` class) in the following code snippet:

```
public enum ItemUseType{
    ITEM_RESTORE_HEALTH(1),
    ITEM_RESTORE_MP(2),
    ITEM_DAMAGE(4),
    WEAPON_ONEHAND(8),
    WEAPON_TWOHAND(16),
    WAND_ONEHAND(32),
    WAND_TWOHAND(64),
    ARMOR_SHIELD(128),
    ARMOR_HELMET(256),
    ARMOR_CHEST(512),
    ARMOR_FEET(1024);

    private int _itemUseType;

    ItemUseType(int itemUseType){
        this._itemUseType = itemUseType;
    }

    public int getValue(){
        return _itemUseType;
    }
}
```

We make sure that each `ItemUseType` has a unique *power of two* integer value for its ID so that we can OR the `ItemUseType` values together for the type of items that each equip slot will accept. This will give us options to add multiple filtered items for one slot, such as the arm slots, where we can have a weapon, shield, or even a wand for magic attacks. If the player tries to drag and drop a weapon like a sword onto the helmet equip slot, then the helmet equip slot will not accept the item because the only type it accepts is `ItemUseType.ARMOR_HELMET`. We also pass in some images that will act as placeholders in the equip slots to communicate to the user what type of items are acceptable for those specific equip slots:

```
_playerSlotsTable.setBackground(new Image(
    new NinePatch(Utility.STATUSUI_TEXTUREATLAS.createPatch(
        "dialog"))).getDrawable());
```

We wrap the inventory slots with a 9-patch texture that we created previously so that there is no tearing or artifacts in the stretchable regions:

```
//layout
for(int i = 1; i <= _numSlots; i++){
    InventorySlot inventorySlot = new InventorySlot();
    _inventorySlotTable.add(
        inventorySlot).size(_slotWidth, _slotHeight);

    if(i % _lengthSlotRow == 0){
        _inventorySlotTable.row();
    }
}
```

We construct all the slots for the inventory, adding them to the table as we create them:

```
_equipSlots.add();
_equipSlots.add(headSlot).size(_slotWidth, _slotHeight);
_equipSlots.row();

_equipSlots.add(leftArmSlot).size(
    _slotWidth, _slotHeight);
_equipSlots.add(chestSlot).size(_slotWidth, _slotHeight);
_equipSlots.add(rightArmSlot).size(
    _slotWidth, _slotHeight);
_equipSlots.row();

_equipSlots.add();
_equipSlots.right().add(legsSlot).size(
    _slotWidth, _slotHeight);
```

As part of the layout, we add the equip-based slots to the equip table, making sure that they maintain their standard size:

```
_playerSlotsTable.add(_equipSlots);

this.add(_playerSlotsTable).padBottom(20).row();
this.add(_inventorySlotTable).row();
this.pack();
}
```

We add the equip-based slot table and the inventory table to the table of InventoryUI, making sure to add a buffer between them for a better looking layout:

```
public Table getInventorySlotTable() {
    return _inventorySlotTable;
}

public Table getEquipSlotTable() {
    return _equipSlots;
}

public void populateInventory(Table targetTable,
    Array<InventoryItemLocation> inventoryItems){
        Array<Cell> cells = targetTable.getCells();
        for(int i = 0; i < inventoryItems.size; i++){
            InventoryItemLocation itemLocation =
                inventoryItems.get(i);
            ItemTypeID itemTypeID = ItemTypeID.valueOf(
                itemLocation.getItemTypeAtLocation());
            InventorySlot inventorySlot =
                ((InventorySlot)cells.get(
                    itemLocation.getLocationIndex()).getActor());
            inventorySlot.clearAllInventoryItems();

            for( int index = 0;
                index < itemLocation.getNumberItemsAtLocation();
                index++ ){
                inventorySlot.add(
                    InventoryItemFactory.getInstance(
                        ).getInventoryItem(itemTypeID));
            }
        }
    }
```

The `populateInventory()` method is used when loading inventory items from a save game profile. It will take an array of `InventoryItem` objects (rewrapped into a POJO class named `InventoryItemLocation`) and a `Table` widget used for storing the `InventoryItem` objects. Then, each of the `InventoryItem` objects will be placed in their corresponding cell in the `Table` widget based on the position saved:

```
public Array<InventoryItemLocation> getInventory(Table
  targetTable){
    Array<Cell> cells = targetTable.getCells();
    Array<InventoryItemLocation> items = new
      Array<InventoryItemLocation>();
    for(int i = 0; i < cells.size; i++){
        InventorySlot inventorySlot =
            ((InventorySlot)cells.get(i).getActor());
        if( inventorySlot == null ) continue;
        int numItems = inventorySlot.getNumItems();
        if( numItems > 0 ){
                items.add(new InventoryItemLocation(i,
                    inventorySlot.getTopInventoryItem(
                        ).getItemTypeID().toString(), numItems));
        }
    }
    return items;
  }
}
```

The `getInventory()` method will take a table and return an array of the POJO `InventoryItemLocation` objects. The `InventoryItemLocation` class includes the location index where the `InventoryItem` object is stored, the type of `InventoryItem`, and the number of items that were stored at that location. This method simply iterates through all the table cells with `InventorySlot` locations, populates an `InventoryItemLocation` object, and adds it to the array.

Drag and drop usage

The following snippet demonstrates how the `DragAndDrop` object is used to register the source and target classes in order to use the drag and drop functionality:

```
public class InventoryUI extends Window {
...
private DragAndDrop _dragAndDrop;
```

```
public InventoryUI(){

    ...
    _dragAndDrop = new DragAndDrop();

    _dragAndDrop.addTarget(new InventorySlotTarget(headSlot));
    _dragAndDrop.addTarget(new InventorySlotTarget
        (leftArmSlot));
    _dragAndDrop.addTarget(new InventorySlotTarget
        (chestSlot));
    _dragAndDrop.addTarget(new InventorySlotTarget
        (rightArmSlot));
    _dragAndDrop.addTarget(new InventorySlotTarget(legsSlot));

    //layout
    for(int i = 1; i <= _numSlots; i++){

        ...
        _dragAndDrop.addTarget(new
            InventorySlotTarget(inventorySlot));
    }
}
```

When adding the `InventorySlotTarget` objects to the `DragAndDrop` member
variable, we need to make sure we pass in a reference to the corresponding
`InventorySlot` object so that once registered, the proper notifications get sent:

```
public void populateInventory(Table targetTable,
    Array<InventoryItemLocation> inventoryItems){
...
    for(int i = 0; i < inventoryItems.size; i++){
        ...
        for( int index = 0; index <
            itemLocation.getNumberItemsAtLocation(); index++ ){
            ...
            _dragAndDrop.addSource(new
                InventorySlotSource(inventorySlot, _dragAndDrop));
        }
    }
}
```

In the `populateInventory()` method, which is used when loading inventory items
from a save game profile, we need to make sure that we pass in an `InventorySlot`
reference when we register `InventorySlotSource` as a source for the `DragAndDrop`
member variable.

Tooltip usage

Finally, we get to the construction and usage of `InventorySlotTooltip`. An excerpted portion of the source for reference is discussed here:

```
public class InventoryUI extends Window {
...
private Array<Actor> _inventoryActors;
private InventorySlotTooltip _inventorySlotTooltip;

public InventoryUI(){
...
_inventoryActors = new Array<Actor>();
```

The array of `Actor` objects is a container primarily for the `InventorySlotTooltip` window, as we need to pass this object back to the parent (`PlayerHUD`) so that the window is displayed correctly on the screen:

```
_inventorySlotTooltip = new InventorySlotTooltip
    (Utility.STATUSUI_SKIN);

    headSlot.addListener(new InventorySlotTooltipListener(
        _inventorySlotTooltip));

    leftArmSlot.addListener(new InventorySlotTooltipListener(
        _inventorySlotTooltip));

    rightArmSlot.addListener(new InventorySlotTooltipListener(
        _inventorySlotTooltip));

    chestSlot.addListener(new InventorySlotTooltipListener(
        _inventorySlotTooltip));

    legsSlot.addListener(new InventorySlotTooltipListener(
        _inventorySlotTooltip));

//layout
for(int i = 1; i <= _numSlots; i++){
    ...
    inventorySlot.addListener(new
        InventorySlotTooltipListener(_inventorySlotTooltip));
}
```

We make sure that all the `InventorySlot` objects register an `InventorySlotTooltipListener` so that they can propagate the notifications to the `InventorySlotTooltip` window when a tooltip event gets triggered (when the mouse hovers over an `InventoryItem`):

```
    _inventoryActors.add(_inventorySlotTooltip);
}
    public Array<Actor> getInventoryActors(){
        return _inventoryActors;
    }
}
```

Menu screens

Taking everything we have learned, we can now apply the knowledge to constructing the screen UIs. The following screenshot (*Figure 13*) shows how we switch between the different screens, depending on which callbacks were triggered (a button widget press event):

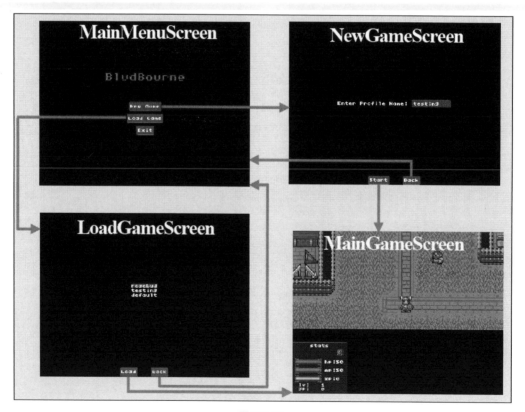

Figure 13

Note that when implementing the logic for the different screens, make sure the appropriate `show()` and `hide()` methods are implemented for each screen. When switching between the different screens, we make a single method call, `setScreen()`, from the main entry point class, `BludBourne.java`. The `setScreen()` method will call the `hide()` method on the currently visible screen and then call `show()` on the new screen. This should cover most use cases for creating interactive screens. In the future, we will learn how to add transition effects when loading different map locations, as well as during screen changes.

Save and load game profiles

There are many different ways to implement the save/restore functionality in a game. There is a spectrum of options in the solution space, with one end of the spectrum for a minimalist approach for save/restore philosophy, specifically a simple name/value pair approach, with values for persisting a high score or the current level number. LibGDX supports this natively through the `Preferences` class in LibGDX that is modeled after preferences on Android. The other end of the save/restore functionality spectrum is a brute force approach where everything in-memory for the current game state is dumped to some binary format. This approach has severe drawbacks with save game sizes and also has a brittle state where one change in a class (patch update) can render previous saves useless. Our philosophy approach for the purpose of this book is one that adopts a little from both ends of the spectrum.

The primary class that will handle all of our serialization and deserialization efforts is `ProfileManager`. This class is implemented as a Singleton as we need a single global point of access when we first start the game for selecting from the existing save game profiles, loading a profile, and accessing the current profile when saving the current state.

Currently, there is one save game location for each profile. *BludBourne* has a shorter game playthrough than what your finished title will have, so having one profile to save to, adds an extra element of challenge for the player. This can be augmented to include multiple save locations per profile, depending on the requirements for your game.

The `ProfileManager` class can be found under the `profiles` directory off the source root project directory. The source for `ProfileManager` is as follows:

```
package com.packtpub.libgdx.bludbourne.profile;

import com.badlogic.gdx.Gdx;
import com.badlogic.gdx.files.FileHandle;
import com.badlogic.gdx.utils.Array;
import com.badlogic.gdx.utils.Json;
import com.badlogic.gdx.utils.ObjectMap;
import java.util.Enumeration;
import java.util.Hashtable;
```

The noteworthy item on the imports for `ProfileManager` is the `ObjectMap` class in LibGDX. Since we are primarily dealing with JSON as the serializing data format (as JSON is built for key/value pairs of data including support for arrays packed with POJO data), LibGDX has a convenience class, `ObjectMap`, which is efficient at storing and retrieving this type of data:

```
public class ProfileManager extends ProfileSubject {
    private Json _json;
    private static ProfileManager _profileManager;
    private Hashtable<String,FileHandle> _profiles = null;
    private ObjectMap<String, Object> _profileProperties = new
            ObjectMap<String, Object>();
    private String _profileName;

    private static final String SAVEGAME_SUFFIX = ".sav";
    public static final String DEFAULT_PROFILE = "default";
```

We will discuss the `ProfileSubject` base class later on as part of the *Observer pattern* implementation. We will be storing two items in `ProfileManager`. The first item we will be storing is `Hashtable` of all the profile file handles available for easy access during loading and saving operations. The second item we will be storing is as an `ObjectMap` of all the key/value pairs of properties we want to persist for the save/restore functionality of our game:

```
    private ProfileManager(){
        _json = new Json();
        _profiles = new Hashtable<String,FileHandle>();
        _profiles.clear();
        _profileName = DEFAULT_PROFILE;
```

```
            storeAllProfiles();
    }

    public static final ProfileManager getInstance(){
        if( _profileManager == null){
            _profileManager = new ProfileManager();
        }
        return _profileManager;
    }
```

The `getInstance()` method is the single point of access using lazy initialization (initialized as late as possible, upon first usage) for the Singleton instance of `ProfileManager`:

```
    public Array<String> getProfileList(){
        Array<String> profiles = new Array<String>();
        for (Enumeration<String> e = _profiles.keys();
            e.hasMoreElements();){
            profiles.add(e.nextElement());
        }
        return profiles;
    }
```

The `getProfileList()` method constructs an array of profile strings to display in our selection UI dialog:

```
    public FileHandle getProfileFile(String profile){
        if( !doesProfileExist(profile) ){
            return null;
        }
        return _profiles.get(profile);
    }
```

The `getProfileFile()` method will return the file handle (if available) for the profile name passed in. We need to make a note to handle the null case if the file handle does not exist:

```
    public void storeAllProfiles(){
        if( Gdx.files.isLocalStorageAvailable() ){
            FileHandle[] files =
                Gdx.files.local(".").list(SAVEGAME_SUFFIX);
```

```
                for(FileHandle file: files) {
                    _profiles.put(file.nameWithoutExtension(), file);
                }
            }else{
                return;
            }
        }
```

The `storeAllProfiles()` method will check to see whether local storage is available, and if it is, store all available profile files into our member `Hashtable` for access later:

```
        public boolean doesProfileExist(String profileName){
            return _profiles.containsKey(profileName);
        }

        public void writeProfileToStorage(String profileName, String
          fileData, boolean overwrite){
            String fullFilename = profileName+SAVEGAME_SUFFIX;

            boolean localFileExists =
                    Gdx.files.internal(fullFilename).exists();

            //If we cannot overwrite and the file exists, exit
            if( localFileExists && !overwrite ){
                return;
            }

            FileHandle file = null;

            if( Gdx.files.isLocalStorageAvailable() ) {
                file = Gdx.files.local(fullFilename);
                file.writeString(fileData, !overwrite);
            }
            _profiles.put(profileName, file);
        }
```

The `writeProfileToStorage()` method will take a profile name string, a serialized JSON string of data, and a `boolean` value whether or not we want to overwrite the file if it exists. We construct the file based on the profile name and see if it exists. If the file exists and we can overwrite the file, then we continue, otherwise we return.

We then write out the serialized JSON string to the file and add this new file handle to our Hashtable of profiles:

```
public void setProperty(String key, Object object){
    _profileProperties.put(key, object);
}

public <T extends Object> T getProperty(String key, Class<T>
  type){
    T property = null;
    if( !_profileProperties.containsKey(key) ){
        return property;
    }
    property = (T)_profileProperties.get(key);
    return property;
}
```

The setProperty() method will add a key/value pair property to the ObjectMap member object, _profileProperties. The convenience of this method cannot be overstated as it allows us to pass in arrays with POJO data, simplifying the storage of different types of properties. The getProperty() method takes a key string and a class type as input parameters. If we cannot find the key in the ObjectMap property, then we return null, otherwise we return the value found cast to the class type:

```
public void saveProfile(){
    notify(this, ProfileObserver.ProfileEvent.SAVING_PROFILE);
    String text = _json.prettyPrint(
            _json.toJson(_profileProperties));
    writeProfileToStorage(_profileName, text, true);
}

public void loadProfile(){
    String fullProfileFileName = _profileName+SAVEGAME_SUFFIX;
    boolean doesProfileFileExist =
            Gdx.files.internal(fullProfileFileName).exists();

    if( !doesProfileFileExist ){
        System.out.println("File doesn't exist!");
        return;
    }

    _profileProperties = _json.fromJson(
        ObjectMap.class, _profiles.get(_profileName));
    notify(this, ProfileObserver.ProfileEvent.PROFILE_LOADED);
}
```

The `saveProfile()` method will first notify all observers with a `SAVING_PROFILE` profile event. The observers that are subscribed to this notification will store their current properties in preparation for serialization. The observer pattern is discussed in more detail in the next section. We will then convert the `ObjectMap` that contains all of our properties into a JSON string and then write it out to the profile file. One item to note here is that the properties in `ObjectMap` should be restricted to simple key/value pairs of objects and simple arrays with POJO data. Otherwise, if the data is too complex, then the chances of having circular references increases, leading to a scenario where the JSON serialization will fail with a stack overflow.

The `loadProfile()` method will verify that the profile file exists, and if it does, deserialize the file into `ObjectMap` for all the properties. A notification with a `PROFILE_LOADED` profile event is sent to all registered observers so that the classes that own those properties can correctly initialize the data.

If we wanted a little obfuscation for the save game profiles, we could add Base64 encoding to the profiles at the serialization and deserialization steps in these methods. For the purposes of this book, it is easier to understand the data we are working with in a more readable format:

```
public void setCurrentProfile(String profileName){
    if( doesProfileExist(profileName) ){
        _profileName = profileName;
    }else{
        _profileName = DEFAULT_PROFILE;
    }
}
}
```

Finally, the `setCurrentProfile()` method will set the profile string passed in as the currently loaded profile (if it exists), otherwise we will load a default profile.

Observer pattern

One piece of this solution that we need to consider is which classes have ownership of the properties we are storing. We want to try to avoid a scenario where we duplicate properties in a class that acts as a property bag for easier serialization. The main problem with this approach is when properties change, or are removed altogether from the main class that uses the property, the changes might not get propagated to the serializing class. So, we want to keep the ownership of the properties with their corresponding classes without duplicating them.

One solution to solving this problem is to implement an observer pattern where we have classes subscribe or register themselves (the observers) with other classes (the subject) in order to look for certain notifications. The overall class diagram structure for this pattern implemented in our game is shown here (*Figure 14*):

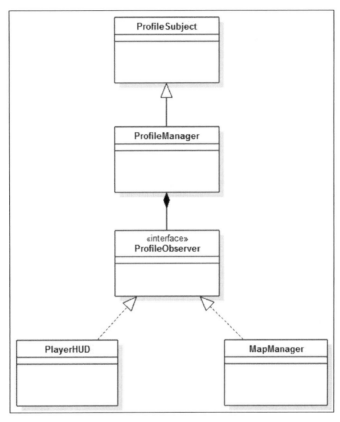

Figure 14

Figure 14 first shows how `ProfileManager` extends from the base class `ProfileSubject`, which is described in the following class diagram in *Figure 15*:

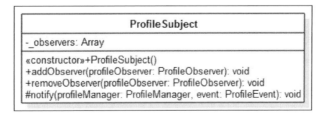

Figure 15

`ProfileSubject` is the subject class in our observer pattern that owns all the observers that register themselves, storing them in an array. Once a notification is created (a profile event in our case), the `ProfileSubject` class will iterate over all registered observers and send them the notifications.

For the classes that wish to receive the `ProfileSubject` notifications (or profile events in our case), they will implement the `ProfileObserver` interface, which is described in the following class diagram (*Figure 16*):

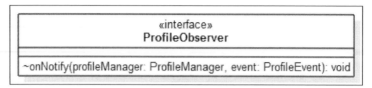

Figure 16

This simplifies the saving/restoring logic because if a class has certain properties it wants to persist, the class simply registers itself first by implementing the `ProfileObserver` interface.

Observer pattern usage example

As an example usage of the observer pattern, let's say we want to save the current map that's loaded so that when the player loads the game profile, they will start from the current map location. We will need to define the property to store which, in our case, will be `currentMapType` that represents the `MapType` enum defined in `MapFactory`. First, we implement the `ProfileObserver` interface in the class that owns the property, which is demonstrated with the following code snippet:

```
import com.packtpub.libgdx.bludbourne.profile.ProfileManager;
import com.packtpub.libgdx.bludbourne.profile.ProfileObserver;

public class MapManager implements ProfileObserver {
...
    @Override
    public void onNotify(ProfileManager profileManager,
        ProfileEvent event) {
        switch(event){
            case PROFILE_LOADED:
                String currentMap = profileManager.getProperty(
                        "currentMapType", String.class);
                MapFactory.MapType mapType;
                if( currentMap == null || currentMap.isEmpty() ){
                    mapType = MapFactory.MapType.TOWN;
```

```
            }else{
                mapType = MapFactory.MapType.valueOf(
                    currentMap);
            }
            loadMap(mapType);
            break;
        case SAVING_PROFILE:
            profileManager.setProperty(
                "currentMapType",
                _currentMap._currentMapType.toString());
            break;
        default:
            break;
        }
    }
}
```

We make sure to handle the events for the `ProfileEvent` types. When saving a profile (a `SAVING_PROFILE` event), we make sure to set the property for the `currentMapType`. When loading the profile (a `PROFILE_LOADED` event), we load the correct map based upon the `currentMapType` property. Second, after we have implemented the logic to deal with the various `ProfileEvent` events for our property, we then need to register it with the subject class, which in our case is `ProfileManager` that implements `ProfileSubject`:

```
public class MainGameScreen implements Screen {
...
    public MainGameScreen(BludBourne game){
        ...
        ProfileManager.getInstance().addObserver(_mapMgr);
    }
}
```

Now whenever a new profile is loaded or the current profile is saved, `MapManager` will know to load the saved map or save the current map property, respectively. The actual save game profile (JSON formatted) from this example will look similar to the following excerpt:

```
{
  currentMapType: {
    class: java.lang.String
    value: TOWN
  }
}
```

This is the approach we will use in order to manage the persistence of all the various properties for our game.

Summary

In this chapter, we first learned the basics of how UIs are created with LibGDX by understanding widget styles, texture atlases, 9-patch images, and creating skins for the widgets. We then took this foundation and implemented a HUD, a UI for player status, a UI for player inventory, screen UIs for the main screen, and loading game profiles. Finally, we implemented a save and restore solution in order to persist our game profiles using the observer pattern.

In the next chapter, we will begin to look at speech windows and dialog trees for NPC interaction and also implement a shop store UI with a buy and sell transaction system.

5
Time to Breathe Some Life into This Town

Up until now we have been building a general foundation for our game that includes loading maps, displaying textures, persisting game state, and developing interactive UIs. At this point, we will start to develop features more specific to RPGs. In this chapter, we will explore conversation trees in order to add lore and backstory to our adventures through the land of *BludBourne*, and also make the NPCs more interactive and interesting. We will also look at developing the store inventory, which can be used for not only dealing with money transactions, but also as a simple trade screen with any NPC (if they have items).

In summary, we will cover the following topics in this chapter:

- Speech windows with dialog trees
- Shop store UI with items and money transactions

There is some theory that we will cover to better understand how conversation trees work and then we will quickly move to the actual design and implementation used in our game. We will take a step-by-step approach. We will first start with the fundamental data structures that compose a conversation tree and then move to the class overview used in our game. The classes include the basic UI dialog, a graph-based data structure that contains the conversations, and event triggering based upon choices made in the conversation. We will then discuss how the conversations themselves will be created in script files for easy modification and localization support.

Speech windows with dialog trees

The following image (*Figure 1*) shows an example of a conversation used in our game, with the basic dialog text at the top-half of the UI window, and the various selectable choices presented at the bottom-half:

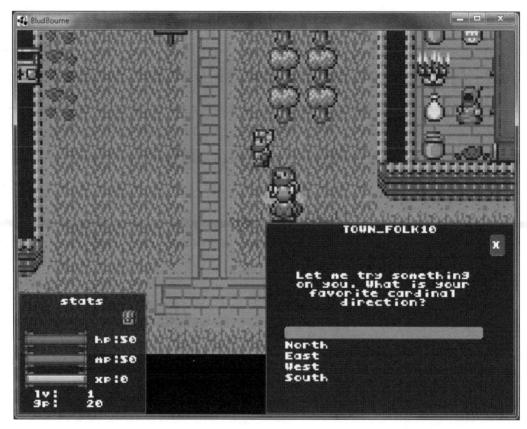

Figure 1

Theory behind conversation trees

In the general parlance of game development, the terms **conversation tree** or **dialog tree** are commonly used to specify the UI dialogs that are presented when interacting with NPC characters in a video game. This is a nice level of immersion because this is a chance for the player to interact directly with an NPC based on choices of dialog, instead of just stealing items from their homes or attacking them. The idea of conversation trees has existed before video games started to use them, such as the *Which Way* or *Choose Your Own Adventure* books, which gave the reader two choices at the end of each chapter. This mechanic of branching dialog choices led to either a good ending where the player was successful or a bad ending where various horrible events befell the reader and forced them to start over.

In more modern games, conversations can include more dynamic choices, ones that affect future interactions with an NPC. One example of these types of choices would be *Fallout 3* by Bethesda Softworks, where answering questions with threats can cause the NPC to never talk to you again. Another example would be the *Mass Effect* series where you could answer questions across a spectrum of intentions, such as "Paragon" for "good" alignment options, "Renegade" for "bad" alignment options, or the safe route with the neutral option. Since our game is in the spirit of older titles that did not always have dynamic choices, we will support multiple dialog choices that allow you to interact with the NPCs but without the persistence.

For our purposes, based on more modern gameplay mechanics, we want the ability for the player to be able to go back to previous points in a conversation, even the beginning, asking different questions or looking for different responses. We also want the ability to have more than two choices, which makes for more interesting dialog choices for the player than just having two clearly distinct choices. For these reasons, we will not be developing a conversation tree, but a **conversation graph**, since a graph supports more than two choices and can contain cycles (the option to go back to a previous conversation).

I will not be going in depth into graph theory, as the book *Algorithms (4th Edition by Robert Sedgewick and Kevin Wayne)*, does an amazing job of describing data structures and algorithms with examples in the Java language. Just as I had to brush up on some basics of constructing graphs, I believe it is important enough to warrant a brief explanation, starting with a basic graph in the following figure (*Figure 2*):

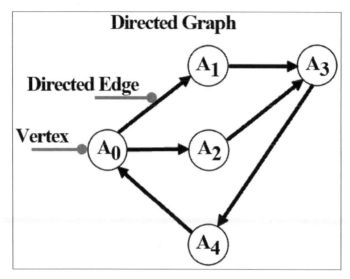

Figure 2

First, in computer science, a graph is defined as a data structure composed of a set (or distinct collection) of vertices or nodes. In *Figure 2*, we have a set of five vertices, designated as *{A0, A1, A2, A3, A4}*. These vertices are connected via edges or arcs that create pairs of vertices or connections. In *Figure 2*, we have the following edges or pairs of vertices: *{(A0,A1), (A0,A2), (A1,A3), (A2,A3), (A3,A4), (A4,A0)}*. Since our edges have a direction, we end up with ordered pairs of vertices, thus making our graph a directed graph. If we used an undirected model instead of a directed model for our conversation graph, then we would lose control over the flow of the conversation because of the bidirectionality of the connections between the vertices. Since we want to maintain a specific, directed flow of logic surrounding each decision that the player makes during a conversation, we want to use a directed graph instead.

The other feature of this graph is that it supports cycles. A cycle is when a series of edges start and end with the same vertex. In *Figure 2*, one of the cycles follows this sequence: *{(A0,A1), (A1,A3), (A3,A4), (A4,A0)}*. As you can see, our root vertex of the graph starts at *A0* and by following the connections, we end up back at *A0*. Supporting cycles is useful; for example, when you have a lot of information that you want the player to explore with the NPC, you can have the conversation cycle back to a previous part of the conversation so the player can choose another path. Cycles in our directed graph differentiates our conversation graph from a regular conversation tree structure, since there are no cycles in a tree.

The next step is to substitute in a conversation into a graph structure to see how everything fits together, as shown in the following figure (*Figure 3*):

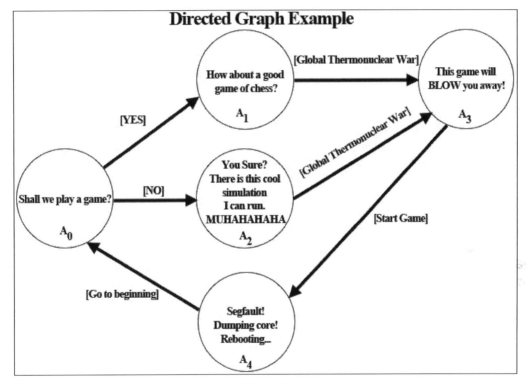

Figure 3

This is a conversation retrofitted into the previous directed graph from *Figure 2*. I did take some artistic license with the conversation that Matthew Broderick had with Joshua in *WarGames*, but I believe it works in our example. As we can see, we still have our vertices designated in the set *{A0, A1, A2, A3, A4}*. Here, each vertex represents a question or statement that the NPC will ask or say, respectively, to you in the process of your conversation. Your response to the NPC will be represented as an edge that connects from the original question or statement to another part of the conversation. As the player answers the question or selects a statement, that connection will determine what the NPC will say or how the NPC will react during the conversation.

Using this example as a model for a conversation graph for our game, we will now take a deep dive into the overall object model and look at the implementation so that we can start breathing some life into the NPCs.

An overview of class hierarchy

The following class diagram (*Figure 4*) gives an overview of the new classes created for the conversation graph and also for a few existing classes used to facilitate notifications throughout the UI:

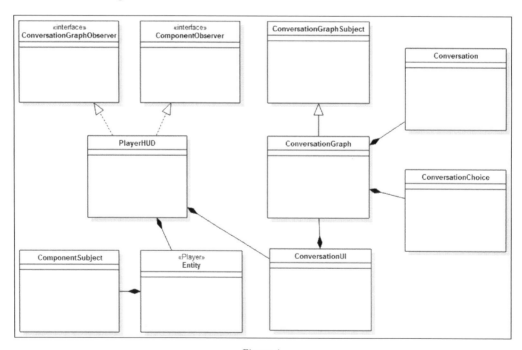

Figure 4

First, the `ConversationGraph` class is the graph data structure that loads new conversations. The following is the class diagram (*Figure 5*) for `ConversationGraph`:

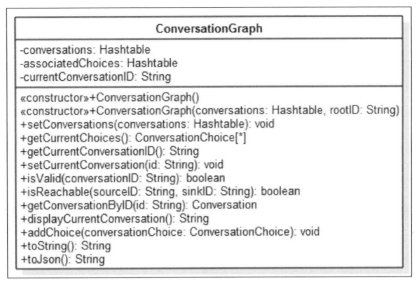

ConversationGraph

-conversations: Hashtable
-associatedChoices: Hashtable
-currentConversationID: String

«constructor»+ConversationGraph()
«constructor»+ConversationGraph(conversations: Hashtable, rootID: String)
+setConversations(conversations: Hashtable): void
+getCurrentChoices(): ConversationChoice[*]
+getCurrentConversationID(): String
+setCurrentConversation(id: String): void
+isValid(conversationID: String): boolean
+isReachable(sourceID: String, sinkID: String): boolean
+getConversationByID(id: String): Conversation
+displayCurrentConversation(): String
+addChoice(conversationChoice: ConversationChoice): void
+toString(): String
+toJson(): String

Figure 5

The `ConversationGraph` class is composed of `Conversation` and `ConversationChoice` objects, each stored in a `Hashtable` for fast retrieval.

Conversation

The class diagram that describes the `Conversation` class is as follows (*Figure 6*):

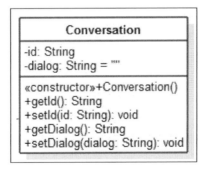

Conversation

-id: String
-dialog: String = ""

«constructor»+Conversation()
+getId(): String
+setId(id: String): void
+getDialog(): String
+setDialog(dialog: String): void

Figure 6

This `Conversation` class represents the vertices of the `ConversationGraph` class. `Conversation` is a POJO (for easy JSON serialization) that contains text for a piece of dialog to be displayed on a particular vertex and also a unique ID for reference.

ConversationChoice

The class diagram that describes the `ConversationChoice` class is as follows (*Figure 7*):

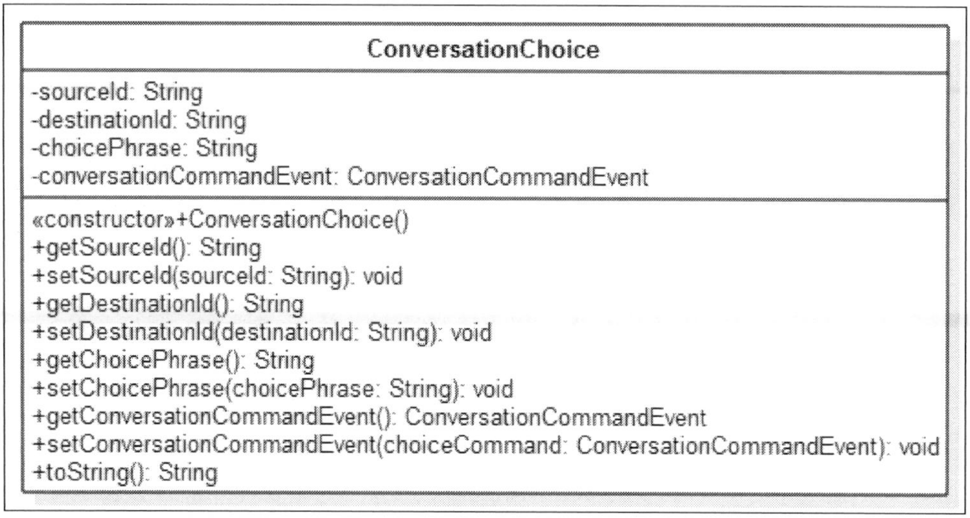

ConversationChoice
-sourceId: String
-destinationId: String
-choicePhrase: String
-conversationCommandEvent: ConversationCommandEvent
«constructor»+ConversationChoice() +getSourceId(): String +setSourceId(sourceId: String): void +getDestinationId(): String +setDestinationId(destinationId: String): void +getChoicePhrase(): String +setChoicePhrase(choicePhrase: String): void +getConversationCommandEvent(): ConversationCommandEvent +setConversationCommandEvent(choiceCommand: ConversationCommandEvent): void +toString(): String

Figure 7

The `ConversationChoice` class represents the edges of the `ConversationGraph` class. `ConversationChoice` is also a POJO, which connects two vertices (source and destination) with a particular choice to be displayed to the player and manages any events (`ConversationCommandEvent`) that occur from a particular choice. The source and destination IDs represent the direction of the connection for our directed graph, which directs the flow of the conversation as the player makes choices at each `Conversation` vertex of the graph.

ConversationGraphSubject and ConversationGraphObserver

The ConversationGraph class extends from the base class ConversationGraphSubject, which is used to send notifications to ConversationGraphObserver as a player moves through the conversation graph selecting different options. These two classes represent the observer pattern that we discussed in *Chapter 4, Where Do I Put My Stuff?*

The following class diagram (*Figure 8*) outlines the interface for the ConversationGraphObserver:

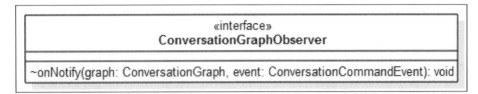

Figure 8

The PlayerHUD class acts as a hub for all the game UI, implementing the various observer interfaces so that it can relay the appropriate notifications to the correct destinations. In this class diagram (*Figure 4*), PlayerHUD implements both the ConversationGraphObserver and ComponentObserver interfaces.

The ConversationGraphObserver interface sends notifications for ConversationCommandEvents, such as when the conversation has ended or the player wants to see a vendor's wares based on their conversation.

The following class diagram (*Figure 9*) outlines the interface for the ConversationGraphSubject class:

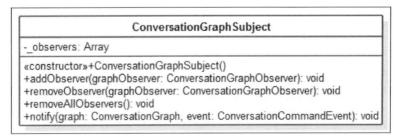

Figure 9

ConversationGraphSubject implements the standard observer pattern as described in *Chapter 4, Where Do I Put My Stuff?*

We will now do a code walkthrough of ConversationGraph (*Figure 5*) to see how all these classes fit together.

ConversationGraph

The source for ConversationGraph is as follows:

```
package com.packtpub.libgdx.bludbourne.dialog;

import com.badlogic.gdx.utils.Json;

import java.util.ArrayList;
import java.util.Hashtable;
import java.util.Set;

public class ConversationGraph extends ConversationGraphSubject {
    private Hashtable<String, Conversation> conversations;
    private Hashtable<String, ArrayList<ConversationChoice>>
            associatedChoices;
    private String currentConversationID = null;

    public ConversationGraph(){
    }
```

Here, ConversationGraph derives from ConversationGraphSubject so that we can hook in ConversationGraphObservers in order to get notifications from the current graph.

The first Hashtable has a String type for a key, which represents the unique ID of the vertex (represented by the Conversation class). As an example from *Figure 3*, conversations would have a size of 5 with the following keys: *{A0, A1, A2, A3, A4}*. Each key would have access to a Conversation object with the dialog for its respective vertex. For instance, the *A0* key would return a Conversation object with the dialog string "Shall we play a game?".

The second `Hashtable`, `associatedChoices`, also has a `String` type for a key, which represents the unique ID of the edge (represented by the `ConversationChoice` class). `associatedChoices` contains an `ArrayList` of the `ConversationChoice` objects. This is an adjacency list (a list of neighboring vertices) that maintains `ConversationChoice` (edge) `ArrayList` indexed by the ID of the `Conversation` objects (vertices). Essentially, this list represents the vertices connected by an edge to each vertex. As another example from *Figure 3*, we can use *A0* as a key value for the `associatedChoices` `Hashtable`, which will return an `ArrayList` with two `ConversationChoice` entries: one with a destination ID of *A1* and a choice phrase of "YES" and the other entry with a destination ID of *A2* and a choice phrase of "NO". Both of these entries would have *A0* as the source ID.

We also keep a `String` ID, `currentConversationID`, around that represents the current `Conversation` vertex for easier bookkeeping:

```
public ConversationGraph(Hashtable<String, Conversation>
    conversations, String rootID){
    setConversations(conversations);
    setCurrentConversation(rootID);
}
```

Here, we can populate the `ConversationGraph` via this constructor by passing in the `Hashtable` already containing all the `Conversation` based vertices:

```
public void setConversations(Hashtable<String, Conversation>
    conversations) {
    if( conversations.size() < 0 ){
        throw new IllegalArgumentException(
            "Can't have a negative amount of conversations");
    }

    this.conversations = conversations;
    this.associatedChoices = new Hashtable<
        String,
        ArrayList<ConversationChoice>>(conversations.size());

    for( Conversation conversation: conversations.values() ){
        associatedChoices.put(
            conversation.getId(),
            new ArrayList<ConversationChoice>());
    }
    this.conversations = conversations;
}
```

```
public ArrayList<ConversationChoice> getCurrentChoices(){
    return associatedChoices.get(currentConversationID);
}


public String getCurrentConversationID(){
    return this.currentConversationID;
}
```

Another option for populating our `ConversationGraph` is to simply call the default constructor and use setter methods to populate the graph. Since we will be using JSON serialization/deserialization to load `ConversationGraph` from script files, we will end up using the default constructor with the setter methods automatically via Java reflection used in conjunction with the LibGDX JSON libraries.

The `setConversations()` method will first make sure we have the `Conversation` objects in the `Hashtable` and then initialize the `associatedChoices` `Hashtable` with empty `ArrayList` containers:

```
public boolean isValid(String conversationID){
    Conversation conversation =
                    conversations.get(conversationID);
    if( conversation == null ) return false;
    return true;
}


public boolean isReachable(String sourceID, String sinkID){
    if( !isValid(sourceID) || !isValid(sinkID) ) return false;
    if( conversations.get(sourceID) == null ) return false;

    //First get edges/choices from the source
    ArrayList<ConversationChoice> list =
        associatedChoices.get(sourceID);
    if( list == null ) return false;
    for(ConversationChoice choice: list){
        if(choice.getSourceId().equalsIgnoreCase(sourceID) &&
            choice.getDestinationId().equalsIgnoreCase(sinkID)
            ){
            return true;
        }
    }
    return false;
}
```

```
public Conversation getConversationByID(String id){
    if( !isValid(id) ){
        System.out.println("Id " + id + " is not valid!");
        return null;
    }
    return conversations.get(id);
}


public void setCurrentConversation(String id){
    Conversation conversation = getConversationByID(id);
    if( conversation == null ) return;
    //Can we reach the new conversation from the current one?

    //Make sure we check case
    //where the current node is checked against itself
    if( currentConversationID == null ||
            currentConversationID.equalsIgnoreCase(id) ||
            isReachable(currentConversationID, id) ){
        currentConversationID = id;
    }else{
        System.out.println("New conversation node [" + id +
            "]is not reachable from current node [" +
            currentConversationID + "]");
    }
}
```

We have two verification methods here. The first verification method is isValid(), which simply uses the ID passed in as a key for the conversations Hashtable, and if the Conversation vertex exists, then we return true, otherwise we return false. The other verification method is isReachable(). We basically pass in two vertex IDs and test whether there is a valid edge connection from the source vertex to the destination vertex. We iterate over the adjacency list of ConversationChoice objects comparing the vertex IDs, and if there is a match, then we know we have an edge connection and will return true. Otherwise, the destination vertex is not reachable from the source vertex and so we return false.

The getConversationByID() method will test to make sure the vertex ID exists, and if it does, return it. Otherwise, if the Conversation vertex does not exist, we will return a null object.

Finally, in the `setCurrentConversation()` method, we will run some validation tests to make sure that the conversation we want to set is reachable (has a valid edge connection) from the current `Conversation`. If we pass the validation tests, then we update our bookkeeping variable `currentConversationID` with the ID passed in:

```
public void addChoice(ConversationChoice conversationChoice){

    ArrayList<ConversationChoice> list =
        associatedChoices.get(conversationChoice.getSourceId());
    if( list == null) return;

    list.add(conversationChoice);
}
```

The `addChoice()` method will add an edge connection between two vertices, contained in the `ConversationChoice` object, to the current `Conversation` objects adjacency list (`ArrayList`):

```
public String displayCurrentConversation(){
    return conversations.get(
        currentConversationID).getDialog();
}
```

The `displayCurrentConversation()` method will return the `String` object that represents the dialog to be displayed from the current `Conversation` vertex:

```
public String toString(){
    StringBuilder outputString = new StringBuilder();
    int numberTotalChoices = 0;

    Set<String> keys = associatedChoices.keySet();
    for( String id: keys){
        outputString.append(String.format("[%s]: ", id));

        for( ConversationChoice choice:
                associatedChoices.get(id)){
            numberTotalChoices++;
            outputString.append(String.format("%s ",
                choice.getDestinationId())));
        }
        outputString.append(
            System.getProperty("line.separator"));
    }
```

```
            outputString.append(
                String.format("Number conversations: %d",
                conversations.size()));
            outputString.append(
                String.format(", Number of choices: %d",
                numberTotalChoices));
            outputString.append(System.getProperty("line.separator"));

            return outputString.toString();
        }

        public String toJson(){
            Json json = new Json();
            return json.prettyPrint(this);
        }
    }
```

The `toString()` method was used in the initial implementation for an interactive conversation session via the command line, before a UI was created to support `ConversationGraph`. The following is a sample session of testing out the `ConversationGraph` from the command line:

com.packtpub.libgdx.bludbourne.tests.ConversationGraphTest

[500]: 601 802

[250]:

[601]: 500

[802]: 500

Number conversations: 4, Number of choices: 4

Do you want to play a game?

601 YES

802 NO

>601

BOOM! Bombs dropping everywhere

500 Go to beginning!

>500

Do you want to play a game?

601 YES

802 NO

>802

```
Too bad!
500 Go to beginning!
>500
Do you want to play a game?
601 YES
802 NO
>250
New conversation node [250] is not reachable from current node [500]
Do you want to play a game?
601 YES
802 NO
>q
```

UI structure

The ConversationUI class is the dialog window that gets displayed when
a player selects an NPC, and that NPC has a conversation (in the form of a JSON
script file) available as shown in *Figure 1*. Each time a player selects an NPC, if
the NPC has a conversation script available, ConversationUI will deserialize the
JSON script and populate its ConversationGraph with the Conversation and
ConversationChoice objects.

The following diagram (*Figure 10*) outlines the important UI components that
ConversationUI is composed of:

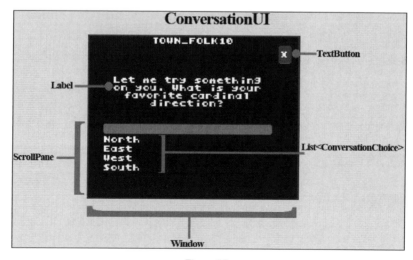

Figure 10

Let's take a look at how all these pieces fit together, between the `ConversationGraph` class and the `ConversationUI` class with the following code:

```
package com.packtpub.libgdx.bludbourne.UI;

import com.badlogic.gdx.Gdx;
import com.badlogic.gdx.scenes.scene2d.InputEvent;
import com.badlogic.gdx.scenes.scene2d.ui.Label;
import com.badlogic.gdx.scenes.scene2d.ui.List;
import com.badlogic.gdx.scenes.scene2d.ui.ScrollPane;
import com.badlogic.gdx.scenes.scene2d.ui.TextButton;
import com.badlogic.gdx.scenes.scene2d.ui.Window;
import com.badlogic.gdx.scenes.scene2d.utils.Align;
import com.badlogic.gdx.scenes.scene2d.utils.ClickListener;
import com.badlogic.gdx.utils.Json;
import com.packtpub.libgdx.bludbourne.EntityConfig;
import com.packtpub.libgdx.bludbourne.Utility;
import com.packtpub.libgdx.bludbourne.dialog.Conversation;
import com.packtpub.libgdx.bludbourne.dialog.ConversationChoice;
import com.packtpub.libgdx.bludbourne.dialog.ConversationGraph;

import java.util.ArrayList;

public class ConversationUI extends Window {
    private static final String TAG =
                ConversationUI.class.getSimpleName();

    private Label _dialogText;
    private List _listItems;
    private ConversationGraph _graph;
    private String _currentEntityID;
    private TextButton _closeButton;
    private Json _json;

    public ConversationUI() {
        super("dialog", Utility.STATUSUI_SKIN, "solidbackground");

        _json = new Json();
        _graph = new ConversationGraph();

        //create
        _dialogText = new Label("No Conversation",
                                Utility.STATUSUI_SKIN);
        _dialogText.setWrap(true);
        _dialogText.setAlignment(Align.center);
```

We have a variable for `Label` that represents the current dialog of the `ConversationGraph` that was previously loaded. To make the dialog more presentable in the `Window` class, we need to make sure that the text is centered and set to wrap:

```
_closeButton = new TextButton("X", Utility.STATUSUI_SKIN);
```

For our `Window`, we will add a `TextButton` widget with the "X" character set as the text:

```
_listItems = new List<ConversationChoice>(
                Utility.STATUSUI_SKIN);
```

The `List` class will contain all the `ConversationChoice` objects to be presented to the player. A `List` is a list box that displays text-based items and highlights the currently selected item. We use this in conjunction with the `ScrollPane` widget for ease of use for the player:

```
ScrollPane scrollPane = new ScrollPane(_listItems,
                Utility.STATUSUI_SKIN, "inventoryPane");
scrollPane.setOverscroll(false, false);
scrollPane.setFadeScrollBars(false);
scrollPane.setScrollingDisabled(true, false);
scrollPane.setForceScroll(true, false);
scrollPane.setScrollBarPositions(false, true);
```

Here, we pass in the `List` of the `ConversationChoice` items to the `ScrollPane` to be displayed to the player. We want to disable some of the features enabled by default, such as the overscroll and fade scroll bar features for better control:

```
//layout
this.add();
this.add(_closeButton);
this.row();
```

Now, we will layout the widgets, since the `Window` class is derived from `Table`. We will place the close button widget in the top-right corner of the window (second column):

```
this.defaults().expand().fill();
this.add(_dialogText).pad(10, 10, 10, 10);
this.row();
this.add(scrollPane).pad(10,10,10,10);
```

We will add the dialog text, which represents the current vertex dialog from
ConversationGraph, to the top-half of the Window class. Then, we will add
ScrollPane to the bottom-half of the Window class:

```
this.pack();

//Listeners
_listItems.addListener(new ClickListener() {
    @Override
    public void clicked (InputEvent event, float x,
                                float y) {
        ConversationChoice choice =
            (ConversationChoice)_listItems.getSelected();
        if( choice == null ) return;

        _graph.notify(_graph,
            choice.getConversationCommandEvent());

        populateConversationDialog(
            choice.getDestinationId());
        }
    }
);
}
```

Here, we add a listener (callback for the widget) for when a ListItem item is
selected. First, we get the ConversationChoice that the selection represents and
then send a notification to all observers if the current ConversationChoice has
some sort of event attached with it. For example, when a player states that they
want to look at the inventory of a vendor, the event for the choice will be sent to all
observers. This allows the PlayerHUD class (which is an observer for this event) to
present the StoreInventoryUI. Finally, we call populateConversationDialog() in
order to make the new destination ID (from the choice) the current Conversation:

```
public TextButton getCloseButton(){
    return _closeButton;
}

public String getCurrentEntityID() {
    return _currentEntityID;
}
```

```
public void loadConversation(EntityConfig entityConfig){
    String fullFilenamePath =
                entityConfig.getConversationConfigPath();
    this.setTitle("");

    clearDialog();

    if( fullFilenamePath.isEmpty() ||
        !Gdx.files.internal(fullFilenamePath).exists() ){
        Gdx.app.debug(TAG,
                    "Conversation file does not exist!");
        return;
    }

    _currentEntityID = entityConfig.getEntityID();
    this.setTitle(entityConfig.getEntityID());

    ConversationGraph graph =
                    _json.fromJson(ConversationGraph.class,
                    Gdx.files.internal(fullFilenamePath));
    setConversationGraph(graph);
}
```

The `loadConversation()` method is a utility method that handles loading the conversation script file (described in the *Script support for conversations* section in more depth) and initializing the `ConversationGraph` object for this dialog window:

```
public void setConversationGraph(ConversationGraph graph){
    if( _graph != null ) _graph.removeAllObservers();
    this._graph = graph;

    populateConversationDialog(
        _graph.getCurrentConversationID());
}

public ConversationGraph getCurrentConversationGraph(){
    return this._graph;
}

private void populateConversationDialog(String
                conversationID){
    clearDialog();
```

```
            Conversation conversation =
                        _graph.getConversationByID(conversationID);
            if( conversation == null ) return;

            _graph.setCurrentConversation(conversationID);
            _dialogText.setText(conversation.getDialog());
            ArrayList<ConversationChoice> choices =
                                    _graph.getCurrentChoices();
            if( choices == null ) return;
            _listItems.setItems(choices.toArray());
            _listItems.setSelectedIndex(-1);
        }
```

The populateConversationDialog() method is the primary driver that manages the business logic for this class. An ID that represents the vertex ID of the Conversation object to load is passed in. We set this Conversation as the current conversation in the ConversationGraph data structure. We then set the dialog text to be displayed in the dialog window from this Conversation object. Next, we set the ListItem object with all the ConversationChoice objects associated with the current Conversation class. Finally, we want to make sure no choice is already selected by default, so we pass in -1 to the selected index of ListItem to indicate that we do not want that default selection set:

```
        private void clearDialog(){
            _dialogText.setText("");
            _listItems.clearItems();
        }
    }
```

Every time we load a new conversation or finish an existing one, we want to make sure to clear the dialog text and all the ConversationChoice items.

Script support for conversations

As mentioned previously in the last section, the loadConversation() method in the ConversationUI class is a utility method that handles loading a conversation from a script file. The script file is a representation of the ConversationGraph object, serialized into JSON format. In your game, as you make more complex conversations, it is advisable to create a utility executable where the user can create the Conversation objects in some visual form, connect them with the ConversationChoice objects, and then serialize them out to a script file to be loaded by our game.

For *BludBourne*, I created a graph by hand to keep track of the objects and then created the JSON script file for `ConversationGraph` making sure to track the conversation. We also update the `EntityConfig` class by adding a `String` property `conversationConfigPath` that represents the full file path to the conversation script file. If the entity does not have a script associated with it, then no conversation dialog will be shown; otherwise, its configured script file will be loaded and presented in the `ConversationUI` dialog window.

The following script file `assets\conversations\conversation003.json` is presented here as an example of the form and structure you can use with the existing implementation:

```
{
conversations: {
      1: {
               id: 1
               dialog: Hello Traveler. Would you like to see my
                 wares?
      }
      2: {
               id: 2
               dialog: Ok
      }
      3: {
               id: 3
               dialog: Ok
      }
}
```

Here, at the beginning of our script, we define all the `Conversation` objects, each representing a vertex of `ConversationGraph`. We make sure that we define a unique ID and the dialog text to be displayed when that vertex of the graph is selected:

```
associatedChoices: {
      1: [
             {
                      class: com.packtpub.libgdx.bludbourne.
                        dialog.ConversationChoice
                      sourceId: 1
                      destinationId: 2
                      choicePhrase: Yes
             conversationCommandEvent: LOAD_STORE_INVENTORY
             }
             {
```

```
          class: com.packtpub.libgdx.bludbourne.
            dialog.ConversationChoice
          sourceId: 1
          destinationId: 3
          choicePhrase: No
     conversationCommandEvent: EXIT_CONVERSATION
          }
     ]
  }
```

In this section, we define all the `ConversationChoice` objects, each representing an edge that connects two vertices of `ConversationGraph`. We define the source vertex ID and the destination source vertex that completes the edge connection. We then add the text to be displayed for this particular `ConversationChoice`, such as a "NO" or "YES" response choice in a standard conversation. Finally, we add a field that defines the `ConversationCommandEvent`. The `ConversationUI` will emit a notification to all observers every time a conversation script is loaded, so when a player clicks on a choice, any observer looking for a particular event based on a conversation will be able to run its business logic:

```
currentConversationID: 1
  }
```

This field in the script file is important as it flags which of the `Conversation` vertices is the root vertex or the vertex where the conversation will start initially.

Triggering events

In the previous section, one of the fields of the `ConversationChoice` class is `ConversationCommandEvent`. This event facilitates communication between a particular choice in the conversation with some event in the game. Let's take an example based on the script file from the last section in this chapter. If a player says "YES" in order to look at the inventory of the vendor, then a LOAD_STORE_INVENTORY notification event gets emitted. The `PlayerHUD`, an observer of `ConversationGraph`, will receive the notification and promptly display the `StoreInventoryUI` to the player. The EXIT_CONVERSATION event is also received by `PlayerHUD`, which in turn will trigger the closing of the `ConversationUI` dialog window.

Another area where these events can get triggered is when to display the `ConversationUI` and figure out how to communicate selections made by the player when clicking on various NPCs. The `ComponentSubject` class bubbles up notifications from the `Component` objects that are owned by the `Entity` class.

These classes include InputComponent, PhysicsComponent, and GraphicsComponent. Once the PlayerHUD class implements the ComponentObserver and registers itself as an observer for the player-based entity object, the PlayerHUD will begin to receive notifications from the player. For our purposes, this includes notifications for when the player selects or deselects an NPC.

As we can see, the power of utilizing the observer pattern for communicating changes and events cannot be overstated, as it decouples the logic from the event and processes the event itself. This frees us up to make updates and changes without worrying about how those pieces will be communicated to the rest of the game. The responsibility will be on the classes that wish to receive the event, and all they need to do is implement the observer interface in order to get those notifications.

Shop store UI with items and money transactions

The final point of discussion in this chapter is the StoreInventoryUI class, as shown the following screenshot (*Figure 11*):

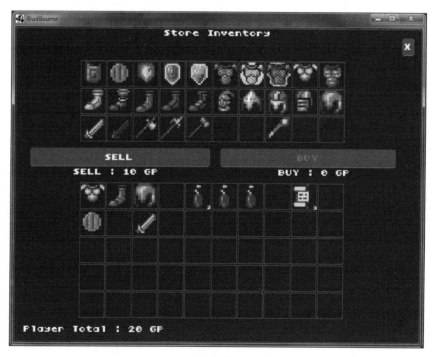

Figure 11

This class allows the player the ability to trade with various NPCs and is a fundamental feature for any RPG. This class is also a good example of how events can be triggered from a conversation, as we have discussed in the previous section, such as when we wish to see the wares of a shopkeeper.

The overall class relationship is represented in the following class diagram (*Figure 12*):

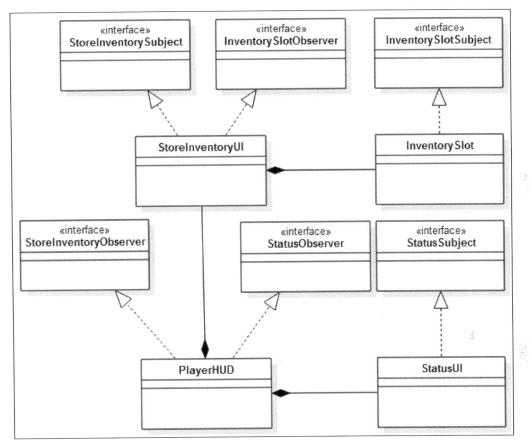

Figure 12

Again, `PlayerHUD` acts as a relay between the different UI windows that it owns, communicating relevant notifications. One such communication is when the player's money (GP) is updated, an event gets triggered. If the money is updated in the `StoreInventoryUI`, the `PlayerHUD` will communicate that change to the `StatusUI` and the player's GP will be updated accordingly, and vice versa. We will also have observers on the `InventorySlot` items to keep track of when items are dropped onto different target slots or removed from source slots. This is how `StoreInventoryUI` will manage the trade-in value of the items for sale (which is lower than the market price) or the market cost of items for the player to buy.

The general layout and widget structure is outlined in the following screenshot (*Figure 13*):

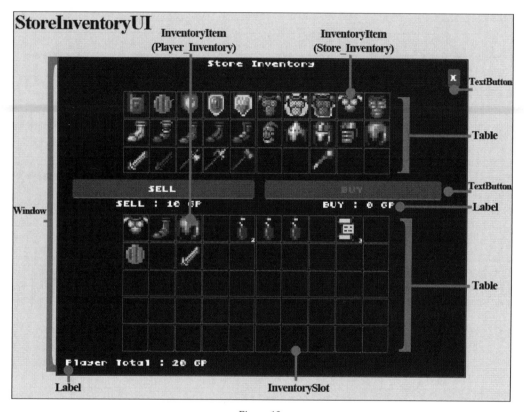

Figure 13

We will now step through the business logic for the `StoreInventoryUI` source here:

```
public class StoreInventoryUI extends Window implements
    InventorySlotObserver, StoreInventorySubject{
    ...
```

Here, the `StoreInventoryUI` class implements the `StoreInventorySubject` class so that the `PlayerHUD` class can add itself as a `StoreInventoryObserver` and relay any changes to the player's total amount of GP to the `StatusUI` class. `StoreInventoryUI` also implements the `InventorySlotObserver` class so that the notifications of player-based items being placed in the store inventory to sell and items from the store being placed in the player's inventory to buy, are captured with the appropriate trade-in value or buy price, respectively, and are updated in the `StoreInventoryUI`:

```
public StoreInventoryUI(){
    super("Store Inventory", Utility.STATUSUI_SKIN,
        "solidbackground");

    _observers = new Array<StoreInventoryObserver>();
    _json = new Json();

    this.setFillParent(true);

    //create
    _dragAndDrop = new DragAndDrop();
    _inventoryActors = new Array<Actor>();
    _inventorySlotTable = new Table();
    _inventorySlotTable.setName(STORE_INVENTORY);

    _playerInventorySlotTable = new Table();
    _playerInventorySlotTable.setName(PLAYER_INVENTORY);
    _inventorySlotTooltip = new InventorySlotTooltip(
                            Utility.STATUSUI_SKIN);
```

For the `StoreInventoryUI`, we are going to have two distinct tables, one for the store-owned items for sale (`_inventorySlotTable`) and one that represents the player's inventory (`_playerInventorySlotTable`):

```
    _sellButton = new TextButton(SELL, Utility.STATUSUI_SKIN,
                            "inventory");
    disableButton(_sellButton, true);

    _sellTotalLabel = new Label(SELL + " : " + _tradeInVal +
```

```
                              GP, Utility.STATUSUI_SKIN);
    _sellTotalLabel.setAlignment(Align.center);


    _buyTotalLabel = new Label(BUY + " : " + _fullValue + GP,
                            Utility.STATUSUI_SKIN);
    _buyTotalLabel.setAlignment(Align.center);


    _playerTotalGP = new Label(PLAYER_TOTAL + " : " +
                         _playerTotal + GP,
                          Utility.STATUSUI_SKIN);


    _buyButton = new TextButton(BUY, Utility.STATUSUI_SKIN,
                                  "inventory");
    disableButton(_buyButton, true);


    _closeButton = new TextButton("X", Utility.STATUSUI_SKIN);


    _buttons = new Table();
    _buttons.defaults().expand().fill();
    _buttons.add(_sellButton).padLeft(10).padRight(10);
    _buttons.add(_buyButton).padLeft(10).padRight(10);


    _totalLabels = new Table();
    _totalLabels.defaults().expand().fill();
    _totalLabels.add(_sellTotalLabel).padLeft(40);
    _totalLabels.add();
    _totalLabels.add(_buyTotalLabel).padRight(40);


    //layout
    for(int i = 1; i <= _numStoreInventorySlots; i++){
        InventorySlot inventorySlot = new InventorySlot();
        inventorySlot.addListener(
           new InventorySlotTooltipListener(
                _inventorySlotTooltip));

        inventorySlot.addObserver(this);
        inventorySlot.setName(STORE_INVENTORY);

        _dragAndDrop.addTarget(new
           InventorySlotTarget(inventorySlot));
```

```
    _inventorySlotTable.add(
        inventorySlot).size(_slotWidth, _slotHeight);

    if(i % _lengthSlotRow == 0){
        _inventorySlotTable.row();
    }
}

for(int i = 1; i <= InventoryUI._numSlots; i++){
    InventorySlot inventorySlot = new InventorySlot();
    inventorySlot.addListener(
        new InventorySlotTooltipListener(
            _inventorySlotTooltip));

    inventorySlot.addObserver(this);
    inventorySlot.setName(PLAYER_INVENTORY);

    _dragAndDrop.addTarget(new
        InventorySlotTarget(inventorySlot));

    _playerInventorySlotTable.add(
        inventorySlot).size(_slotWidth, _slotHeight);

    if(i % _lengthSlotRow == 0){
        _playerInventorySlotTable.row();
    }
}
```

Here, we first initialize the respective inventories, one for the store and one for the player. There are two important pieces to keep in mind when initializing these inventories. The first piece is that we need to make sure that every InventorySlot registers itself as an observer, so that notifications of the InventoryItem objects being added and removed from them can be handled by the StoreInventoryUI class. The second piece is that we need to set the ownership for each of the InventorySlot slots. This allows us to differentiate between the player-owned InventoryItem objects being placed on the store-based InventorySlot slots that will trigger a sale of an item, or the store-owned InventoryItem objects being placed on the player-based InventorySlot slots that will trigger a purchase of an item:

```
    _inventoryActors.add(_inventorySlotTooltip);

    this.add();
    this.add(_closeButton);
```

```
                    this.row();

                    this.defaults().expand().fill();
                    this.add(_inventorySlotTable).pad(10, 10, 10, 10).row();
                    this.add(_buttons).row();
                    this.add(_totalLabels).row();
                    this.add(
                        _playerInventorySlotTable).pad(10, 10, 10, 10).row();
                    this.add(_playerTotalGP);
                    this.pack();

                    //Listeners
                    _buyButton.addListener(new ClickListener() {

                    @Override
                        public void clicked(InputEvent event, float x, float y) {
                        if( _fullValue > 0 && _playerTotal >= _fullValue) {
                            _playerTotal -= _fullValue;
                            StoreInventoryUI.this.notify(
                                Integer.toString(_playerTotal),
                                StoreInventoryEvent.PLAYER_GP_TOTAL_UPDATED);

                            _fullValue = 0;
                            _buyTotalLabel.setText(BUY  + " : " +  _fullValue +
                                              GP);
                            checkButtonStates();

                            InventoryUI.setInventoryItemNames(
                                _playerInventorySlotTable, PLAYER_INVENTORY);

                            savePlayerInventory();
                    }
                }
            }
        }
    );
```

If the buy button is enabled and the player has clicked on the button, then we follow the business logic for purchase. We do another check that the player indeed has enough money for the transaction and then subtract the purchase amount from the player's total. We will then send out a notification for any observers that the player's GP amount has changed, and reset the buy button.

Finally, we update the ownership of the `InventoryItem` by setting the name to `PLAYER_INVENTORY` and then serialize the player's inventory so that the player's own inventory can get updated:

```
_sellButton.addListener(new ClickListener() {
    @Override
    public void clicked(InputEvent event, float x, float y) {
    if( _tradeInVal > 0 ) {
        _playerTotal += _tradeInVal;
        StoreInventoryUI.this.notify(
                Integer.toString(_playerTotal),
                StoreInventoryEvent.PLAYER_GP_TOTAL_UPDATED);
        _tradeInVal = 0;

        _sellTotalLabel.setText(SELL  + " : " +  _tradeInVal +
                             GP);

        checkButtonStates();

        Array<Cell> cells = _inventorySlotTable.getCells();

        for( int i = 0; i < cells.size; i++){
            InventorySlot inventorySlot =
                         (InventorySlot)cells.get(i).getActor();
            if( inventorySlot == null ) continue;
            if( inventorySlot.hasItem() &&
                inventorySlot.getTopInventoryItem().getName().
                equalsIgnoreCase(PLAYER_INVENTORY)){
                    inventorySlot.clearAllInventoryItems(false);
            }
        }
        savePlayerInventory();
    }
  }
 }
);
}
```

The business logic for the sell button is similar to that of the buy button. If the sell button is enabled and the player has clicked on the button, then we follow the business logic for sale. We add the trade-in value amount of the item to the player's total. We will then send out a notification for any observers that the player's GP amount has changed, and reset the sell button. Finally, we remove any of the player's items from the store inventory and then serialize the player's inventory so that the player's own inventory can get updated:

```
public TextButton getCloseButton(){
    return _closeButton;
}

public Table getInventorySlotTable() {
    return _inventorySlotTable;
}

public Array<Actor> getInventoryActors(){
    return _inventoryActors;
}

public void loadPlayerInventory(Array<InventoryItemLocation>
                                playerInventoryItems){
    InventoryUI.populateInventory(
      _playerInventorySlotTable, playerInventoryItems,
      _dragAndDrop);
}

public void loadStoreInventory(Array<InventoryItemLocation>
                               storeInventoryItems){
    InventoryUI.populateInventory(
      _inventorySlotTable, storeInventoryItems,
      _dragAndDrop);
}

public void savePlayerInventory(){
    Array<InventoryItemLocation> playerItemsInPlayerInventory =
        InventoryUI.getInventory(_playerInventorySlotTable,
        PLAYER_INVENTORY);
    Array<InventoryItemLocation> playerItemsInStoreInventory =
        InventoryUI.getInventory(_playerInventorySlotTable,
        _inventorySlotTable, PLAYER_INVENTORY);
```

```
        playerItemsInPlayerInventory.addAll(
            playerItemsInStoreInventory);

    StoreInventoryUI.this.notify(
        _json.toJson(playerItemsInPlayerInventory),
        StoreInventoryEvent.PLAYER_INVENTORY_UPDATED);

}
```

The `savePlayerInventory()` method is important to note, as this method covers edge cases in the `StoreInventoryUI`. Specifically, when the player leaves their items in the store inventory and then exits the store without selling them. The first step is to capture those items by iterating through the store inventory slots, looking for items owned by the player. The second step is a little more cumbersome, in that we don't know where to place these items back into the player's inventory. One solution is to check for all available slots in the player's inventory (empty cells) and then iterate over the list of empty cells, placing the items as the empty cells become available. Finally, after we have finished with combining the current player `InventoryItem` objects with the player's items left in the store, we serialize the items into a JSON string and send a notification out that the player's inventory has changed:

```
        public void cleanupStoreInventory(){
            InventoryUI.removeInventoryItems(
                STORE_INVENTORY, _playerInventorySlotTable);
            InventoryUI.removeInventoryItems(
                PLAYER_INVENTORY, _inventorySlotTable);
        }

        @Override
        public void onNotify(InventorySlot slot, SlotEvent event) {
            switch(event)
            {
                case ADDED_ITEM:
                    if( slot.getTopInventoryItem().getName(
                        ).equalsIgnoreCase(PLAYER_INVENTORY) &&

                        slot.getName().equalsIgnoreCase(
                            STORE_INVENTORY) ) {

                        _tradeInVal += slot.getTopInventoryItem(
                                        ).getTradeValue();
                        _sellTotalLabel.setText(SELL + " : " +
```

```
                                          _tradeInVal + GP);
            }
            if( slot.getTopInventoryItem().getName(
                ).equalsIgnoreCase(STORE_INVENTORY) &&
                slot.getName().equalsIgnoreCase(
                    PLAYER_INVENTORY) ) {
                _fullValue += slot.getTopInventoryItem(
                            ).getItemValue();
                _buyTotalLabel.setText(BUY + " : " +
                                    _fullValue + GP);
            }
            break;
        case REMOVED_ITEM:
            if( slot.getTopInventoryItem().getName(
                ).equalsIgnoreCase(PLAYER_INVENTORY) &&
                slot.getName().equalsIgnoreCase(
                    STORE_INVENTORY) ) {
                _tradeInVal -= slot.getTopInventoryItem(
                            ).getTradeValue();
                _sellTotalLabel.setText(SELL + " : " +
                                    _tradeInVal + GP);
            }
            if( slot.getTopInventoryItem().getName(
                ).equalsIgnoreCase(STORE_INVENTORY) &&
                slot.getName().equalsIgnoreCase(
                    PLAYER_INVENTORY) ) {
                _fullValue -= slot.getTopInventoryItem(
                            ).getItemValue();
                _buyTotalLabel.setText(BUY + " : " +
                                    _fullValue + GP);
            }
            break;
    }
        checkButtonStates();
}
```

The onNotify() method handles the different events based on how the
InventoryItem objects are dragged and dropped around the StoreInventoryUI.

The first event we need to check for is when an item is added. There are two specific scenarios that we need to cover. The first scenario is when an `InventoryItem` moves from the player's inventory to the store's inventory, which would trigger a sell event so we increment the total trade-in value. The second scenario is when an `InventoryItem` moves from the store's inventory to the player's inventory, which would trigger a buy event, so we increment the total buy price.

The second event we need to check for is when an item is removed. There are two scenarios to check. The first scenario is when a player-owned `InventoryItem` is removed from the store inventory. In this situation, we need to update the trade-in value by removing the trade-in value of the item from the total sell price. The second scenario is when a store-owned `InventoryItem` is removed from the player inventory. In this situation, we need to update the purchase price by removing the purchase price of the item from the total buy price:

```
public void checkButtonStates(){
    if( _tradeInVal <= 0 ) {
        disableButton(_sellButton, true);
    }else{
        disableButton(_sellButton, false);
    }

    if( _fullValue <= 0 || _playerTotal < _fullValue) {
        disableButton(_buyButton, true);
    }else{
        disableButton(_buyButton, false);
    }
}

private void disableButton(Button button, boolean disable){
    if( disable ){
        button.setDisabled(true);
        button.setTouchable(Touchable.disabled);
    }else{
        button.setDisabled(false);
        button.setTouchable(Touchable.enabled);
    }
}
public void setPlayerGP(int value){
    _playerTotal = value;
    _playerTotalGP.setText(PLAYER_TOTAL + " : " +
                            _playerTotal + GP);
}
```

The `disableButton()` deserves a note because the `setDisabled()` method for a button widget will only trigger a visual change to the button in a disabled state, but will not disable the button callbacks themselves. In order to disable the callbacks as well, you need to call `setTouchable()` and pass in an enum value `Touchable.disabled`.

As we stepped through the code for the store inventory UI, we can see that there are many edge cases to think of when developing such a feature, such as how we would handle items that the player left in the store when exiting. The complexity is compounded by item management across two different inventories and the support for transactions with these items. The divide and conquer approach when developing a feature with these complexities includes taking a step back and solving the smaller pieces first, as we begin to build on the previous features.

First, we outlined the overall design and placed our widgets in their respective cells in the layout. We then added notifications for when the items were dropped into the inventory slots. After this, we started to build out the business logic for the transactions via the sell and buy button listeners. Finally, we added cleanup code for edge cases when exiting the `StoreInventoryUI` and serializing the player inventory out for persistence.

Summary

In this chapter, we learned the fundamentals of a conversation graph, `ConversationGraph`, and then implemented one for our game. We also implemented a store inventory, `StoreInventoryUI`, which can be used for trade amongst the NPCs. Finally, we developed a way to trigger events from the conversations themselves.

In the next chapter, we will begin to explore quests for *BludBourne*, including creating quests, enabling NPCs to give quests, handling triggers and events for quests, and giving quest rewards.

6
So Many Quests, So Little Time...

As we begin to flesh out the remaining features of *BludBourne*, this chapter in particular will focus on a core staple in most RPGs—the quest system. A quest system defines the parameters for leveling a player character, with adventures such as saving a princess or collecting animal carcasses. The quest rewards for completion typically include gold, experience points, and other items in the game world. In this chapter, you will learn a data structure used for quests, the dependency graph, and also a few types of implemented quests to give you reference implementations for your own game.

In summary, we will cover the following topics in this chapter:

- The theory of dependency graphs
- The dependency graph implementation
- QuestUI
- The steps involved in creating a quest

We will start by first describing the theory behind the dependency graph and explain why this data structure is applicable for quest management. After discussing the theory, we will then walk through the implementation and further explain the details in order to hook the quest system up for *BludBourne*.

The following screenshot (*Figure 1*) shows the final product implemented in this chapter:

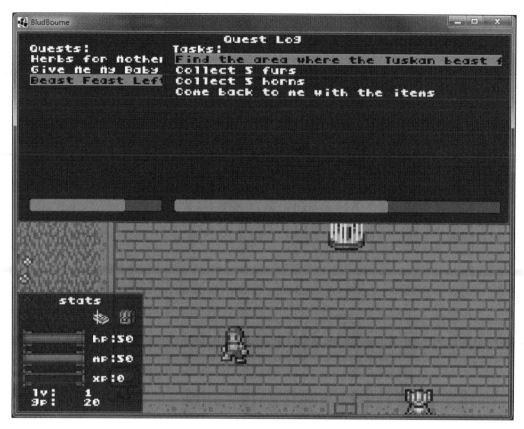

Figure 1

The theory of dependency graphs

We are going to extend what we learned with the previous chapter when constructing a conversation graph, and with a few (but significant) changes, create a quest dependency graph that will store the completion state of its corresponding tasks. A **dependency graph** is essentially a directed graph representing dependencies of several objects with each other. The key difference of this graph from the conversation graph is that the dependency graph does not contain any cycles. A graph with circular dependencies would lead to a situation where no valid evaluation order exists, since none of the vertices can be evaluated first. Without cycles in a graph, we will end up using a **directed acyclic graph** (DAG).

As explained later, we will make sure that we check for cycles every time we add a new dependency, and if any of them are found, disregard that particular dependency.

The following diagram (*Figure 2*) represents a sample dependency graph with four total vertices and four total directed edge connections (dependencies):

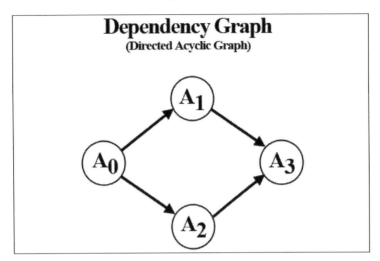

Figure 2

In *Figure 2*, we have a set of four vertices, designated as {A0, A1, A2, A3}. You can think of each vertex as a discrete autonomous task, one that can only be started once its dependencies have been evaluated and completed. Dependency graphs are used in all types of applications, such as spreadsheet calculators (to figure out dependencies between cells for calculations), software installers, and software project build systems. In *Figure 2*, A0 cannot be started until A1 and A2 have been completed. A1 and A2 cannot be completed until A3 is finished. The vertex A3 does not have any dependencies, and so this will be the first task to be completed. Once A3 is complete, the A1 and A2 dependencies will have been satisfied, and so A1 and A2 can begin their tasks concurrently since they do not depend on each other. Finally, once A1 and A2 have both finished their tasks, A0 can begin its task since all other vertices have been evaluated.

To put this data structure in more concrete terms, the following diagram (*Figure 3*) demonstrates the same graph, but with tasks, designated as vertices {A0,A1, A2, A3}, associated with a quest:

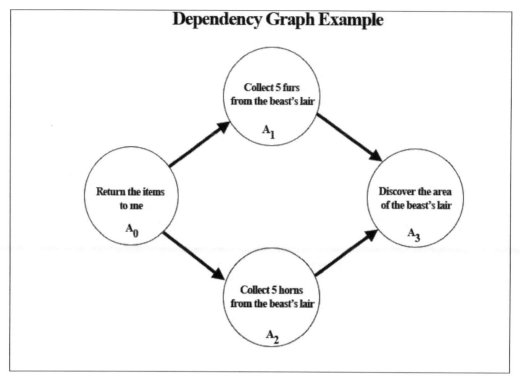

Figure 3

So, in *Figure 3*, based on the evaluation order of dependencies, the first task to be completed will be task A3, since A3 does not have any dependencies. The player will roam the countryside looking for the general area where the beast's lair will be located. Once the player has walked over the area location, A3 will be complete. This will trigger the next tasks to be started, which in our example would be the tasks A1 and A2. The player will be able to collect the items for these quests in any order since neither of them depends on the other. Even if the player gets all the furs and completes the A1 task, the A0 task will not be unlocked or ready to be evaluated, since A0 still has a dependency on A2, which has not been completed yet. Once the player finds all the horns and completes A2, with both A1 and A2 completed, the final task A0 will be ready to start.

The dependency graph implementation

With the fundamentals of the dependency graph covered, we will now take a look at the high-level class diagram (*Figure 4*), which describes the new classes and relationships for implementing the quest system:

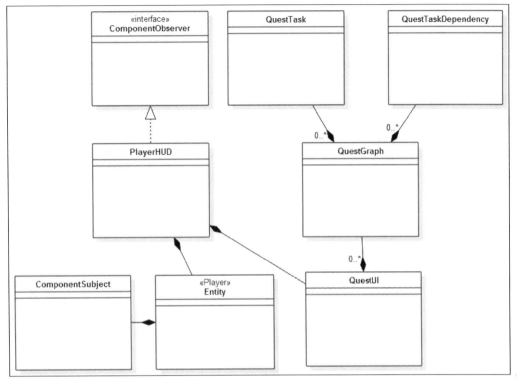

Figure 4

The left-half of this class diagram represents the notification propagation via the observer pattern. For instance, when the player entity selects a quest item or walks over a designated quest task area, those notifications bubble up to the PlayerHUD, which is an observer for those ComponentEvent notifications. Depending on the type of notification trigger, this will get passed to the QuestUI to update the current quests. This mechanism has been described in more detail in the previous chapters.

From *Figure 4*, we can see how QuestUI loads QuestGraph, one graph for each quest. Each QuestGraph is composed of multiple QuestTask and QuestTaskDependency objects. The QuestTask objects represent the dependency graph vertices. The QuestTaskDependency objects represent the edge connection dependencies between vertices.

QuestTask

We will now take a dive into the implementation of this design starting with the two POJO classes that together form `QuestGraph`. The following class diagram (*Figure 5*) represents the first POJO class, `QuestTask`:

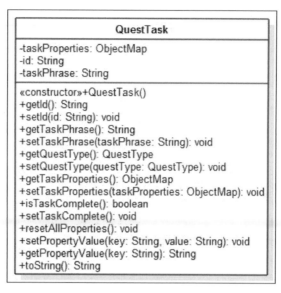

Figure 5

As stated previously, the `QuestTask` class represents the vertex of a dependency graph, a task that needs to be completed in order to continue or finish a quest. Each `QuestTask` has a unique ID (`id`) which clearly differentiates it from the other quest tasks in the graph. The `taskPhrase` string type object represents the text displayed in the quest log that clearly identifies the objective of that particular task, such as "Collect 5 horns from the beast's lair". We also have a field for checking whether the task is complete and also for setting the task complete.

The `QuestType` field identifies the general purpose of the task. The reference implementation for this chapter currently supports the FETCH, RETURN, and DISCOVER `QuestType` fields. The FETCH task is the type of task where the objective is to collect some number of a particular item. The RETURN tasks have an objective to go back to the quest giver in order to finish a quest or receive some item. The DISCOVER tasks have an objective to go find a particular area in some map.

Other `QuestType` types defined are KILL (objective to slay any number of a particular beast), DELIVERY (bring some item to someone else), GUARD (defend some outpost usually with a wave of enemies), and ESCORT (protect some NPC going to some other location); this could easily be extended later.

The `taskProperties` member variable is an `ObjectMap` that maintains all the `QuestTaskPropertyType` properties associated with any particular task. Currently, the following `QuestTaskPropertyType` values are used: IS_TASK_COMPLETE, TARGET_TYPE, TARGET_NUM, and TARGET_LOCATION. We also have methods for getting and setting any particular property value for a given task.

QuestTaskDependency

The next class diagram (*Figure 6*) represents the other POJO class that the `QuestGraph` class contains:

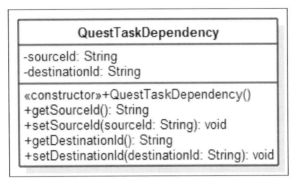

Figure 6

The `QuestTaskDependency` class plays a vital role in maintaining the evaluation order of the `QuestGraph` by establishing dependencies between different `QuestTask` objects. The simplicity of this class is also important as the only fields that need defining are the source ID of the `QuestTask` and the destination ID of `QuestTask` that the source depends on.

QuestGraph

The `QuestGraph` class is the heart of the quest system, tying together `QuestTask` and `QuestTaskDependency` and creating a single point of access for all related queries for the data structure.

The following snippet of source for `QuestGraph` will be explained in detail here:

```
...
public class QuestGraph {
    private static final String TAG =
            QuestGraph.class.getSimpleName();

    private Hashtable<String, QuestTask> questTasks;
    private Hashtable<String, ArrayList<QuestTaskDependency>>
            questTaskDependencies;
    private String questTitle;
    private String questID;
    private boolean isQuestComplete;
    private int goldReward;
    private int xpReward;
```

First, we will describe the member variables that get serialized in the JSON format when creating a quest. The `questTitle` string type variable represents the text displayed in the quest log for the name of the particular quest (on the left pane). The `questID` represents the unique identifier for this particular quest, which can be used as a reference value in order to map quest-related positions on a TMX map to their item spawn placement for the quest. The `isQuestComplete` variable represents a simple `boolean` value that gets set to `true` once all the tasks are completed. The `goldReward` and `xpReward` represent two values for quest rewards once this particular quest is finished.

The `questTasks Hashtable` contains all the tasks that need to be completed in order to finish the particular quest, with the `QuestTask` unique ID used as a key value. The `questTaskDependencies Hashtable` has a container of the `QuestTaskDependency` objects that represent all the dependencies that a particular `QuestTask` needs to satisfy in order to be considered complete. The `questTaskDependencies Hashtable` uses a `QuestTask` unique ID as a key value, which will also be the `sourceID` for each of its dependencies:

```
    . . .
    public void setTasks(Hashtable<String, QuestTask> questTasks) {
        if( questTasks.size() < 0 ){
            throw new IllegalArgumentException(
                "Can't have a negative amount of conversations");
        }

        this.questTasks = questTasks;
        this.questTaskDependencies = new Hashtable<
```

```
        String, ArrayList<QuestTaskDependency>>
            (questTasks.size());

    for( QuestTask questTask: questTasks.values() ){
        questTaskDependencies.put(questTask.getId(), new
            ArrayList<QuestTaskDependency>());
    }
}
```

The setTasks() method is used in the QuestGraphTest class under tests/ in order to initialize the QuestGraph data structure. The QuestGraphTest shows how to programmatically create the QuestTask and QuestTaskDependency objects that compose a QuestGraph:

```
public ArrayList<QuestTask> getAllQuestTasks(){
    Enumeration<QuestTask> enumeration =
        questTasks.elements();
    return Collections.list(enumeration);
}
```

The getAllQuestTasks() method is a simple getter that returns a container of all the QuestTask objects associated with the current QuestGraph object:

```
public void clear(){
    questTasks.clear();
    questTaskDependencies.clear();
}
```

The clear() method simply removes any of the QuestTask and QuestTaskDependency objects associated with the current QuestGraph:

```
public boolean isValid(String taskID){
    QuestTask questTask = questTasks.get(taskID);
    if( questTask == null ) return false;
    return true;
}
```

The isValid() method is a safety check mechanism to make sure a particular unique ID actually exists as a valid QuestTask in the current QuestGraph:

```
public QuestTask getQuestTaskByID(String id){
    if( !isValid(id) ){
        System.out.println("Id " + id + " is not valid!");
        return null;
    }
    return questTasks.get(id);
}
```

The getQuestTaskByID() will first check to make sure that the ID is valid, and if it is, return the QuestTask object associated with the ID:

```
public boolean doesCycleExist(
                    QuestTaskDependency questTaskDep){
    Set<String> keys = questTasks.keySet();
    for( String id: keys ){
        if( doesQuestTaskHaveDependencies(id) &&
            questTaskDep.getDestinationId().equalsIgnoreCase(
                id)){
                System.out.println("ID: " + id + " destID: " +
                    questTaskDep.getDestinationId());
                return true;
            }
        }
    return false;
}
```

The doesCycleExist() method will check whether the QuestTaskDependency object passed in creates a cycle in the current graph. In order to determine this, we iterate over all the current QuestTask IDs, checking all the QuestTask objects for dependencies, and if they do have dependencies, check whether the QuestTaskDependency destination ID passed in matches. If we match a destination ID with a current QuestTask ID, then we know we have a cycle, and because of this back reference, we will return true. This is an important method as the dependency graph will fail the evaluation order if we do not catch circular dependencies early:

```
public void addDependency(
                    QuestTaskDependency questTaskDependency){
    ArrayList<QuestTaskDependency> list = questTaskDependencies.
        get(questTaskDependency.getSourceId());

    if( list == null) return;

    //Will not add if creates cycles
    if( doesCycleExist(questTaskDependency) ){
        System.out.println("Cycle exists! Not adding");
        return;
    }

    list.add(questTaskDependency);
}
```

The addDependency() method is used to add the QuestTaskDependency object to the Hashtable of QuestTaskDependency objects associated with the QuestGraph. The important point here is that we check the object passed in to see if a cycle exists. If a cycle exists, then we will ignore the QuestTaskDependency object:

```
public boolean doesQuestTaskHaveDependencies(String id){
    QuestTask task = getQuestTaskByID(id);
    if( task == null) return false;

    ArrayList<QuestTaskDependency> list =
        questTaskDependencies.get(id);

    if( list.isEmpty() || list.size() == 0){
        return false;
    }else{
        return true;
    }
}
```

The doesQuestTaskHaveDependencies() method checks whether the QuestTask is associated with any dependencies:

```
public boolean isQuestTaskAvailable(String id){
    QuestTask task = getQuestTaskByID(id);
    if( task == null) return false;
    ArrayList<QuestTaskDependency> list =
        questTaskDependencies.get(id);

    for(QuestTaskDependency dep: list){
        QuestTask depTask = getQuestTaskByID(
                    dep.getDestinationId());
        if( depTask == null || depTask.isTaskComplete() ){
            continue;
        }

        if( dep.getSourceId().equalsIgnoreCase(id) ){
            return false;
        }
    }
    return true;
}
```

The `isQuestTaskAvailable()` method will look at all the `QuestTaskDependency` objects associated with a specific `QuestTask` and determine if all of the dependencies are satisfied (completed dependency tasks):

```
public void setQuestTaskComplete(String id){
    QuestTask task = getQuestTaskByID(id);
    if( task == null) return;
    task.setTaskComplete();
}
```

The `setQuestTaskComplete()` method is a convenience method to set a particular `QuestTask` as completed:

```
public void update(MapManager mapMgr){
    ArrayList<QuestTask> allQuestTasks = getAllQuestTasks();

    for( QuestTask questTask: allQuestTasks ) {

        if( questTask.isTaskComplete() ) continue;

        //We first want to make sure the task is available and
        //is relevant to current location
        if (!isQuestTaskAvailable(questTask.getId()))
          continue;

        String taskLocation = questTask.getPropertyValue(
                QuestTask.QuestTaskPropertyType.
                  TARGET_LOCATION.toString());

        if (taskLocation == null ||
            taskLocation.isEmpty() ||
            !taskLocation.equalsIgnoreCase(
              mapMgr.getCurrentMapType().toString()))
                continue;

        switch (questTask.getQuestType()) {
            case FETCH:
              String taskConfig = questTask.getPropertyValue(
                      QuestTask.QuestTaskPropertyType.
                        TARGET_TYPE.toString());
              if( taskConfig == null || taskConfig.isEmpty() )
                  break;
```

```
                     EntityConfig config = Entity.getEntityConfig(
                                  taskConfig);

                     Array<Vector2> questItemPositions =
                        ProfileManager.getInstance().getProperty(
                           config.getEntityID(), Array.class);

                     if( questItemPositions == null ) break;

                     //Case where all the items have been picked up
                     if( questItemPositions.size == 0 ){
                        questTask.setTaskComplete();
                        Gdx.app.debug(TAG, "TASK : " +
                                       questTask.getId() +
                                       " is complete of Quest:" +
                                       questID);
                        Gdx.app.debug(TAG, "INFO : " + QuestTask.
                                       QuestTaskPropertyType.
                                       TARGET_TYPE.toString());
                     }
                     break;
                  case KILL:
                     break;
                  case DELIVERY:
                     break;
                  case GUARD:
                     break;
                  case ESCORT:
                     break;
                  case RETURN:
                     break;
                  case DISCOVER:
                     break;
               }
         }
      }
```

The `update()` method is called when a particular event related to quests is triggered, such as accepting a quest. We look at all the `QuestTask` objects, filtering out those that are completed or not available (meaning they have dependencies that have not been completed yet), and check whether a particular `QuestTask` is associated with the current area. If all of these conditions have been satisfied, then we can check the `QuestTask` objects for specific criteria.

Currently, for FETCH type quests, we check to see whether all the items
have been picked up. If all the items have been collected, then we can mark
the quest as completed:

```
public boolean updateQuestForReturn(){
    ArrayList<QuestTask> tasks = getAllQuestTasks();
    QuestTask readyTask = null;

    //First, see if all tasks are available, meaning no
    //blocking dependencies
    for( QuestTask task : tasks){
        if( !isQuestTaskAvailable(task.getId())){
            return false;
        }

        if( !task.isTaskComplete() ){
            if( task.getQuestType().equals(
                    QuestTask.QuestType.RETURN) ){
                readyTask = task;
            }else{
                return false;
            }
        }
    }
    if( readyTask == null ) return false;

    readyTask.setTaskComplete();
    return true;
}
```

The updateQuestForReturn() is one additional sanity check that is
made when returning a quest to the quest giver. Here, we check to make sure
that all the QuestTask objects have been completed, except for the RETURN type
QuestTask. If all the other tasks have been completed, and the only task left is
a RETURN task, then we set the final QuestTask as complete and return, as the
QuestGraph graph is ready for completion:

```
public void init(MapManager mapMgr){
    ArrayList<QuestTask> allQuestTasks = getAllQuestTasks();

    for( QuestTask questTask: allQuestTasks ) {

        if( questTask.isTaskComplete() ) continue;
```

```
//We first want to make sure the task is available and
//is relevant to current location
if (!isQuestTaskAvailable(questTask.getId()))
   continue;

String taskLocation = questTask.getPropertyValue(
        QuestTask.QuestTaskPropertyType.
          TARGET_LOCATION.toString());

if (taskLocation == null ||
    taskLocation.isEmpty() ||
    !taskLocation.equalsIgnoreCase(
      mapMgr.getCurrentMapType().toString()))
  continue;

switch (questTask.getQuestType()) {
    case FETCH:
        Array<Entity> questEntities = new
                    Array<Entity>();
        Array<Vector2> positions = mapMgr.
          getQuestItemSpawnPositions(
            questID, questTask.getId());

        String taskConfig = questTask.
                getPropertyValue(
                  QuestTask.QuestTaskPropertyType.
                  TARGET_TYPE.toString());
        if(taskConfig == null || taskConfig.isEmpty())
          break;

        EntityConfig config = Entity.getEntityConfig(
                    taskConfig);

        Array<Vector2> questItemPositions =
          ProfileManager.getInstance().getProperty(
            config.getEntityID(), Array.class);

        if( questItemPositions == null ){
            questItemPositions = new Array<Vector2>();

            for( Vector2 position: positions ){
                questItemPositions.add(position);
```

```
                          Entity entity = Map.initEntity(
                                  config, position);
                          entity.getEntityConfig().
                             setCurrentQuestID(questID);
                          questEntities.add(entity);
                      }
                  }else{
                      for( Vector2 questItemPosition:
                            questItemPositions ){

                          Entity entity = Map.initEntity(
                                  config, questItemPosition);
                          entity.getEntityConfig().
                             setCurrentQuestID(questID);
                          questEntities.add(entity);
                      }
                  }

                  mapMgr.addMapQuestEntities(questEntities);
                  ProfileManager.getInstance().
                     setProperty(config.getEntityID(),
                         questItemPositions);
                  break;
              case KILL:
                  break;
              case DELIVERY:
                  break;
              case GUARD:
                  break;
              case ESCORT:
                  break;
              case RETURN:
                  break;
              case DISCOVER:
                  break;

              }
          }
      }
```

```
    public String toString(){
        return questTitle;
    }

    public String toJson(){
        Json json = new Json();
        return json.prettyPrint(this);
    }

}
```

The `init()` method is called when a quest is initially accepted and when the portal system is activated with a new map location loaded. Every time we leave a particular map, such as `TOWN`, we want to clear all items and events associated with the tasks there. So, when loading a new map location, we want to check and load any quest tasks specific to that location. Similar to the `update()` method, and as previously stated, we look at all the `QuestTask` objects, filtering out those that are completed or not available (meaning they have dependencies that have not been completed yet), and check whether a particular `QuestTask` is associated with the current area. If all of these conditions have been satisfied, then we can check the `QuestTask` objects for specific criteria.

For instance, for the `FETCH` type quests, this is where we will take map spawn positions that match the current `QuestTask`, use these positions as the starting positions for the quest items, initialize the items, and then add them to the current map location.

QuestUI

We need some way to communicate to the player what quests they have accepted so they know what to finish and to whom to return the quest.

The `QuestUI` is composed of two primary panes. The left `ScrollPane` represents all the quests the player currently has accepted or finished, where the `QuestGraph` (each one representing a separate quest) is stored in a `List`. The right `ScrollPane` represents all the tasks associated with a selected quest, where the `QuestTask` is also stored in a `List`.

`QuestUI` can easily be extended with additional features that fit your specifications. We will discuss a very basic quest log, `QuestUI`, starting with the following diagram (*Figure 7*), which outlines the components of the quest log:

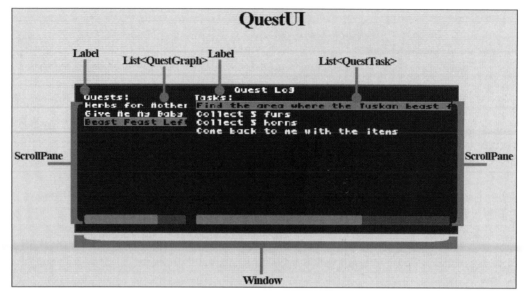

Figure 7

The following source snippet of `QuestUI` will outline some important functionality that you may want to add to your own implementation:

```
package com.packtpub.libgdx.bludbourne.UI;
...
public class QuestUI extends Window {
    private static final String TAG =
                        QuestUI.class.getSimpleName();

    public static final String RETURN_QUEST =
                    "conversations/return_quest.json";
    public static final String FINISHED_QUEST =
                    "conversations/quest_finished.json";
    private List _listQuests;
    private List _listTasks;
    private Json _json;
    private Array<QuestGraph> _quests;
    private Label _questLabel;
    private Label _tasksLabel;
```

```
public QuestUI() {
    super("Quest Log", Utility.STATUSUI_SKIN,
        "solidbackground");

    _json = new Json();
    _quests = new Array<QuestGraph>();

    //create
    _questLabel = new Label("Quests:", Utility.STATUSUI_SKIN);
    _tasksLabel = new Label("Tasks:", Utility.STATUSUI_SKIN);

    _listQuests = new List<QuestGraph>(Utility.STATUSUI_SKIN);

    ScrollPane scrollPane = new ScrollPane(
        _listQuests, Utility.STATUSUI_SKIN, "inventoryPane");
    scrollPane.setOverscroll(false, false);
    scrollPane.setFadeScrollBars(false);
    scrollPane.setForceScroll(true, false);
```

Here, we set up the left `ScrollPane` to store all the quests (the `QuestGraph` objects) the player currently has accepted:

```
    _listTasks = new List<QuestTask>(Utility.STATUSUI_SKIN);

    ScrollPane scrollPaneTasks = new ScrollPane(
        _listTasks, Utility.STATUSUI_SKIN, "inventoryPane");
    scrollPaneTasks.setOverscroll(false, false);
    scrollPaneTasks.setFadeScrollBars(false);
    scrollPaneTasks.setForceScroll(true, false);
```

Here, we set up the right `ScrollPane` to store all the tasks associated with a quest (the `QuestTask` objects) that the player must complete for a given quest:

```
    //layout
    this.add(_questLabel).align(Align.left);
    this.add(_tasksLabel).align(Align.left);
    this.row();
    this.defaults().expand().fill();
    this.add(scrollPane).padRight(15);
    this.add(scrollPaneTasks).padLeft(5);

    this.pack();
```

```
//Listeners
_listQuests.addListener(new ClickListener() {

@Override
public void clicked(InputEvent event, float x, float y) {
   QuestGraph quest = (QuestGraph) _listQuests.getSelected();

   if (quest == null) return;
                                    populateQuestTaskDialog(quest);
   }
 }
);
}
```

This listener will be triggered when the player selects a quest from the left
ScrollPane widget of the quest log. We will populate the right pane with all the
QuestTask objects associated with QuestGraph that the player has selected:

```
public void questTaskComplete(String questID,
                                   String questTaskID){
     for( QuestGraph questGraph: _quests ){
         if( questGraph.getQuestID().equalsIgnoreCase
            (questID)){
            if( questGraph.isQuestTaskAvailable(questTaskID) ){
                questGraph.setQuestTaskComplete(questTaskID);
            }else{
                return;
            }
         }
      }
   }
```

The questTaskComplete() is a convenience method for certain triggers. In the
current implementation, this method is called when the player has discovered
a new area. The discovery of a new area triggers a ComponentEvent (QUEST_
LOCATION_DISCOVERED) when the player walks over the designated area in the
map. The QUEST_LOCATION_DISCOVERED event contains both the QuestGraph ID
and the QuestTask ID, and these values are passed into questTaskComplete().
If the QuestTask associated with the ID is available (meaning all dependencies are
satisfied), then the QuestTask object is set to complete:

```
public QuestGraph loadQuest(String questConfigPath){
     if( questConfigPath.isEmpty() ||
```

```
               !Gdx.files.internal(questConfigPath).exists() ){
                   Gdx.app.debug(TAG, "Quest file does not exist!");
                   return null;
               }

               QuestGraph graph = _json.fromJson(QuestGraph.class,
                               Gdx.files.internal(questConfigPath));
               if( doesQuestExist(graph.getQuestID()) ){
                   return null;
               }

               clearDialog();
               _quests.add(graph);
               updateQuestItemList();
               return graph;
           }
```

The `loadQuest()` method is a utility method that will load a `QuestGraph` (in JSON serialized format) from disk based on the file path passed into the method. The `QuestGraph` is then added to the `Hashtable` and the `QuestUI` is updated accordingly:

```
           public boolean isQuestReadyForReturn(String questID){
               if( questID.isEmpty()){
                   Gdx.app.debug(TAG, "Quest ID not valid");
                   return false;
               }

               if( !doesQuestExist(questID) ) return false;

               QuestGraph graph = getQuestByID(questID);
               if( graph == null ) return false;

               if( graph.updateQuestForReturn() ){
                   graph.setQuestComplete(true);
               }else{
                   return false;
               }
               return true;
           }
```

The `isQuestReadyForReturn()` method is specific to when the player is returning a quest to a quest giver. Here, we check to make sure the `QuestGraph` exists, is valid, and verify that the final `QuestTask` is in fact a RETURN type task. Once these conditions are met, we set the entire `QuestGraph` to complete:

```
public QuestGraph getQuestByID(String questGraphID){
    for( QuestGraph questGraph: _quests ){
        if( questGraph.getQuestID().equalsIgnoreCase(
            questGraphID)){
            return questGraph;
        }
    }
    return null;
}
```

The `getQuestByID()` method is a convenience method that returns the `QuestGraph` associated with the specific ID:

```
public boolean doesQuestExist(String questGraphID){
    for( QuestGraph questGraph: _quests ){
        if( questGraph.getQuestID().equalsIgnoreCase(
            questGraphID)){
            return true;
        }
    }
    return false;
}
```

The `doesQuestExist()` is a check used to make sure the current `QuestGraph` ID is in fact valid and is part of our quest log:

```
public Array<QuestGraph> getQuests() {
    return _quests;
}

public void setQuests(Array<QuestGraph> quests) {
    this._quests = quests;
    updateQuestItemList();
}

public void updateQuestItemList(){
    clearDialog();
```

```
        _listQuests.setItems(_quests);
        _listQuests.setSelectedIndex(-1);
    }

    private void clearDialog(){
        _listQuests.clearItems();
    }
```

The `updateQuestItemList()` method is called whenever changes are made, such as adding an additional quest to the quest log. Here, we clear the current dialog and then add the updated container for the `QuestGraph` object:

```
    private void populateQuestTaskDialog(QuestGraph graph){
        _listTasks.clearItems();

        ArrayList<QuestTask> tasks =  graph.getAllQuestTasks();
        if( tasks == null ) return;

        _listTasks.setItems(tasks.toArray());
        _listTasks.setSelectedIndex(-1);
    }
```

The `populateQuestTaskDialog()` method is called whenever a player has selected a new `QuestGraph` object from the left pane `List` items. This will clear the current `QuestTask` objects in the right pane and populate the `List` with the `QuestTask` objects associated with the currently selected `QuestGraph`:

```
    public void initQuests(MapManager mapMgr){
        mapMgr.clearAllMapQuestEntities();

        //populate items if quests have them
        for( QuestGraph quest : _quests ){
            if( !quest.isQuestComplete() ){
                quest.init(mapMgr);
            }
        }
        ProfileManager.getInstance().setProperty(
            "playerQuests", _quests);
    }
```

The `initQuests()` method is called when specific events happen, such as accepting a quest, changing map locations, or discovering a location. This basically resets all the previous quest items and reinitializes all of them, including the new quest items:

```
public void updateQuests(MapManager mapMgr){
    for( QuestGraph quest : _quests ){
        if( !quest.isQuestComplete() ){
            quest.update(mapMgr);
        }
    }
    ProfileManager.getInstance().setProperty(
        "playerQuests", _quests);
}
}
```

The `updateQuests()` method is a more lightweight method than `init()`, basically used to check up on the status of the `QuestTask` items. For instance, `updateQuests()` is called whenever the player picks up a quest item and adds it to their inventory. This method is called so that the current map removes the quest item from the field of play.

The steps involved in creating a quest

This section will briefly review the steps involved in creating a quest using this quest system implementation. We will discuss how to create the conversation that initiates the quest, the quest script that defines the parameters set in the quest, create the quest items for both the map and player's inventory, and finally return the quest once completed.

First, we should identify who will be the quest giver for a particular quest and then create their conversation graph to signify to the player that they are being asked to complete a quest.

The following screenshot (*Figure 8*) is an in-game screenshot of the conversation created from the assets/conversations/conversation006.json file:

Figure 8

Second, we need to draw out (preferably create a quest builder application) the quest tasks and their associated dependencies and create a serialized JSON version of the QuestGraph. This following quest script is a simple FETCH quest and can be found in the assets/quests/quest003.json file:

```
{
questTitle : "Give Me My Baby Back!"
questID : 3
goldReward : 20
xpReward : 20
```

```
isQuestComplete : FALSE
questTasks: {
  2: {
    taskProperties: {
      IS_TASK_COMPLETE: {
        class: java.lang.String
        value: "false"
      }
      TARGET_TYPE: {
        class: java.lang.String
        value: "scripts/quest003_task002.json"
      }
      TARGET_NUM: {
        class: java.lang.String
        value: "1"
      }
      TARGET_LOCATION: {
        class: java.lang.String
        value: "TOWN"
      }

    }
    id: 2
    taskPhrase: Please find my missing baby!
    questType : FETCH
  }
  1: {
    taskProperties: {
      IS_TASK_COMPLETE: {
        class: java.lang.String
        value: "false"
      }
      TARGET_TYPE: {
        class: java.lang.String
        value: "TOWN_FOLK2"
      }
      TARGET_LOCATION: {
        class: java.lang.String
        value: "TOWN"
      }
    }
    id: 1
    taskPhrase: Give me my baby!
    questType : RETURN
  }
}
questTaskDependencies: {
  1: [
    {
```

```
            class: com.packtpub.libgdx.bludbourne.
              quest.QuestTaskDependency
            sourceId: 1
            destinationId: 2
          }
      ]
      2: []
    }
  }
```

One interesting feature of the current project is that we currently support the Entity Component System for our player character and NPCs. When I was originally creating the quest system, I was curious about using the ECS for quest items that display on the map as well. I created an EntityConfig JSON script to define the quest item, and the item showed up on the map with all the selection and popup dialog features that I needed. This is another example of the power of using the ECS model when developing a video game.

In the previous quest003.json script file, the TARGET_TYPE property for the quest item is defined as scripts/quest003_task002.json. This is the EntityConfig script for the quest item mentioned earlier, and is defined as follows:

```
{
entityID : QUEST003_TASK002
state : IMMOBILE
direction : DOWN
conversationConfigPath : "conversations/conversation005.json"
questConfigPath : ""
currentQuestID : ""
itemTypeID: BABY001
inventory : [
  ]
animationConfig: [
  {
      frameDuration: 1.0
    animationType: IMMOBILE
    texturePaths: [
        sprites/characters/Player0.png
        sprites/characters/Player1.png
    ]
    gridPoints: [
      {
        x: 1
        y: 1
      }
      {
```

```
            x: 1
            y: 1
        }
    ]
}
]
}
```

Another benefit of being able to use `EntityConfig` is that I can easily add animation for the quest item on the map screen, as demonstrated in the `quest003_task002.json` file. The other interesting item of note is that I was able to use `ConversationGraph` with a special `ConversationCommandEvent` called `ADD_ENTITY_TO_INVENTORY`, to trigger the event to take the item on the map and add it to the player's inventory. The following screenshot (*Figure 9*) is an in-game screenshot that shows not only the quest item (defined as `Entity`), but also the item pickup conversation:

Figure 9

Third, we need to hook the conversation from the first step and the quest itself defined in the second step with the quest giver. We need to update the associated properties in the `EntityConfig` script file for the NPC that will be the quest giver. The following is a snippet with the changes from the `assets/scripts/town_folk.json` file:

```
{
    entityID : TOWN_FOLK2
    ...
    conversationConfigPath : "conversations/conversation006.json"
    questConfigPath : "quests/quest003.json"
    ...
}
```

Fourth, we need to create the positions on the game map location where the items will spawn. The following instructions will be specific to the setup using Tiled:

1. We start by creating an object layer named `MAP_QUEST_ITEM_SPAWN_LAYER`.
2. We then place a rectangle object in a position where you want the item to spawn.
3. After setting the position, we need to set the name of the object to the `QuestGraph` unique ID, which in our case would be 3.
4. You will need to create a custom property named `taskID` with the value that represents the `QuestTask` unique ID, which in our case would be 2.

The following screenshot (*Figure 10*) contains a portion of map area in Tiled with the object layer visible:

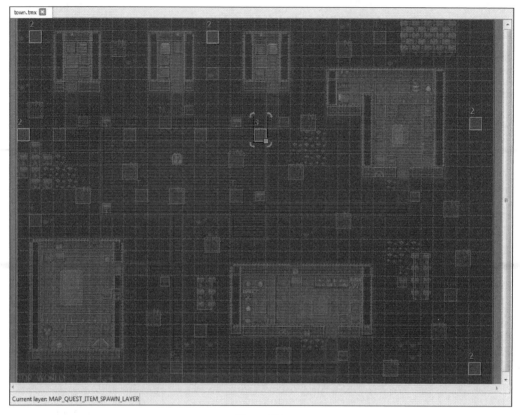

Figure 10

Fifth, for items that we pick up for the FETCH quests, we will need a version that is compatible with InventoryItem objects. This will require a few small updates:

1. Update the ItemTypeID enum in src/com/packtpub/libgdx/bludbourne/ InventoryItem.java with the identifier for the quest item, which in our case would be BABY001.

2. Update the script for inventory properties, assets/scripts/inventory_ items.json, which in our case would be as follows:

```
{
    itemAttributes: 4
    itemUseType: 2048
    itemTypeID: BABY001
```

```
    itemShortDescription: Quest Item Baby
    itemValue: -1
},
```

3. Finally, add an image of the quest item to the item texture atlas, core/
    assets/skins/items.atlas, by creating the image with the ItemTypeID as
    BABY001 and using the libgdx-texturepacker-gui tool (version 3.2.0) to update
    the atlas files.

The following in-game screenshot (*Figure 11*) shows how the quest item would look
once configured as an appropriate InventoryItem:

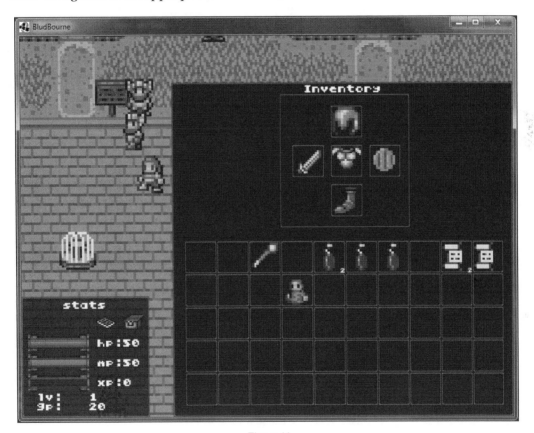

Figure 11

As we can see in the preceding screenshot, the quest item or, in our case, the poor woman's baby is safely stowed away under the protection of the current caretaker, the player, until safely returned to his mother. When returning to the baby's mother, the quest giver will ask a simple question of whether you have finished the quest or not. Once the items are verified as complete, the selection will progress to the next step. This conversation is already configured for quests, but could be easily modified if your requirements change, as shown in the following in-game screenshot (*Figure 12*):

Figure 12

Once you have successfully given the baby back to his mother, she will give the player the quest rewards, which include gold and experience. The GP and XP amounts will increase with a visual indication on the **XP** bar in the `StatusUI`. All of these are also persisted in the save game profile. The quest giver will also be forever grateful for your efforts, as shown in the following screenshot (*Figure 13*):

Figure 13

We reviewed the five-step procedure for creating a quest with the current quest system. First, we developed a conversation to start a quest. Second, we wrote a script that defines the parameters set for the quest. Third, we created the quest items for both the map players' inventory. Fourth, for fetch quests, we needed to make sure to create positions for the quest items on the map. Fifth and finally, we generated a mechanism for the player to return the quest once finished. This gives us a nice overview of the steps involved in creating quests and sets up a framework for creating other types of quests.

Summary

In this chapter, we learned the theory of dependency graphs and how they apply to a quest system for an RPG. We then quickly moved into the practical implementation of a dependency graph. First, we started with an overview of the new classes involved and then looking into the `QuestGraph` in more detail. We then went through an explanation of a very basic quest log, `QuestUI`, to help the player better manage their quest experiences. Finally, we walked through the steps involved when creating a quest for the current source so that we can better handle the content creation from the start.

In the next chapter, we will get our hands dirty with battle mechanics and finally start fighting some monsters to help free the people from their evil grasp.

7
Time to Show These Monsters Who's the Boss

A core component of any RPG is a battle system in which a player's character fights an enemy (or enemies) in hostile territory for the purpose of gaining experience and gold and completing quests. This chapter will cover the topics involved in creating this system, starting with the look and feel of the battle system as it relates to *BludBourne*. Our retro look and feel is inspired by elements of *Dragon Warrior* with a simple, but effective UI design. Other topics covered include handling leveling for the player as they progress, updating status during a battle, creating randomized monsters, and creating a flexible script for adding monsters in specific battle zones.

In summary, we will cover the following topics in this chapter:

- A battle system with enemy NPC creation and battle mechanics
- A battle UI used for encounters with monsters
- HUD updates tied with state changes in an environment such as damage (health bar, magic bar, and experience bar)
- Consuming items from the inventory
- The leveling system
- The game over screen

The battle system implementation

There are many moving parts in implementing a battle system for an RPG, but we will walk through the implementation step by step, starting with a high-level overview of the relationships between the new classes for this chapter and delving into specific details when warranted.

We will start with the following screenshot (*Figure 1*), which represents the battle screen when a player encounters a monster in *BludBourne*:

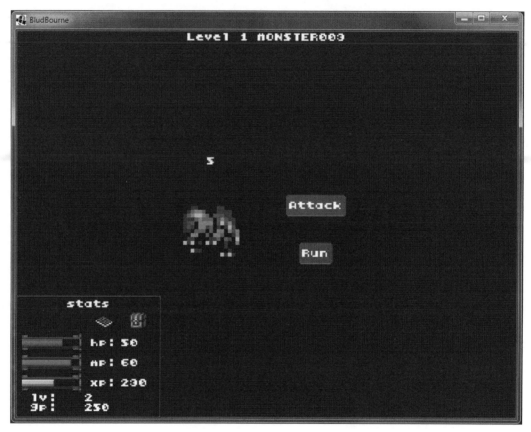

Figure 1

The classes that make this interaction from *Figure 1* happen are outlined in this chapter, taking you step by step in its implementation. There are some extra features, such as consuming health potions, which are discussed in further detail as well. The following class diagram (*Figure 2*) represents the relationships between the new classes for the implementation of our battle system:

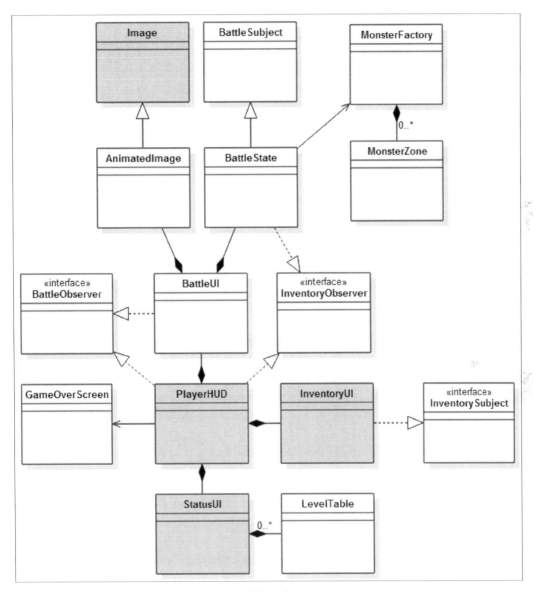

Figure 2

The grey-colored classes represent classes that we have already discussed in the previous chapters, and are added to fully describe the relationships with the new classes created specifically for the battle system. The first class that we will discuss is `BattleState`, the primary driver for the logic involved during a player's battle with a monster. The `BattleUI` class, shown previously in *Figure 1*, contains one `BattleState` object to handle all the business logic such as calculating damage, calculating the chance of running away, and sending notifications of changes to the player's status. The `BattleState` uses the `MonsterFactory` to create a monster for a particular battle, either with a specific reference to a `MonsterEntityType`, or to return a random monster based on the particular `MonsterZone` (explained later). Finally, `BattleState` also implements an observer pattern with `BattleSubject` and `BattleObserver` so that the relevant `BattleEvent` notifications get propagated to the correct classes. One note is that the `BattleState` class also implements the `InventoryObserver`, which is another observer pattern created for the battle system in order to get the currently equipped values for the attack and defense points. This is important for this implementation, since a player can equip and unequip items even during battle.

We will then discuss the `AnimatedImage` class that extends the LibGDX core class, `Image`, which allows an actor to render animations when added to a UI layout.

We will also talk about how the `StatusUI` determines the level changes for the player as they gain experience by using the `LevelTable` class as a reference for certain attributes of each of the levels.

Finally, we will discuss the `GameOverScreen` that will be called when our player falls in battle and also discuss how it connects with the `LoadGameScreen`.

BattleState

We will first look at the primary business logic that maintains the state and calculations involved in determining the outcome of a particular player's battle with an enemy. The following code snippet represents the `BattleState` class, which can be found at `core\src\com\packtpub\libgdx\bludbourne\battle\BattleState.java`:

```
package com.packtpub.libgdx.bludbourne.battle;

import com.badlogic.gdx.math.MathUtils;
import com.packtpub.libgdx.bludbourne.Entity;
import com.packtpub.libgdx.bludbourne.EntityConfig;
import com.packtpub.libgdx.bludbourne.UI.InventoryObserver;
```

```
import com.packtpub.libgdx.bludbourne.profile.ProfileManager;

public class BattleState extends BattleSubject implements
    InventoryObserver {
```

We need a way to communicate changes that occur during a battle turn, such as loss of HP or MP, a finished turn, or an escape attempt. We will use an observer pattern, consisting of `BattleSubject` and `BattleObserver`, to send the relevant notifications during a battle session. Here, `BattleState` extends from the `BattleSubject` base class in order to create the mechanism to send notifications to the relevant classes.

BattleSubject

The following (*Figure 3*) is a class diagram of `BattleSubject`:

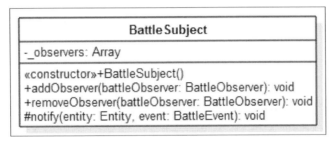

Figure 3

The observer pattern has been explained at length in the previous chapters, but the essence is that, whenever the `BattleState` class wants to communicate changes in state information to other classes, a simple `notify()` method will be called with the appropriate information.

BattleObserver

The complement class to `BattleSubject` is represented by the following class diagram (*Figure 4*):

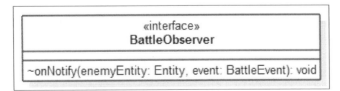

Figure 4

The `BattleObserver` is simply an interface that will be implemented by the relevant classes that wish to receive updates from the `BattleSubject` or the `BattleState` class in our case. The classes that will use the state change information from `BattleObserver`, for this chapter, are `BattleUI` and `PlayerHUD`. `BattleUI` will use the information to make damage indications to the player and also disable or enable buttons based on the current turn (for instance, once a player attacks, the attack button will be disabled until the opponent finishes their turn, so the player can't keep using the attack button). The `PlayerHUD` will use the information to determine the flow as it relates to the game, such as changing screens to the `GameOverScreen` if the player loses all their HP, updating rewards such as gold and experience for conquering a foe, or even handling escaping if a battle gets too difficult.

The last piece of this observer pattern includes the definitions for the various types of notifications that the `BattleSubject` can send during a session, as defined with the following code snippet of the `BattleEvent` enum:

```
public static enum BattleEvent{
    OPPONENT_ADDED,
    OPPONENT_HIT_DAMAGE,
    OPPONENT_DEFEATED,
    OPPONENT_TURN_DONE,
    PLAYER_HIT_DAMAGE,
    PLAYER_RUNNING,
    PLAYER_TURN_DONE,
    PLAYER_TURN_START,
    PLAYER_USED_MAGIC,
    NONE
}
```

The following definitions are the different options available in this class:

- `OPPONENT_ADDED`: This is an initial condition used to signal that a battle zone has been triggered and that a monster is queued up and ready for battle

- `OPPONENT_HIT_DAMAGE`: This is used to signal that the monster has been successfully hit and has sustained a certain amount of damage

- `OPPONENT_DEFEATED`: This is used to signal that the monster has been vanquished, in order to dismiss the `BattleUI` and give the player their just rewards

- `OPPONENT_TURN_DONE`: This is a notification that the monster has finished attacking, and the next round starts with the player's turn

- PLAYER_HIT_DAMAGE: This is used to signal that the player has sustained damage from the monster, in order to update the player's HP bar, and is the point at which we can make a determination if the player has been killed

- PLAYER_RUNNING: This is used to signal that the player has successfully escaped from the monster

- PLAYER_TURN_DONE: This is used to signal that the player has finished attacking, and the second-half of the battle round starts with the opponent's turn

- PLAYER_TURN_START: This is used to signal the beginning of a battle round starting with the player's turn first

- PLAYER_USED_MAGIC: This is used to signal that the player has used magic during the battle so that we can update the MP bar with the appropriate value of magic used

The last part of the BattleState class declaration implements the InventoryObserver interface. The InventoryObserver and InventorySubject together compose an observer pattern for notifications sent from the InventoryUI. For the purposes of our battle system, we need to determine the attack points of weapons equipped and also the defense points of armor equipped, in order to make the correct calculations to determine damage done in any one battle turn.

InventorySubject

The following class diagram (*Figure 5*) represents the first part of this observer pattern, InventorySubject:

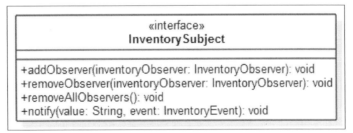

Figure 5

The `InventoryUI` class contains the drag and drop inventory of the user and also includes the ability to equip certain items. The `InventoryUI` implements `InventorySubject` and sends notifications when certain `InventoryEvent` type events occur. The following class diagram (*Figure 6*) represents the `InventoryObserver`:

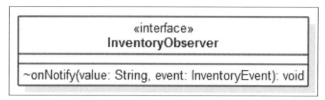

Figure 6

The `InventoryObserver` class is the complement to `InventorySubject`, which is needed to complete this observer pattern. The `InventoryObserver` class is implemented by `BattleState` in order to keep track of the total attack points (AP) tallied up with the currently equipped weapons and also the total defense points (DP) with all the equipped armor. We want these notifications to be dynamic since a player can equip and unequip during battle. Otherwise, if we set the values at the start of the battle and the player changes armor or weapons, our AP or DP values would be stale and therefore incorrect. The other class that implements the `InventoryObserver` is `PlayerHUD`, in order to update the relevant status when a player consumes an item from the inventory.

The following snippet is the complete enum for `InventoryEvent`:

```
public static enum InventoryEvent {
    UPDATED_AP,
    UPDATED_DP,
    ITEM_CONSUMED,
    ADD_WAND_AP,
    REMOVE_WAND_AP,
    NONE
}
```

The following definitions are the different options available in this class:

- `UPDATED_AP`: This represents a notification that the attack points have changed, either from the player adding a new weapon, or removing a previously equipped one

- `UPDATED_DP`: This represents a signal that the defense points have changed, either from the player adding a new piece of armor, or removing a previously equipped one

- `ITEM_CONSUMED`: This is a notification that the player has consumed an item from the inventory, such as a scroll to heal HP or a flask to replenish MP
- `ADD_WAND_AP`: This is a more specific notification of when a wand is added so that we can track the amount of MP consumed during an attack
- `REMOVE_WAND_AP`: This is the complementary notification to signal when a wand has been unequipped

One important note is related to the `ITEM_CONSUMED` enum that deserves an explanation in the following section.

Consuming items

There are multiple ways to implement a feature that allows the player to use or consume an item. Initially, I was checking for a mouse-click event from the player's `InputProcessor`, but the better approach used in *BludBourne* is to add a listener on the `InventorySlot`.

The first change is in `InventoryUI`, which can be found at `core\src\com\packtpub\libgdx\bludbourne\UI\InventoryUI.java`. In the `InventoryUI` constructor, for every `InventorySlot` that we create, we add the following listener:

```
. . .
public class InventoryUI extends Window implements
    InventorySubject, InventorySlotObserver{
   . . .
  public InventoryUI(){
   . . .
      inventorySlot.addListener(new ClickListener() {
        @Override
        public void touchUp (InputEvent event, float x, float y,
                         int pointer, int button) {
          super.touchUp(event, x, y, pointer, button);
            if( getTapCount() == 2 ){
              InventorySlot slot = (InventorySlot)event.
                getListenerActor();
              if( slot.hasItem() ){
                InventoryItem item = slot.
                  getTopInventoryItem();

                if( item.isConsumable() ){
                    String itemInfo = item.getItemUseType()
                      + Component.MESSAGE_TOKEN +
                      item.getItemUseTypeValue();
                    InventoryUI.this.notify(itemInfo,
                      InventoryObserver.InventoryEvent.
                      ITEM_CONSUMED);
                    slot.remove(item);
```

```
                    }
                }
            }
        }
    }
    );
}
}
```

We override the default `ClickListener` class method `touchUp()`, which occurs on a release, but only when a touch (or press) down event is successfully returned from the `touchdown()` method. We first pass the values through to the base class for processing. We then get a counter value indicating how many times a `touchUp()` event has occurred in succession, using the `getTapCount()` method. Since we are looking for a double tap, we check for two successive taps. If we have a double tap event, we check whether the `InventorySlot` contains an `InventoryItem`, otherwise we ignore the event. If there is an item, we check whether the item has a consumable attribute, otherwise we ignore. If these conditions are satisfied, we will construct a notification message for an `InventoryEvent` event that contains the item use type and value, send the message on its way, and then remove said item from the `InventorySlot` location. If the items are stacked, then just the counter will be updated, otherwise the slot will be shown as empty.

The `PlayerHUD` implements the `InventoryObserver` and checks specifically for the `ITEM_CONSUMED` message. The following snippet of code represents the logic for handling this event in `PlayerHUD`:

```java
@Override
public void onNotify(String value, InventoryEvent event) {
    switch(event){
        case ITEM_CONSUMED:
            String[] strings =
                value.split(Component.MESSAGE_TOKEN);

            if( strings.length != 2) return;

            int type = Integer.parseInt(strings[0]);
            int typeValue = Integer.parseInt(strings[1]);

            if( InventoryItem.doesRestoreHP(type) ){
                _statusUI.addHPValue(typeValue);
            }else if( InventoryItem.doesRestoreMP(type) ){
                _statusUI.addMPValue(typeValue);
            }
            break;
        default:
            break;
    }
}
```

Here, we parse out the item type and item type value from the message. We check whether the item type restores HP or MP and we update the proper status value using the item use type value accordingly.

After discussing the class definition of BattleState, we continue on to look at the class body:

```
private Entity _currentOpponent;
private int _currentZoneLevel = 0;
private int _currentPlayerAP;
private int _currentPlayerDP;
private int _currentPlayerWandAPPoints = 0;
private final int _chanceOfAttack = 25;
private final int _chanceOfEscape = 40;
private final int _criticalChance = 90;
```

We have an assortment of variables to maintain during any one battle, and they will be discussed in turn. First, we keep an Entity object, _currentOpponent, which represents the monster that the player will fight. The logic to select a particular monster will be discussed later. We keep an int value, _currentZoneLevel, which represents the current zone level that the player has entered. A zone level represents an area of a map designated by a particular value, such as 1 or 5. Each zone will be configured to have particular monsters, and so every time the player enters a new zone, this value gets set; otherwise, if the player is not in a designated zone, the value will be set to 0. The next three int values, _currentPlayerAP, _currentPlayerDP, and _currentPlayerWandAPPoints, represent the currently equipped attack points, defense points, and attack points from the wand, respectively, which will be used when determining damage done to the monster and damage taken from the monster. We then have the three int values, _chanceOfAttack, _chanceOfEscape, and _criticalChance, which add some chance values to encounters. The first int represents the chance that a monster will attack the player, which for now, we set to 25 for a 25% chance of having an encounter. The next value represents a 40% chance that the player will be successful when they try to escape. The final value represents a value where anything over 90% will be considered a critical value:

```
public void setCurrentZoneLevel(int zoneLevel){
    _currentZoneLevel = zoneLevel;
}

public int getCurrentZoneLevel(){
    return _currentZoneLevel;
}
```

The `setCurrentZoneLevel()` and `getCurrentZoneLevel()` represent the setter and getter for the zone level that the player has entered into. As stated previously, this value is important for determining the type of enemy that should fight the player at any particular moment on the map:

```
public void setCurrentOpponent(){
    Entity entity = MonsterFactory.getInstance().
        getRandomMonster(_currentZoneLevel);
    if( entity == null ) return;
    this._currentOpponent = entity;
    notify(entity, BattleObserver.BattleEvent.OPPONENT_ADDED);
}
```

The `setCurrentOpponent()` method will be called when the determination has been made that the player will fight a monster. We first get a random monster from the `MonsterFactory` based on the current zone level passed in. We set this entity as our current opponent and then send a notification that we are ready for battle.

Before describing more of the `BattleState` source, now is a good time to discuss the `MonsterFactory` class and one of its components, `MonsterZone`.

MonsterFactory

The following code snippet represents `MonsterFactory`, which can be found at `core\src\com\packtpub\libgdx\bludbourne\battle\MonsterFactory.java`:

```
package com.packtpub.libgdx.bludbourne.battle;

import com.badlogic.gdx.math.MathUtils;
import com.badlogic.gdx.utils.Array;
import com.packtpub.libgdx.bludbourne.Entity;
import com.packtpub.libgdx.bludbourne.EntityConfig;

import java.util.Hashtable;

public class MonsterFactory {
    public static enum MonsterEntityType{
        MONSTER001,MONSTER002,MONSTER003,MONSTER004,MONSTER005,
        MONSTER006,MONSTER007,MONSTER008,MONSTER009,MONSTER010,
        MONSTER011,MONSTER012,MONSTER013,MONSTER014,MONSTER015,
        MONSTER016,MONSTER017,MONSTER018,MONSTER019,MONSTER020,
        MONSTER021,MONSTER022,MONSTER023,MONSTER024,MONSTER025,
        MONSTER026,MONSTER027,MONSTER028,MONSTER029,MONSTER030,
        MONSTER031,MONSTER032,MONSTER033,MONSTER034,MONSTER035,
        MONSTER036,MONSTER037,MONSTER038,MONSTER039,MONSTER040,
        MONSTER041, MONSTER042,
        NONE
    }
```

In order to maintain a list of monster definitions, we add the monster types to the `MonsterEntityType` enum:

```
private static MonsterFactory _instance = null;
```

The `MonsterFactory` is implemented as a singleton with lazy initialization, so we will save the static instance with the `_instance` variable:

```
private Hashtable<String, Entity> _entities;
```

We will maintain a `Hashtable` of entities, where `entityID` is the key and the `Entity` object itself is the value. The monsters defined in the `MonsterEntityType` enum will be implemented as `Entity` objects. The following section briefly discusses their configuration.

Monster entity

We define these monster `Entity` objects in a separate JSON script file called `monsters.json`, which can be found at `core\assets\scripts\`. The following is an excerpt from the script representing the first monster:

```
[
{
entityID : MONSTER001
state : IMMOBILE
direction : DOWN
conversationConfigPath : ""
questConfigPath : ""
currentQuestID : ""
itemTypeID: NONE
entityProperties: {
  ENTITY_HEALTH_POINTS: {
    class: java.lang.String
    value: 15
  }
  ENTITY_ATTACK_POINTS: {
    class: java.lang.String
    value: 40
  }
  ENTITY_DEFENSE_POINTS: {
    class: java.lang.String
    value: 5
  }
  ENTITY_XP_REWARD: {
    class: java.lang.String
    value: 5
  }
  ENTITY_GP_REWARD: {
    class: java.lang.String
```

```
            value: 5
        }
    }
    animationConfig: [
        {
            frameDuration: .5
            animationType: IMMOBILE
            texturePaths: [
                sprites/characters/Demon0.png
                sprites/characters/Demon1.png
            ]
            gridPoints: [
                {
                    x: 0
                    y: 0
                }

                {
                    x: 0
                    y: 0
                }
            ]
        }
    ]
    },
    ]
```

As we can see, the definition of the monster type `Entity` is similar to that of the NPCs and the player character. The only items that are new for the monster `Entity` would be the properties. The `entityProperties` value is an `ObjectMap` of name value pairs for any given `Entity`. Here, we define important properties for a monster `Entity`: `ENTITY_HEALTH_POINTS`, `ENTITY_ATTACK_POINTS`, `ENTITY_DEFENSE_POINTS`, `ENTITY_XP_REWARD`, and `ENTITY_GP_REWARD`. The `ENTITY_HEALTH_POINTS` represents the total HP that the monster starts with at the beginning of the battle. The `ENTITY_ATTACK_POINTS` represents the offensive strength that the monster has in total. The `ENTITY_DEFENSE_POINTS` represents the total defensive capability of the monster during the battle. The `ENTITY_XP_REWARD` and `ENTITY_GP_REWARD` properties represent the rewards that the player receives once a particular monster is vanquished.

Now that we see how the monster `Entity` objects are defined, we can continue with the source for `MonsterFactory`:

```
        private Hashtable<String, Array<MonsterEntityType>>
                _monsterZones;
```

Here, we maintain a `Hashtable` where the level of the monster zone is the key and an `Array` container of the monster types are the values. This is a good place to discuss exactly what I mean by a monster-level zone.

MonsterZone

First, conceptually, a `MonsterZone` is an area of a map that contains certain types of monsters. We first create these zones with Tiled, by defining an object layer called `MAP_ENEMY_SPAWN_LAYER`. We then add rectangular objects on the map that represent the different regions where certain types of monsters roam. The following screenshot (*Figure 7*) shows a subregion of the `TOP_WORLD` map with an assortment of zones:

Figure 7

Each region or zone has a name defined that represents their level, such as 1 or 2, all the way up to 10 (since 10 is the level cap for *BludBourne*). When a player walks over any of these areas, a notification is triggered that the player is in a particular area and the `setCurrentZoneLevel()` method of `BattleState` is called.

Second, we look at the mapping between the Tiled map values of the different zone levels and how they relate to the game world. We define a POJO class called `MonsterZone`. A class diagram (*Figure 8*) of `MonsterZone` is shown here:

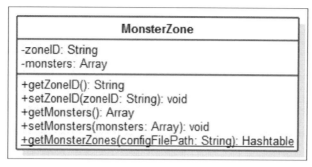

Figure 8

Each `MonsterZone` object contains a unique `zoneID`, such as the zone named 1 in the Tiled TOP_WORLD map in *Figure 7*. The other class member represents a container of the different assorted `MonsterEntityType` types that an area is configured to have roaming around in that particular area.

We define these POJO instances with a JSON-based script file `monster_zones.json`, which can be found at `core\assets\scripts\`. This script file maps the different zone levels with the different `MonsterEntityType` entities. The following excerpt shows how the first zone is currently configured:

```
[
{
zoneID : 1
monsters: [
   {
     value: MONSTER001
   }
   {
     value: MONSTER002
   }
   {
     value: MONSTER003
   }
   {
     value: MONSTER004
   }
   {
     value: MONSTER005
   }
   ]
},
]
```

So, from this example, we state that any region on the map named 1 for the `zoneID` has the following `MonsterEntityType` entities roaming around inside: MONSTER001, MONSTER002, MONSTER003, MONSTER004, and MONSTER005. This allows easy configuration when playing with different combinations in order to give the player a challenge, while at the same time minimizing the steep ramp up of difficulty. As a small design choice, it is recommended that lower level enemies are localized near the town, with an incremental difficulty increase as the maps expand out when the player ventures out.

Now that we have reviewed the monster `Entity` and `MonsterZone` objects, the construction of the `MonsterFactory` should make more sense in context:

```
private MonsterFactory(){
    Array<EntityConfig> configs = Entity.getEntityConfigs(
        "scripts/monsters.json");
    _entities =  Entity.initEntities(configs);

    _monsterZones = MonsterZone.getMonsterZones(
        "scripts/monster_zones.json");
}
```

Here, in the `MonsterFactory` constructor, we initialize the monster entities defined in the `monster.json` file and also the `MonsterZone` objects defined in the `monster_zones.json` file:

```
public static MonsterFactory getInstance() {
    if (_instance == null) {
        _instance = new MonsterFactory();
    }

    return _instance;
}
```

The `getInstance()` gives us access to the static instance of our singleton class, `MonsterFactory`:

```
public Entity getMonster(MonsterEntityType monsterEntityType){
    Entity entity = _entities.get(
        monsterEntityType.toString());
    return new Entity(entity);
}
```

The getMonster() method is a helper method to give us a deep copy instance of the type of monster passed in. By using the copy constructor, this deep copy allows us to have a unique instance for a particular battle without worrying about the values persisting in case we had a reference instead:

```
public Entity getRandomMonster(int monsterZoneID){
    Array<MonsterEntityType> monsters = _monsterZones.get(
        String.valueOf(monsterZoneID));
    int size = monsters.size;
    if( size == 0 ){
        return null;
    }
    int randomIndex = MathUtils.random(size - 1);

    return getMonster(monsters.get(randomIndex));
    }
}
```

The getRandomMonster() method is the primary method used to determine the type of monster that the player will fight. Here, we first use the monster zone ID passed in to access the container of monsters available for that particular area. Once we have a container of available monsters, we then choose a random index in order to retrieve a random monster from the Array. We then return the randomly chosen monster Entity object.

With the MonsterFactory, the monster-based Entity objects, and the MonsterZone objects covered, the use of these classes in BattleState should make much more sense:

```
public boolean isOpponentReady(){
    if( _currentZoneLevel == 0 ) return false;
    int randomVal = MathUtils.random(1,100);

    if( _chanceOfAttack > randomVal  ){
        setCurrentOpponent();
        return true;
    }else{
        return false;
    }
}
```

Here, in the `isOpponentReady()` method, we first check to see whether the zone level was set. `0` is a special case that indicates that the player is currently not in a zone with monsters. If the player is in a zone that contains monsters, then we check to see whether the player encounters a monster based on a check against the chance of attack value. If we fall within the chance of attack, then we will set the monster and get ready for battle:

```
public void playerAttacks(){
    if( _currentOpponent == null ){
        return;
    }
    //Check for magic if used in attack;
    //If we don't have enough MP, then return
    int mpVal = ProfileManager.getInstance().getProperty(
        "currentPlayerMP", Integer.class);
    if( _currentPlayerWandAPPoints > mpVal ){
        return;
    }else{
        mpVal -= _currentPlayerWandAPPoints;
        ProfileManager.getInstance().setProperty(
            "currentPlayerMP", mpVal);
        notify(_currentOpponent, BattleObserver.BattleEvent.
                PLAYER_USED_MAGIC);
    }

    notify(_currentOpponent, BattleObserver.BattleEvent.
            PLAYER_TURN_START);

    int currentOpponentHP = Integer.parseInt(_currentOpponent.
        getEntityConfig().getPropertyValue(
            EntityConfig.EntityProperties.
            ENTITY_HEALTH_POINTS.toString()));
    int currentOpponentDP = Integer.parseInt(_currentOpponent.
        getEntityConfig().getPropertyValue(
            EntityConfig.EntityProperties.
            ENTITY_DEFENSE_POINTS.toString()));

    int damage = MathUtils.clamp(
        _currentPlayerAP - currentOpponentDP, 0,
        _currentPlayerAP);

    currentOpponentHP = MathUtils.clamp(
        currentOpponentHP - damage, 0,
```

```
                        currentOpponentHP);

            _currentOpponent.getEntityConfig().setPropertyValue(
                EntityConfig.EntityProperties.
                ENTITY_HEALTH_POINTS.toString(),
                String.valueOf(currentOpponentHP));

            _currentOpponent.getEntityConfig().setPropertyValue(
                EntityConfig.EntityProperties.
                ENTITY_HIT_DAMAGE_TOTAL.toString(),
                String.valueOf(damage));

            notify(_currentOpponent,
                BattleObserver.BattleEvent.OPPONENT_HIT_DAMAGE);

            if( currentOpponentHP == 0 ){
                notify(_currentOpponent,
                    BattleObserver.BattleEvent.OPPONENT_DEFEATED);
            }

            notify(_currentOpponent,
                BattleObserver.BattleEvent.PLAYER_TURN_DONE);
    }
```

The `playerAttacks()` method represents the turn in the battle round for the player, when they actually attack the monster. First, we do a quick sanity check that a monster `Entity` has been initialized. We then check whether the player has enough MP for a magic attack, which is enabled when the player equips a wand. If the player does not have enough MP, then the attack fails. Otherwise, we subtract the cost of using the wand from the MP and send a notification that the status for the MP has changed (that is, gone down). We then send a notification with the `PLAYER_TURN_START` BattleEvent that the player's turn has officially started and get the current values for the monster's current health and defensive points. We want to keep the damage calculation simple for this implementation so we subtract the monster's DP from the player's AP total. We make sure to clamp the values in a range to prevent errors. We then subtract the damage calculation from the health of the monster. For this round, we save the updated HP of the monster entity, along with the damage that the monster sustained. We send a notification that the monster sustained some damage. Next, we check whether the monster is still alive, and if not, send a notification that the monster has been defeated with the `OPPONENT_DEFEATED` BattleEvent:

```
        public void opponentAttacks(){
            if( _currentOpponent == null ){
                return;
            }
```

```
    int currentOpponentAP = Integer.parseInt(
        _currentOpponent.getEntityConfig().
        getPropertyValue(EntityConfig.EntityProperties.
        ENTITY_ATTACK_POINTS.toString()));

    int damage = MathUtils.clamp(
        currentOpponentAP - _currentPlayerDP, 0,
        currentOpponentAP);

    int hpVal = ProfileManager.getInstance().getProperty(
        "currentPlayerHP", Integer.class);

    hpVal = MathUtils.clamp( hpVal - damage, 0, hpVal);
    ProfileManager.getInstance().setProperty(
    "currentPlayerHP", hpVal);

    notify(_currentOpponent,
        BattleObserver.BattleEvent.PLAYER_HIT_DAMAGE);

    notify(_currentOpponent,
        BattleObserver.BattleEvent.OPPONENT_TURN_DONE);
}
```

The `opponentAttacks()` method is similar to the `playerAttacks()`, but without most of the bookkeeping. First, we verify that the monster `Entity` has been initialized. Since this is the part of the round that the monster attacks, we get the monster's attack points and calculate the damage by subtracting the player's defensive points. Again, we clamp the values to make sure they are in a valid range. Then, we subtract the monster's damage from the player's health and update the player's HP property. We then send a notification via `BattleEvent` that the player was damaged and that the monster's turn is over:

```
public void playerRuns(){
    int randomVal = MathUtils.random(1,100);
    if( _chanceOfEscape > randomVal  ) {
        notify(_currentOpponent,
            BattleObserver.BattleEvent.PLAYER_RUNNING);
    }else if (randomVal > _criticalChance){
        opponentAttacks();
    }else{
        return;
    }
}
```

Here, the `playerRuns()` method is called when, during a battle, the player presses the **Run** button. Since there is a small chance of escape, we check the chance of escape value against a random number. If satisfied, then the player successfully escapes and we send the `PLAYER_RUNNING` `BattleEvent` notification, in order to differentiate this from a successful defeat of the monster (so no quest rewards). Finally, if the player does not successfully escape, we then do another check to see whether the monster has a chance to get a free attack on our hero by checking against the critical chance value:

```
@Override
public void onNotify(String value, InventoryEvent event) {
    switch(event) {
        case UPDATED_AP:
            int apVal = Integer.valueOf(value);
            _currentPlayerAP = apVal;
            break;
        case UPDATED_DP:
            int dpVal = Integer.valueOf(value);
            _currentPlayerDP = dpVal;
            break;
        case ADD_WAND_AP:
            int wandAP = Integer.valueOf(value);
            _currentPlayerWandAPPoints += wandAP;
            break;
        case REMOVE_WAND_AP:
            int removeWandAP = Integer.valueOf(value);
            _currentPlayerWandAPPoints -= removeWandAP;
            break;
        default:
            break;
    }
}
```

The `onNotify()` method implementation here is to enable the `BattleState` to be an observer for the `InventorySubject`, looking for specific `InventoryEvent` notifications. Since the player can swap out equipment during battle, we always want to receive updates whenever the AP and DP values change, including whether or not the player has equipped a wand in order to keep track of MP.

We covered an assortment of topics in this section, including how we determine calculations and monsters to fight in `BattleState`, how monsters are created as `Entity` objects with the `MonsterFactory` class, how battle zones are configured with the `MonsterZone` objects, and even how consuming items in the player's inventory is implemented with a double click. Next, we look at how this business logic gets used in the UI for battling these monsters.

BattleUI

As mentioned previously, *BludBourne* uses a simple interface for fighting monsters, inspired from the first person's perspective of *Dragon Warrior*. The following screenshot (*Figure 9*) represents the individually labeled components of the `BattleUI` class:

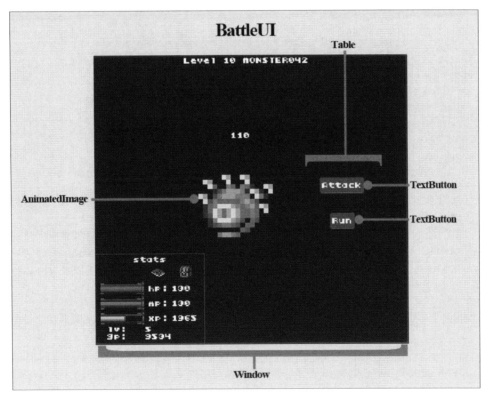

Figure 9

The `BattleUI` class is composed primarily of an `AnimatedImage` custom class and a `Table` with action `TextButton` widgets used by the player during the battle. The `BattleUI` window is configured so that the player's `StatusUI` is always on top, which gives the player access to their inventory so that they can equip items or use consumables during battle. The `StatusUI` also indicates the current HP and MP left.

We will now walk through the source of the `BattleUI` implementation, which can be found at `core\src\com\packtpub\libgdx\bludbourne\UI\BattleUI.java`:

```
package com.packtpub.libgdx.bludbourne.UI;

import com.badlogic.gdx.scenes.scene2d.InputEvent;
import com.badlogic.gdx.scenes.scene2d.Touchable;
import com.badlogic.gdx.scenes.scene2d.ui.Label;
import com.badlogic.gdx.scenes.scene2d.ui.Table;
import com.badlogic.gdx.scenes.scene2d.ui.TextButton;
import com.badlogic.gdx.scenes.scene2d.ui.Window;
import com.badlogic.gdx.scenes.scene2d.utils.Align;
import com.badlogic.gdx.scenes.scene2d.utils.ClickListener;
import com.packtpub.libgdx.bludbourne.Entity;
import com.packtpub.libgdx.bludbourne.EntityConfig;
import com.packtpub.libgdx.bludbourne.Utility;
import com.packtpub.libgdx.bludbourne.battle.BattleObserver;
import com.packtpub.libgdx.bludbourne.battle.BattleState;

public class BattleUI extends Window implements BattleObserver {
```

The `BattleUI` class derives from the `Window` widget class. In order to receive notifications from the `BattleState` object, `BattleUI` also implements the `BattleObserver` interface. As mentioned previously, the `BattleUI` class will use the information to make damage indications to the player and also disable/enable buttons based on the current turn (for instance, once a player attacks, the attack button will be disabled until the opponent finishes their turn, so the player can't keep using the attack button):

```
private AnimatedImage _image;
```

The `AnimatedImage` class is a simple subclass of `Image` in order to get a nice effect of the monster moving with their idle animation. We will take a short detour in order to discuss the `AnimatedImage` class.

AnimatedImage

The following code snippet represents the `AnimatedImage` class and can be found at `core\src\com\packtpub\libgdx\bludbourne\UI\AnimatedImage.java`:

```
package com.packtpub.libgdx.bludbourne.UI;

import com.badlogic.gdx.graphics.g2d.Animation;
import com.badlogic.gdx.scenes.scene2d.ui.Image;
import com.badlogic.gdx.scenes.scene2d.utils.Drawable;
import com.badlogic.gdx.scenes.scene2d.utils.
    TextureRegionDrawable;

public class AnimatedImage extends Image {
```

The `AnimatedImage` class derives from `Image`, which is an Actor (widget) that displays a `Drawable` object:

```
protected Animation _animation = null;
private float _frameTime = 0;
```

The two member variables that we need to keep track of is the actual `Animation` object itself and also the current frame time so that we know which animation frame to update to the screen:

```
public AnimatedImage(){
    super();
}

public AnimatedImage(Animation animation){
    super(animation.getKeyFrame(0));
    this._animation = animation;
}
```

The default `AnimatedImage()` constructor simply delegates to the super class. The other `AnimatedImage()` constructor takes a specific `Animation` as a parameter, passing the first frame to the base class constructor and setting the value:

```
public void setAnimation(Animation animation){
    super.setDrawable(new TextureRegionDrawable(
        animation.getKeyFrame(0)));
    this._animation = animation;
}
```

The setAnimation() method is a helper method for convenience so that we can simply construct an AnimatedImage with a default constructor and set the Animation object later. Again, we set the Drawable of the base class with the first frame in the animation and then set the member variable:

```
@Override
public void act(float delta){
    Drawable drawable = this.getDrawable();
    if( drawable == null ) return;
    _frameTime = (_frameTime + delta)%5;

    ((TextureRegionDrawable)drawable).
        setRegion(_animation.getKeyFrame(_frameTime, true));
    super.act(delta);
    }
}
```

Finally, we override the act() method. This method is called every frame by the Stage class that owns the Actor object. We grab the Drawable (and check to make sure it's valid) and then update the _frameTime value. We then update the Drawable region with the frame based on the current _frameTime value and then the delegate to the base class implementation by passing the delta value to the super class.

Now that we have a better understanding of the AnimatedImage class, we can continue to take a look at the BattleUI class:

```
private final int _enemyWidth = 96;
private final int _enemyHeight = 96;

private BattleState _battleState = null;
private TextButton _attackButton = null;
private TextButton _runButton = null;
private Label _damageValLabel = null;

private float _battleTimer = 0;
private final float _checkTimer = 1;

private float _origDamageValLabelY = 0;
```

We first set the size constraints of the `AnimatedImage` by defining the width and height values. We will be using the `BattleState` class to calculate the business logic for the battle, and so the `BattleUI` will own the `BattleState` object. We will have two action `TextButton` buttons, one for attacking and one for trying to run away. A `Label` object, `_damageValLabel`, will be used to display the monster damage sustained from the player as a nice visual indication to the user that their attack was successful. Also, because the `_damageValLabel` member variable will be moving vertically up during each frame update, we will reset this value with the `_origDamageValLabelY` variable. Finally, we will maintain a simple float value, `_battleTimer`, which represents the timer to check for an enemy periodically, defined by `_checkTimer`:

```
public BattleUI(){
    super("BATTLE", Utility.STATUSUI_SKIN, "solidbackground");

    _battleTimer = 0;
    _battleState = new BattleState();
    _battleState.addObserver(this);

    _damageValLabel = new Label("0", Utility.STATUSUI_SKIN);
    _damageValLabel.setVisible(false);

    _image = new AnimatedImage();
    _image.setTouchable(Touchable.disabled);

    Table table = new Table();
    _attackButton = new TextButton("Attack",
        Utility.STATUSUI_SKIN, "inventory");
    _runButton = new TextButton("Run", Utility.STATUSUI_SKIN);
    table.add(_attackButton).pad(20, 20, 20, 20);
    table.row();
    table.add(_runButton).pad(20, 20, 20, 20);

    //layout
    this.add(_damageValLabel).align(Align.left).
        padLeft(_enemyWidth / 2).row();
    this.add(_image).size(_enemyWidth, _enemyHeight).
        pad(10, 10, 10, _enemyWidth / 2);
    this.add(table);

    this.pack();
```

```
            _origDamageValLabelY = _damageValLabel.getY() +
              _enemyHeight;

         _attackButton.addListener(
               new ClickListener() {
                  @Override
                  public void clicked(InputEvent event, float x,
                                       float y) {
                      _battleState.playerAttacks();
                  }
               }
         );
         _runButton.addListener(
               new ClickListener() {
                  @Override
                  public void clicked(InputEvent event, float x,
                                       float y) {
                      _battleState.playerRuns();
                  }
               }
         );
      }
```

In the `BattleUI()` constructor, we initialize our member variables and put our `TextButton` objects in a `Table`. We then construct the layout, by placing the damage label in the first row (set to be over the center of the `AnimatedImage` object), placing the `AnimatedImage` in the second row with the `TextButton Table` placed in the second column next to the `AnimatedImage`. We then implement two listeners, one for the `TextButton` **Attack** that calls the `BattleState` method `playerAttacks()` and the second one for the `TextButton` **Run** that calls the `BattleState` method `playerRuns()`:

```
         public void battleZoneTriggered(int battleZoneValue){
            _battleState.setCurrentZoneLevel(battleZoneValue);
         }
```

The `battleZoneTriggered()` method relays messages from the `PlayerHUD` UI to the `BattleState` member variable that the player has entered or exited a battle zone area:

```
         public boolean isBattleReady(){
            if( _battleTimer > _checkTimer ){
               _battleTimer = 0;
               return _battleState.isOpponentReady();
            }else{
```

```
            return false;
        }
    }
```

Here, the isBattleReady() method is called every time the player moves in a zone populated by monsters. We use the _battleTimer to reduce the frequency that a check for a monster encounter is made. This gives the player a chance to explore without battling enemies at every step. Once a certain amount of time has transpired, we check whether the player has come across a monster or not, based on chance criteria values previously discussed in the BattleState section:

```
    public BattleState getCurrentState(){
        return _battleState;
    }


    @Override
    public void onNotify(Entity entity, BattleEvent event) {
        switch(event){
            case PLAYER_TURN_START:
                _attackButton.setDisabled(true);
                _attackButton.setTouchable(Touchable.disabled);
                break;
            case OPPONENT_ADDED:
                _image.setAnimation(entity.getAnimation(
                    Entity.AnimationType.IMMOBILE));
                this.setTitle("Level " +
                    _battleState.getCurrentZoneLevel() + " " +
                    entity.getEntityConfig().getEntityID());
                break;
            case OPPONENT_HIT_DAMAGE:
                int damage = Integer.parseInt(entity.
                    getEntityConfig().getPropertyValue(
                    EntityConfig.EntityProperties.
                    ENTITY_HIT_DAMAGE_TOTAL.toString()));
                _damageValLabel.setText(String.valueOf(damage));
                _damageValLabel.setY(_origDamageValLabelY);
                _damageValLabel.setVisible(true);
                break;
            case OPPONENT_DEFEATED:
                _damageValLabel.setVisible(false);
                _damageValLabel.setY(_origDamageValLabelY);
                break;
            case OPPONENT_TURN_DONE:
                _attackButton.setDisabled(false);
                _attackButton.setTouchable(Touchable.enabled);
```

```
                    break;
            case PLAYER_TURN_DONE:
                _battleState.opponentAttacks();
                break;
            default:
                break;
        }
    }
```

The onNotify() method is overridden for the BattleObserver implementation so
that the BattleUI can look for notifications relating to the BattleEvent events. If
we receive a PLAYER_TURN_START notification, then we disable the **Attack** button
until the next round starts, designated by the OPPONENT_TURN_DONE notification.
The OPPONENT_ADDED notification initializes the BattleUI with the new monster for
the encounter. The OPPONENT_HIT_DAMAGE notification gives us the value to display
over the AnimatedImage object when the player successfully hits the monster. We do
some cleanup with the OPPONENT_DEFEATED notification. Finally, when we receive
the PLAYER_TURN_DONE event, we initiate the monster's turn for attack:

```
    @Override
    public void act(float delta){
        _battleTimer = (_battleTimer + delta)%60;
        if( _damageValLabel.isVisible() &&
            _damageValLabel.getY() < this.getHeight()){
            _damageValLabel.setY(_damageValLabel.getY()+5);
        }
        super.act(delta);
    }
}
```

We override the act() method in order to do two things. First, we maintain a battle
timer that increments every frame. Second, if the monster damage Label is visible,
we display the Label, incrementing the vertical direction every frame for a nice
effect. We then delegate to the base class.

In this section, we learned how the BattleUI maintains a simple, yet intuitive
interface for battling monsters, and also how all the pieces from the BattleState
section work in conjunction with the UI. We also learned how we can create nice
effects such as an AnimatedImage for the monster and an animated damage label
moving over the monster.

LevelTable

While completing quests that we learned to implement in *Chapter 6, So Many Quests, So Little Time…*, and defeating legions of monsters on the battle field, the player will receive experience points for helping out the local NPCs and making *BludBourne* a better place overall. For the purposes of this chapter, a simple leveling system was developed to reward and communicate to the player that they are in fact progressing as their character develops.

The first part for handling the leveling is to develop the attributes that will change according to the different levels. LevelTable is a POJO class that represents all of these attributes for a level, including all the accessor methods. The following class diagram (*Figure 10*) represents the LevelTable class (which can be found at core\src\com\packtpub\libgdx\bludbourne\battle\LevelTable.java):

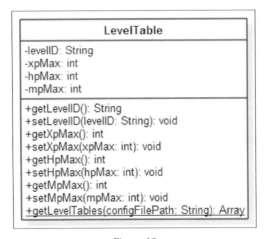

Figure 10

The primary attributes that we care about for *BludBourne*, and which could be easily extended by you for your game, are the current level, the maximum experience points for the level before we move onto the next level, and the maximum HP and MP amounts for the current level.

When defining a `LevelTable` for each of the levels that your game supports, we will update a configuration file in JSON format, which is `core\assets\scripts\level_tables.json`. The following excerpt represents the values for these attributes for level 1 and 2:

```
[
{
levelID : 1
xpMax : 200
hpMax : 50
mpMax : 50
},
{
levelID : 2
xpMax : 400
hpMax : 70
mpMax : 70
},
]
```

You will notice in the `level_tables.json` file that we only define up to level 10. For *BludBourne*, being a shorter game, we set the level cap at level 10. As you start to add different battle zones with different types of enemies, you may want to increase the level cap in order to allow more progression for the player as they level up.

As an example of how to use this in practice, we can now take a look at the `StatusUI.java` class for this chapter. The following represents the relevant snippets of code for using the `LevelTable` objects in practice:

```
public class StatusUI extends Window implements StatusSubject {
...
    private Array<LevelTable> _levelTables;
    private static final String LEVEL_TABLE_CONFIG =
        "scripts/level_tables.json";

    public StatusUI(){
    ...
        _levelTables =
            LevelTable.getLevelTables(LEVEL_TABLE_CONFIG);
    }
```

Here, in the `StatusUI()` constructor, we call a static convenience method in the `LevelTable` class that will load the file, deserialize the JSON, and return a container of the `LevelTable` objects:

```
public void addXPValue(int xpValue){
    this._xpVal += xpValue;

    if( _xpVal > _xpCurrentMax ){
        updateToNewLevel();

    }
    ...
}
```

In the `addXPValue()` method, we add a check to see whether the current experience value, `_xpVal`, is greater than the current level maximum. If it is, then we know that we need to update our current level, and so we call `updateToNewLevel()`:

```
public void updateToNewLevel(){
    for( LevelTable table: _levelTables ){
        if( _xpVal > table.getXpMax() ){
            continue;
        }else{
            setXPValueMax(table.getXpMax());

            setHPValueMax(table.getHpMax());
            setHPValue(table.getHpMax());

            setMPValueMax(table.getMpMax());
            setMPValue(table.getMpMax());

            setLevelValue(Integer.parseInt(table.getLevelID()));
            return;
        }
    }
}
    ...
}
```

The `updateToNewLevel()` method will walk through the container of the `LevelTable` objects, checking to see which `LevelTable` contains the highest ceiling value for the experience max value. This check will determine which level should we be based on the current amount of experience points. Once this `LevelTable` is found, we set all the values from this table, including the new level value and return.

This section gave us a concise overview of the leveling feature in *BludBourne*, and it is a nice starting place for augmenting your own.

GameOverScreen

Finally, we need a mechanism to enable the game to end and allow the player to reload from a previous save, since the element of the player character death naturally comes with adding a battle system. The following screenshot (*Figure 11*) represents the game over screen for *BludBourne* when the HP for the player's character reaches 0:

Figure 11

This screen will load the `LoadGameScreen` when the **Continue** button is pressed, allowing the user to reload from a previous save game. The screen will also load the `MainMenuScreen` when the **Main Menu** button is pressed. The workflow for enabling this screen starts with `PlayerHUD` receiving a notification that the player has been damaged, as shown in the following code snippet:

```
public void onNotify(Entity enemyEntity, BattleEvent event) {
    switch (event) {
    ...
    case PLAYER_HIT_DAMAGE:
        int hpVal = ProfileManager.getInstance().getProperty(
            "currentPlayerHP", Integer.class);
        _statusUI.setHPValue(hpVal);

        if( hpVal <= 0 ){
            _battleUI.setVisible(false);
            MainGameScreen.setGameState(
                MainGameScreen.GameState.GAME_OVER);
        }
    break;
    }
}
```

Here, once the player's HP has reached 0, we set the `GameState` to `GAME_OVER`. This sets a flag in `MainGameScreen`:

```
@Override
public void render(float delta) {
    if( _gameState == GameState.GAME_OVER ){
        _game.setScreen(_game.getScreenType(
            BludBourne.ScreenType.GameOver));
    }
    ...
}
```

Since the `render()` method gets called every frame, we check for `GAME_OVER` at the beginning, and if this value is set, we switch to the `GameOverScreen` (which hides the current `MainGameScreen` and shows the `GameOverScreen`).

This section showed us a straightforward process for exiting from the current `MainGameScreen`.

Summary

You now have the power to put down even the fiercest monsters in *BludBourne*, and now it's up to you to be the hero that the town needs.

In this chapter, we went through the process of developing a battle system. We started by implementing the business logic class, `BattleState`, to handle damage calculations, chance calculations for an encounter, and also calculating chances for escape. We then wrapped a UI, `BattleUI`, around this core logic, creating random monster encounters for the player for gold, experience, and honor. We added a leveling feature, using `LevelTable`, so that the player experiences progression as they discover the world of *BludBourne* and also enable the player to consume health scrolls and magic flasks to recover lost health and magic, respectively. Finally, we walked through the code path flow to display a game over screen when the player dies with `GameOverScreen`.

In the next chapter, we will add the final features to *BludBourne* with sound and music and also add support for cutscenes.

8
Oh, No! Looks Like Drama!

What are some of the elements that players will talk about long after they have beaten your game? The right music that plays at a critical moment, a sound that makes an attack sound more powerful, or a cutscene that evokes some core emotion for the player are just a few examples. With the foundation of knowledge that we have learned over the course of developing *BludBourne*, there is something special to be said for adding the finishing touches of sound, music, and even cutscenes to tell your story. This chapter will show you how to add these important components to your videogame, in order to give a nice polish to your final product. Luckily, for us, LibGDX provides the tools that make this particular piece of your game simple to implement.

In summary, we will cover the following topics in this chapter:

- Sound and music
- Creating cutscenes

Class diagram overview

The following class diagram (*Figure 1*) represents the classes involved with implementing sound, music, and cutscene support:

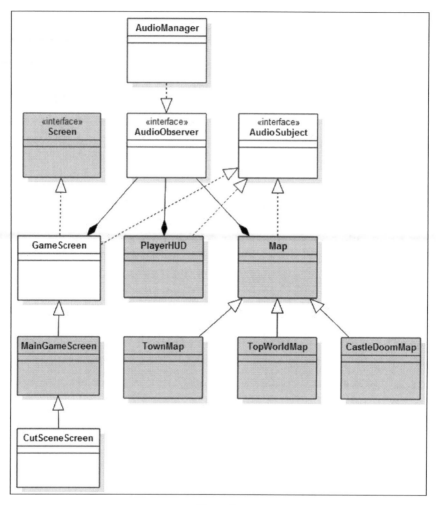

Figure 1

As a note, the classes shaded in as grey are classes we have discussed in the previous chapters, so we will not be discussing them in depth.

The `AudioManager` class implements the `AudioObserver` interface and manages the various commands, such as loading and playing music and sounds. The corresponding `AudioObserver` objects are owned by the `GameScreen`, `PlayerHUD`, and `Map` classes, which in turn send notification events when music or sound files are involved.

The `Map` class implements the `AudioSubject` interface so that all the derived classes, such as `TownMap`, `TopWorldMap`, and `CastleDoomMap`, have access to the music and sound resources. `PlayerHUD` implements the `AudioSubject` interface as well so that the appropriate sounds can be played, for instance, when the player is hit and loses health or the player purchases items from the store. Finally, we have the `GameScreen` class that implements the `Screen` interface and the `AudioSubject` interface, and it is a new class that all current screens will extend.

The `CutSceneScreen` is derived from the base class `MainGameScreen` in order to take advantage of loading different maps and camera settings for the various views.

Sound and music

The first item to note for this section is how the audio resources are managed within the LibGDX framework. As explained in the previous chapters, the implementation of the `Application` interface for the desktop is `LwjglApplication`, which is part of the LibGDX backend package called **LWJGL** (`com.badlogic.gdx.backends.lwjgl`). LWJGL not only includes OpenGL support for graphics, but also audio support via OpenAL.

OpenAL was developed with a 3D environment in mind, and so velocity, position, direction, and intensity are all parameters supported by this API. These parameters allow more naturally sounding audio as the player moves through their environment. Under the covers, the actual audio buffers contain audio data in raw PCM format, in either mono or stereo format. As powerful as OpenAL is for handling audio, the process of learning a new API, initializing devices, and monitoring audio buffers can be daunting at first. Luckily, LibGDX abstracts away all the underlying complexities into a nice, simple package, `com.badlogic.gdx.audio`. The platform-specific implementation of these interfaces for the desktop can be found in `com.badlogic.gdx.backends.lwjgl.audio`. Also, the audio library for LibGDX supports the following container formats: MP3, OGG, and WAV.

The second item to note is that there may be times when you will need to edit either the music or sound files. The editor that I used during the creation of *BludBourne* is **Audacity** (version 2.0.3), which you can get at http://audacityteam.org/download/. This is a great open source alternative that allows you to edit OGG, MP3, and WAV container files, easily bring the dB volume down, and edit the bitrate, among many other features. The following is a screenshot of Audacity in action (*Figure 2*):

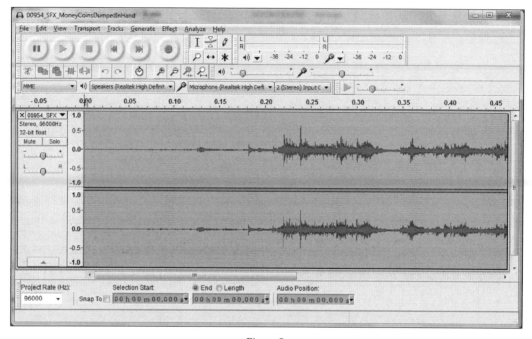

Figure 2

The third item to note for this section is that we have changed the standard use of the observer pattern. Instead of having one subject class with various observer objects waiting for changes, we now have one observer object with multiple subject classes. This use of the observer pattern allows us to centralize all the sound and music resources to one class, AudioManager.

We will discuss the audio-related classes for this chapter, AudioObserver, AudioSubject, and AudioManager, in the following sections.

AudioObserver

The following class diagram (*Figure 3*) represents the `AudioObserver` interface:

Figure 3

This interface is streamlined, but the parameters, `AudioCommand` and
`AudioTypeEvent`, deserve further explanation, starting with the following
`AudioObserver` source (which can be found at `core\src\com\packtpub\libgdx\`
`bludbourne\audio\AudioObserver.java`):

```
package com.packtpub.libgdx.bludbourne.audio;

public interface AudioObserver {
    public static enum AudioTypeEvent{
        MUSIC_TITLE("audio/10112013.wav"),
        MUSIC_TOWN("audio/Magic Town_0.mp3"),
        MUSIC_TOPWORLD("audio/n3535n5n335n35nj.ogg"),
        MUSIC_CASTLEDOOM("audio/Dark chamber.mp3"),
        MUSIC_BATTLE("audio/Random Battle.mp3"),
        MUSIC_INTRO_CUTSCENE("audio/Takeover_5.mp3"),
        MUSIC_LEVEL_UP_FANFARE(
            "audio/4 Open Surge score jingle - B.ogg"),

        SOUND_CREATURE_PAIN(
            "audio/27780_SFX_CreatureGruntInPain1.wav"),
        SOUND_PLAYER_PAIN(
            "audio/27678_SFX_ComicalSoundsTiredGrunt1.wav"),
        SOUND_PLAYER_WAND_ATTACK(
            "audio/26230_SFX_ProductionElementReverseWhoosh19.wav"),
        SOUND_EATING(
            "audio/17661_SFX_HumanEatingPotatoChips1.wav"),
        SOUND_DRINKING(
            "audio/27677_SFX_ComicalSoundsSwallowLiquid1.wav"),
        SOUND_COIN_RUSTLE(
            "audio/00954_SFX_MoneyCoinsDumpedInHand_final.wav"),
        NONE("");
```

```
        private String _audioFullFilePath;

        AudioTypeEvent(String audioFullFilePath){
            this._audioFullFilePath = audioFullFilePath;
        }
        public String getValue(){
            return _audioFullFilePath;
        }
    }
```

An `AudioTypeEvent` enum type represents a specific sound or music file to run a command on. In order to maintain type safety for the different audio files, we will implement them as an enum. There can be issues with defining the locations for these files elsewhere, with the potential to load the wrong file location for a particular `AudioTypeEvent`. In order to mitigate this potential issue, we will be storing the file locations alongside their filename counterparts. So, for each defined `AudioTypeEvent` enum type, we will pass a string that represents the file location into its corresponding constructor. In order to access a particular `AudioTypeEvent` file location, the `getValue()` method is provided as a convenient accessor for that value.

The following list gives a brief explanation of where the music and sounds are used:

- `MUSIC_TITLE`: This retro track is played when the game starts up at the **Main Menu** screen, and throughout the screens, until a game is loaded

- `MUSIC_TOWN`: This uplifting track is played as the player is walking around the `Town` map

- `MUSIC_TOPWORLD`: This somber track is played as the player is walking outside of town, on the `TOP_WORLD` map

- `MUSIC_CASTLEDOOM`: This ominous track is played as the player is walking around the scene for the final fight, at the Castle of Doom

- `MUSIC_BATTLE`: This upbeat track is played when the player encounters an enemy in the field of battle

- `MUSIC_INTRO_CUTSCENE`: This suspenseful track is played when a cutscene is playing

- `MUSIC_LEVEL_UP_FANFARE`: This track is played when the player levels up or completes a quest

- `SOUND_CREATURE_PAIN`: This sound is played when the player successfully attacks the monster and the monster sustains damage

- `SOUND_PLAYER_PAIN`: This sound plays when the player was successfully attacked by the monster and the player sustains damage

- SOUND_PLAYER_WAND_ATTACK: This sound plays when the player successfully attacks the monster with a wand and the monster sustains damage

- SOUND_EATING: This sound plays when the player consumes a scroll (yummy) to heal their HP

- SOUND_DRINKING: This sound plays when the player consumes a vial to recover their MP

- SOUND_COIN_RUSTLE: This sound plays when any money exchanges hands, such as buying, selling, or receiving quest rewards

- NONE: This is a default enum for commands that do not require a specific AudioTypeEvent

Take a look at the following snippet:

```
public static enum AudioCommand {
    MUSIC_LOAD,
    MUSIC_PLAY_ONCE,
    MUSIC_PLAY_LOOP,
    MUSIC_STOP,
    MUSIC_STOP_ALL,
    SOUND_LOAD,
    SOUND_PLAY_ONCE,
    SOUND_PLAY_LOOP,
    SOUND_STOP
}
    void onNotify(AudioCommand command, AudioTypeEvent event);
}
```

An AudioCommand enum type represents a specific command to run on the AudioTypeEvent enum type passed in. The following list describes each command in detail:

- MUSIC_LOAD: This represents the command to load a specific music file. The separation between loading and playing a specific music file allows the front loading of resources upon construction so that the music can be played later.

- MUSIC_PLAY_ONCE: This represents the command to only play the music file once.

- MUSIC_PLAY_LOOP: This represents the command to continue to play the music file on a continuous loop.

- MUSIC_STOP: This represents the command to stop a specific music file currently playing.

- `MUSIC_STOP_ALL`: This represents the command to stop all music currently playing. The `AudioTypeEvent` enum type to use in conjunction with this command would be `NONE`, since the second parameter is not used.

- `SOUND_LOAD`: This represents the command to load a specific sound file. The separation from loading and playing a specific sound file allows you to front load the resources on construction and then play the sound later.

- `SOUND_PLAY_ONCE`: This represents the command to only play the sound file once.

- `SOUND_PLAY_LOOP`: This represents the command to continue to play the sound file on a continuous loop.

- `SOUND_STOP`: This represents the command to stop a specific sound file currently playing.

The `AudioObserver` is slightly different than the other observer classes that we have previously implemented because there are two enum type parameters in the signature for `onNotify()`. This design allows us to issue simple commands on specific files without worrying about the underlying details and makes issuing commands throughout our game straightforward.

AudioSubject

The following class diagram (*Figure 4*) represents the `AudioSubject` interface:

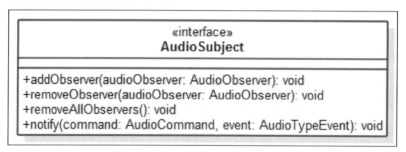

Figure 4

For this chapter, the classes that implement the `AudioSubject` interface are `Map`, `PlayerHUD`, and `GameScreen`.

`PlayerHUD` implements the `AudioSubject` interface so that the appropriate sounds can be played, for instance, when the player is hit and loses health or the player purchases items from the store. The following code snippet is a quick review of how we would implement the subject class for an observer pattern and also register the observer:

```
...
public class PlayerHUD implements AudioSubject {
...
    private Array<AudioObserver> _observers;

    public PlayerHUD(Camera camera, Entity player,
                     MapManager mapMgr) {
        _observers = new Array<AudioObserver>();
        ...
        this.addObserver(AudioManager.getInstance());
    }
```

Here, we initialize an empty array for the `AudioObserver` objects in the `PlayerHUD` constructor and then add the `AudioManager` instance (which implements the `AudioObserver` class) to this array by calling `addObserver()`:

```
    ...
    @Override
    public void addObserver(AudioObserver audioObserver) {
        _observers.add(audioObserver);
    }

    @Override
    public void removeObserver(AudioObserver audioObserver) {
        _observers.removeValue(audioObserver, true);
    }

    @Override
    public void removeAllObservers() {
        _observers.removeAll(_observers, true);
    }

    @Override
    public void notify(AudioObserver.AudioCommand command,
                       AudioObserver.AudioTypeEvent event) {
        for(AudioObserver observer: _observers){
            observer.onNotify(command, event);
        }
    }
}
```

This is a pretty standard implementation for the `AudioSubject`, and it is pretty much all a class would need to implement in order to access the capabilities of the `AudioManager` class via notifications.

The `Map` class implements the `AudioSubject` interface as well so that all derived classes such as `TownMap`, `TopWorldMap`, and `CastleDoomMap` have access to the music and sound resources. The one item to note is that a simple abstract interface was created for `Map` so that each derived `Map` class can manage their own specific music. The following is a snippet of this interface in `Map`:

```
public abstract class Map implements AudioSubject{
    ...
    abstract public void unloadMusic();
    abstract public void loadMusic();
}
```

The following is an example from `TownMap` that implements this interface:

```
public class TownMap extends Map{
    ...
    @Override
    public void unloadMusic() {
        notify(AudioObserver.AudioCommand.MUSIC_STOP,
            AudioObserver.AudioTypeEvent.MUSIC_TOWN);
    }

    @Override
    public void loadMusic() {
        notify(AudioObserver.AudioCommand.MUSIC_LOAD,
            AudioObserver.AudioTypeEvent.MUSIC_TOWN);
        notify(AudioObserver.AudioCommand.MUSIC_PLAY_LOOP,
            AudioObserver.AudioTypeEvent.MUSIC_TOWN);
    }
}
```

As we can see, every time a new map loads in `MapManager`, `MapManager` will first call `unloadMusic()`. This sends a notification to the `AudioManager` (which implements the `AudioObserver` interface) to stop the currently playing music. Then, a `loadMusic()` call is made on the new map to be loaded. This sends a notification to the `AudioManager` to first load the music file and then start playing on a continuous loop.

Finally, we have the `GameScreen` class that implements the `Screen` interface and the `AudioSubject` interface, and it is a new class that all current screens will extend.

Now that we understand the observer pattern for handling music and sound, we can now look at the concrete implementation of the AudioObserver interface, that is, AudioManager.

AudioManager

The following is the source from AudioManager, which can be found at core\src\com\packtpub\libgdx\bludbourne\audio\AudioManager.java:

```
package com.packtpub.libgdx.bludbourne.audio;

import com.badlogic.gdx.Gdx;
import com.badlogic.gdx.audio.Music;
import com.badlogic.gdx.audio.Sound;
import com.packtpub.libgdx.bludbourne.Utility;
import java.util.Hashtable;
```

The primary classes from LibGDX that the AudioManager will use to manage the music and sound files are Music and Sound from the com.badlogic.gdx.audio library.

A Music object (which supports the Music interface and the corresponding concrete backend implementation) represents an audio file streamed from disk, instead of loading the file into memory at once. This interface provides standard play, pause, and stop functionality, and also has methods for panning, changing position, and volume control.

A Sound object (which supports the Sound interface and the corresponding concrete backend implementation) represents a short audio file that is fully loaded into memory. This interface provides standard play, pause, and stop functionality, and also pitch, panning, and volume control:

```
public class AudioManager implements AudioObserver {
    private static final String TAG =
                        AudioManager.class.getSimpleName();

    private static AudioManager _instance = null;

    private Hashtable<String, Music> _queuedMusic;
    private Hashtable<String, Sound> _queuedSounds;

    private AudioManager(){
        _queuedMusic = new Hashtable<String, Music>();
        _queuedSounds = new Hashtable<String, Sound>();
    }
```

We are implementing the `AudioManager` as a Singleton instance to guarantee that all notifications are funneled to this one manager type class. The only other member variables that we will maintain are the two `Hashtable` data structures, `_queuedMusic` and `_queuedSounds`, which will contain any music or sound files, respectively, that we have previously loaded. This gives us a cache of the `Music` and `Sound` objects that we can access later without reloading from disk. This also provides us an easy method to dispose of the resources later. As your game grows and the assets increase, one consideration is that you can implement functionality to clear the cache on every load of a map, in order to minimize the memory footprint:

```
public static AudioManager getInstance() {
    if (_instance == null) {
        _instance = new AudioManager();
    }

    return _instance;
}
```

This `getInstance()` implements a lazy style initialization for the Singleton instance of the `AudioManager`:

```
@Override
public void onNotify(AudioCommand command,
                     AudioTypeEvent event) {
    switch(command){
        case MUSIC_LOAD:
            Utility.loadMusicAsset(event.getValue());
            break;
        case MUSIC_PLAY_ONCE:
            playMusic(false, event.getValue());
            break;
        case MUSIC_PLAY_LOOP:
            playMusic(true, event.getValue());
            break;
        case MUSIC_STOP:
            Music music = _queuedMusic.get(event.getValue());
            if( music != null ){
                music.stop();
            }
            break;
        case MUSIC_STOP_ALL:
            for( Music musicStop: _queuedMusic.values() ){
                musicStop.stop();
            }
            break;
```

```
            case SOUND_LOAD:
                Utility.loadSoundAsset(event.getValue());
                break;
            case SOUND_PLAY_LOOP:
                playSound(true, event.getValue());
                break;
            case SOUND_PLAY_ONCE:
                playSound(false, event.getValue());
                break;
            case SOUND_STOP:
                Sound sound = _queuedSounds.get(event.getValue());
                if( sound != null ){
                    sound.stop();
                }
                break;
            default:
                break;
        }
    }
```

This onNotify() method is the single interface that needs to be implemented
for the AudioObserver. This method implements all the various AudioCommand
enum objects discussed in the previous section, where the commands wrap the
actual functionality from the Music and Sound classes. The second parameter,
AudioTypeEvent, provides the actual full file path, and is used as the key for the two
Hashtable member variables that act as a cache:

```
private Music playMusic(boolean isLooping,
                        String fullFilePath){
    Music music = _queuedMusic.get(fullFilePath);
    if( music != null ){
        music.setLooping(isLooping);
        music.play();
    }else if(Utility.isAssetLoaded(fullFilePath)){
        music = Utility.getMusicAsset(fullFilePath);
        music.setLooping(isLooping);
        music.play();
        _queuedMusic.put(fullFilePath, music);
    }else{
        Gdx.app.debug(TAG, "Music not loaded");
        return null;
    }
    return music;
}
```

The playMusic() method will essentially try to play the music file based on the String file path passed in as a parameter. First, we check to see whether the Music object is in the cache, and if it is, we use that to play the music file. If the Music object was not previously used, or not cached, then we call a Utility method to see whether it was loaded and is ready for use. If the music file was not cached or is not loaded, then we send a message:

```
private Sound playSound(boolean isLooping,
                        String fullFilePath){
    Sound sound = _queuedSounds.get(fullFilePath);
    if( sound != null ){
        long soundId = sound.play();
        sound.setLooping(soundId, isLooping);
    }else if( Utility.isAssetLoaded(fullFilePath) ) {
        sound = Utility.getSoundAsset(fullFilePath);
        long soundId = sound.play();
        sound.setLooping(soundId, isLooping);
        _queuedSounds.put(fullFilePath, sound);
    }else{
        Gdx.app.debug(TAG, "Sound not loaded");
        return null;
    }
    return sound;
}
```

The playSound() method will try to play the sound file based on the String file path passed in as a parameter. First, we check to see whether the Sound object is in the cache, and if it is, we use that to play the sound file. If the Sound object was not previously used or not cached, then we call a Utility method to see whether it was loaded and is ready for use. One difference from the Music class is that in order to set properties on the Sound object after playing, we need to use a sound ID value. If the sound file was not cached or is not loaded, then we send a message noting that we don't have a valid sound:

```
public void dispose(){
    for(Music music: _queuedMusic.values()){
        music.dispose();
    }

    for(Sound sound: _queuedSounds.values()){
        sound.dispose();
    }
}
```

Here, in the `dispose()` method, we iterate over our cache of the `Music` and `Sound` objects and call their respective `dispose()` methods. Since these objects are a managed resource, it is a good idea that once we are finished using them, we call their appropriate `dispose()` method.

So, in this section, we have covered the basics of the audio library in LibGDX, specifically with the use of the `Music` and `Sound` classes. We have also learned how the observer pattern can be effectively used for a simple notification-based use of the `Music` and `Sound` objects, using the `AudioSubject` and `AudioObserver` classes. We have also covered how the `AudioManager` implements the `AudioObserver` and simplifies the process of implementing music and sound support in your game.

Creating cutscenes

In any video game, cutscenes play an important part in order to convey emotion to the player. They help to progress the story and immerse the players in your world. This is even more important in an RPG, as the player needs to react to world events and feel that they are making an impact in the world you are creating. For this section, we will implement a cutscene that explains the influx of monsters over the lands of *BludBourne*, but also leaves some unanswered questions to entice the player to continue playing.

The basic idea is that we create a `Screen` class that renders a `Stage` object. We have previously discussed the `Stage` class in *Chapter 4, Where Do I Put My Stuff?*. Basically, the `Stage` class manages all the different aspects of an `Actor` object lifecycle, such as drawing the `Actor` and distributing the relevant input events. The individual nodes that compose the Scene2D scene graph are referred to as `Actor` objects and they contain their own position, size, origin, scale, rotation, and color. In order to manipulate the `Actor` objects on `Stage`, we will use classes from the `Action` class in the LibGDX library `com.badlogic.gdx.scenes.scene2d`. These `Action` objects are run during a `Stage` class method call, `act()`, on all the relevant `Actor` objects. These actions happen over time, and so this `act()` call is made every frame, based on the latest delta time between frames (the topic of frame update deltas is covered in more detail in *Chapter 2, Welcome to the Land of BludBourne*).

Action

The `Action` class gives us the ability to run some task (small autonomous piece of code) over time, such as moving objects around the screen or generating special effects at a certain time. There are myriad types of `Action` objects available that cover the full gamut of the types of tasks you may need done.

The following are top-level `Action` objects that apply to other `Action` objects:

- `AddAction`: This task will add a specific `Action` object to an `Actor`
- `RemoveAction`: This task will remove a specific `Action` object from an `Actor`
- `DelayAction`: This task delays the execution of an `Action` object for a certain amount of time
- `TimeScaleAction`: This task multiplies the delta of an `Action` object, thus speeding up or slowing down specific actions
- `RepeatAction`: This task will rerun an `Action` object a specified number of times, or forever
- `RunnableAction`: This task will run a specific piece of code in a `Runnable` object

The following are `Action` objects that manipulate some property of an `Actor`:

- `MoveToAction`: This task moves an `Actor` to a specific position
- `MoveByAction`: This task moves an `Actor` to a position relative to its current position
- `SizeToAction`: This task resizes the width and height of an `Actor`
- `SizeByAction`: This task resizes the width and height an `Actor` relative to its current size
- `ScaleToAction`: This task changes the scale of the x and y coordinates of an `Actor`
- `ScaleByAction`: This task changes the scale of the x and y coordinates of an `Actor` relative to its current scale values
- `RotateToAction`: This task changes the rotation angle of an `Actor`
- `RotateByAction`: This task changes the rotation angle of an `Actor` relative to its current rotation
- `ColorAction`: This task changes the color of an `Actor`
- `AlphaAction`: This task changes the alpha channel of an `Actor`. It is useful for fade in and fade out effects
- `VisibleAction`: This task changes whether an `Actor` is visible or not
- `TouchableAction`: This task changes whether an `Actor` is touchable or not
- `RemoveActorAction`: This task removes an `Actor` from the stage
- `LayoutAction`: This task will either enable or disable the layout of an `Actor`
- `AfterAction`: This task will run once all the other tasks associated with the `Actor` have finished

- AddListenerAction: This task will add a `Listener` object to an `Actor`
- RemoveListenerAction: This task will remove a `Listener` object from an `Actor`

The following are `Action` objects that are composed of other `Action` objects:

- SequenceAction: This task will execute the `Action` objects in sequence, one after the other
- ParallelAction: This task will execute the `Action` objects in parallel, all at once

With a brief explanation of the `Action` library behind us, we can now look at the implementation that uses some of these `Action` objects.

CutSceneScreen

For this section, we will be focusing on the `CutSceneScreen` class that can be found at `core\src\com\packtpub\libgdx\bludbourne\screens\CutSceneScreen.java`. The following is the source for `CutSceneScreen`:

```
public class CutSceneScreen extends MainGameScreen {
    private BludBourne _game;
    private Stage _stage;
    private Viewport _viewport;
    private Stage _UIStage;
    private Viewport _UIViewport;
    private Actor _followingActor;
    private boolean _isCameraFixed = true;
    private Dialog _messageBoxUI;
    private Label _label;
    private Image _transitionImage;
```

`CutSceneScreen` derives from the base class `MainGameScreen` so that we can get access to an initialized `MapManager` for loading the different maps and also some convenience methods.

Here, we create two `Stage` objects. One `Stage` object, `_stage`, will contain all the `Actor` objects that will be in the cutscene. The other `Stage` object, `_UIStage`, will contain any UI components that we need for the cutscene. In our case, we will be using a simple `Dialog` object to act as the message box when the characters are talking during the cutscene. We will also maintain a reference to the current `Actor` in the scene, `_followingActor`, so that the camera can lock its coordinates to those coordinates of the `Actor`. Otherwise, we will just keep the `boolean` member variable, `_isCameraFixed`, set to `true`.

The only other variable of note would be the `Image` object, `_transitionImage`. This will be explained more in depth a little further down, but in essence, this is an `Image` that will cover the entire screen with a filled color during transitions between scenes:

```
private Action _screenFadeOutAction;
private Action _screenFadeInAction;
private Action _introCutSceneAction;
private Action _switchScreenAction;
private Action _setupScene01;
private Action _setupScene02;
private Action _setupScene03;
private Action _setupScene04;
private Action _setupScene05;
```

Here, we list out the important `Action` object member variables that we will use during the cutscene. The `Action` object `_screenFadeOutAction` will use the `AlphaAction` class to transition the `_transitionImage` Actor from transparent to filled. The `Action` object `_screenFadeInAction` will use the `AlphaAction` class to transition the `_transitionImage` Actor from filled to transparent. The `Action` object `_introCutSceneAction` is a `SequenceAction` composed of everything that will happen during the cutscene. The `Action` object `_switchScreenAction` will be used in an `AfterAction` object that will be run after the cutscene finishes, in order to switch to the main menu. The last five `Action` objects are all `RunnableAction` objects that will set up each of the different scenes:

```
private AnimatedImage _animBlackSmith;
private AnimatedImage _animInnKeeper;
private AnimatedImage _animMage;
private AnimatedImage _animFire;
private AnimatedImage _animDemon;
```

The last five member variables are all `AnimatedImage` objects. The `AnimatedImage` class was discussed in *Chapter 7, Time to Show These Monsters Who's the Boss*, and we will be using it here to represent the different characters in the cutscene:

```
public CutSceneScreen(BludBourne game) {
    super(game);

    _game = game;

    _viewport = new ScreenViewport(_camera);
    _stage = new Stage(_viewport);

    _UIViewport = new ScreenViewport(_hudCamera);
```

```
_UIStage = new Stage(_UIViewport);

_label = new Label("Test", Utility.STATUSUI_SKIN);
_label.setWrap(true);

_messageBoxUI = new Dialog("",
    Utility.STATUSUI_SKIN, "solidbackground");
_messageBoxUI.setVisible(false);
_messageBoxUI.getContentTable().add(_label).
    width(_stage.getWidth()/2).pad(10, 10, 10, 0);
_messageBoxUI.pack();
_messageBoxUI.setPosition(
    _stage.getWidth() / 2 - _messageBoxUI.getWidth() / 2,
    _stage.getHeight() - _messageBoxUI.getHeight());

_followingActor = new Actor();
_followingActor.setPosition(0, 0);

notify(AudioObserver.AudioCommand.MUSIC_LOAD,
        AudioObserver.AudioTypeEvent.MUSIC_INTRO_CUTSCENE);
```

In the `CutSceneScreen` constructor, we will first initialize the `Stage` objects for our `Actor` objects and UI components. We will also send a notification to load the music for this cutscene:

```
Pixmap pixmap = new Pixmap(1, 1, Pixmap.Format.RGBA8888);
pixmap.setColor(Color.BLACK);
pixmap.fill();
Drawable drawable = new TextureRegionDrawable(
    new TextureRegion(new Texture(pixmap)));

_transitionImage = new Image();
_transitionImage.setFillParent(true);
_transitionImage.setDrawable(drawable);
```

We then construct `Pixmap`. A `Pixmap` object is an image represented in memory. Here, we programmatically create an image with a width and height of 1 (a pixel). We then set the `Pixmap` object's color to black and fill the pixel with said color. This gives us a `Drawable` that we can then pass into our `Image` object, `_transitionImage`. Since the parent of `_transitionImage` will be the `Stage` object `_stage`, we make sure to set the size of the `Image` to the entire screen. Now we have an `Actor`, `_transitionImage`, which covers the entire screen with black:

```
_screenFadeOutAction = new Action() {
    @Override
```

```
                public boolean act(float delta) {
                    _transitionImage.addAction(
                            Actions.sequence(
                                    Actions.alpha(0),
                                    Actions.fadeIn(3)
                            ));
                    return true;
                }
        };

        _screenFadeInAction = new Action() {
            @Override
            public boolean act(float delta) {
                _transitionImage.addAction(
                        Actions.sequence(
                                Actions.alpha(1),
                                Actions.fadeOut(3)
                        ));
                return true;
            }
        };
```

After creating _transitionImage, we can now create two different Action objects to manipulate this Image at various times. The Action object _screenFadeOutAction will use the AlphaAction to transition the _transitionImage Actor from transparent to filled. This will simulate the effect of the cutscene screen fading to black over three seconds. The Action object _screenFadeInAction will use the AlphaAction to transition the _transitionImage Actor from filled to transparent. This will simulate the effect of the black screen fading to the cutscene screen over three seconds.

This is a nice simple trick in order to get the effect of screen transitions without the complexity of overriding the Scene class and implementing your own draw() calls:

```
            _animBlackSmith = getAnimatedImage(EntityFactory.
                EntityName.TOWN_BLACKSMITH);
            _animInnKeeper = getAnimatedImage(EntityFactory.
                EntityName.TOWN_INNKEEPER);
            _animMage = getAnimatedImage(EntityFactory.
                EntityName.TOWN_MAGE);
            _animFire = getAnimatedImage(EntityFactory.
```

```
            EntityName.FIRE);
    _animDemon = getAnimatedImage(MonsterFactory.
        MonsterEntityType.MONSTER042);


    //Actions
    _switchScreenAction = new RunnableAction(){
        @Override
        public void run() {
            _game.setScreen(_game.getScreenType(
                BludBourne.ScreenType.MainMenu));
        }
    };
```

Here, we construct RunnableAction for _switchScreenAction that will set the screen to the main menu when run:

```
        _setupScene01 = new RunnableAction() {
            @Override
            public void run() {
                hideMessage();
                _mapMgr.loadMap(MapFactory.MapType.TOWN);
                _mapMgr.disableCurrentmapMusic();
                setCameraPosition(10, 16);

                _animBlackSmith.setVisible(true);
                _animInnKeeper.setVisible(true);
                _animMage.setVisible(true);

                _animBlackSmith.setPosition(10, 16);
                _animInnKeeper.setPosition(12, 15);
                _animMage.setPosition(11, 17);

                _animDemon.setVisible(false);
                _animFire.setVisible(false);
            }
        };
```

The RunnableAction scene objects are meant to demonstrate the initial setup for each of the scenes. These different scene objects could have used other Action objects, such as MoveToAction instead of setPosition(), but for the purposes of clarity, they are implemented this way.

For our first scene, we will start by hiding the dialog box. We will load the TOWN map and disable any default music for that particular map. We will then set a static camera at a specific position, near the town square. This scene will include three `Actor` objects, so we position them within the scene and then hide the other two `Actor` objects that will come later:

```
_setupScene02 = new RunnableAction() {
    @Override
    public void run() {
        hideMessage();
        _mapMgr.loadMap(MapFactory.MapType.TOP_WORLD);
        _mapMgr.disableCurrentmapMusic();
        setCameraPosition(50, 30);

        _animBlackSmith.setPosition(50, 30);
        _animInnKeeper.setPosition(52, 30);
        _animMage.setPosition(50, 28);

        _animFire.setPosition(52, 28);
        _animFire.setVisible(true);
    }
};
```

For the second scene, we hide the dialog to start because we don't know if previous `Action` objects already displayed the dialog box. We then load the TOP_WORLD map and again disable the default map music. Again, we set a static camera to a specific location. This scene takes place in a cemetery where our three characters are conspiring to raise someone from the dead. In this scene, not only do we see our three villagers, but also a mystical fire used in the spell:

```
_setupScene03 = new RunnableAction() {
    @Override
    public void run() {
        _animDemon.setPosition(52, 28);
        _animDemon.setVisible(true);
        hideMessage();
    }
};
```

For the third scene setup, we now set the boss demon as visible:

```
_setupScene04 = new RunnableAction() {
    @Override
```

```
        public void run() {
            hideMessage();
            _animBlackSmith.setVisible(false);
            _animInnKeeper.setVisible(false);
            _animMage.setVisible(false);
            _animFire.setVisible(false);

            _mapMgr.loadMap(MapFactory.MapType.TOP_WORLD);
            _mapMgr.disableCurrentmapMusic();

            _animDemon.setVisible(true);
            _animDemon.setScale(1, 1);
            _animDemon.setSize(16 * Map.UNIT_SCALE,
                16 * Map.UNIT_SCALE);
            _animDemon.setPosition(50, 40);

            followActor(_animDemon);
        }
    };
```

For the fourth scene, we hide any messages displayed and also the three villagers and their mystical fire. We now load the TOP_WORLD map (we don't want to assume that it was previously loaded, and if it was, we will return right away as it's already loaded) and disable the default music. This time, we reset the demon's scale and size to its original settings, reposition it over some trees after the cemetery, and then set the camera to follow the demon:

```
    _setupScene05 = new RunnableAction() {
        @Override
        public void run() {
            hideMessage();
            _animBlackSmith.setVisible(false);
            _animInnKeeper.setVisible(false);
            _animMage.setVisible(false);
            _animFire.setVisible(false);

            _mapMgr.loadMap(MapFactory.
                MapType.CASTLE_OF_DOOM);
            _mapMgr.disableCurrentmapMusic();
            followActor(_animDemon);

            _animDemon.setVisible(true);
            _animDemon.setPosition(15, 1);
        }
    };
```

For the fifth and final scene, we again hide the message box and make sure all other characters are hidden. We load the CASTLE_OF_DOOM map and disable the default music. We then reposition the demon to the bottom of the map and set the camera to follow the demon:

```
//layout
_stage.addActor(_animMage);
_stage.addActor(_animBlackSmith);
_stage.addActor(_animInnKeeper);
_stage.addActor(_animFire);
_stage.addActor(_animDemon);
_stage.addActor(_transitionImage);
_transitionImage.toFront();

_UIStage.addActor(_messageBoxUI);
}
```

We add all of our characters to the Stage object, making sure that the Image object, _transitionImage, is always at the front since it will be used to transition in and out of the different scenes:

```
private Action getCutsceneAction(){
    _setupScene01.reset();
    _setupScene02.reset();
    _setupScene03.reset();
    _setupScene04.reset();
    _setupScene05.reset();
    _screenFadeInAction.reset();
    _switchScreenAction.reset();
```

There are two important points regarding the use of Action objects that deserve an explanation here. First, every time an Action object is finished, it is removed from the Actor it was associated with. Therefore, the Action object will not be run again unless it is added back. The second point is that, even if you add an Action object back to an Actor, if it was previously completed, it will not run again because a completed flag was set. In order to reset the Actor object as if it was newly created, you need to use reset() on the Action object before adding. These two points are important if you wish to reuse Action objects, since these points are not obvious when first using them.

The following is the entire cutscene example for *BludBourne*, encapsulated in SequenceAction:

```
return Actions.sequence(
        Actions.addAction(_setupScene01),
```

```
Actions.addAction(_screenFadeInAction),
Actions.delay(3),
Actions.run(
  new Runnable() {
    @Override
    public void run() {
    showMessage("BLACKSMITH: We have planned this
      long enough. The time is now! I have had
      enough
      talk...");
    }
  }),
Actions.delay(7),
```

Here, we add the first scene `Action` object and also add the `Action` that will fade from a black screen to the currently loaded map. We add a delay as well to make sure the fade transition finishes before continuing. We then show the first piece of dialog, and this sequence of actions can be seen in the following screenshot (*Figure 5*):

Figure 5

Consider the following code snippet:

```
Actions.run(
  new Runnable() {
    @Override
    public void run() {
    showMessage("MAGE: This is dark magic you
      fool. We must proceed with caution, or this
      could end badly for all of us");
          }
      }),
Actions.delay(7),
Actions.run(
    new Runnable() {
      @Override
      public void run() {
        showMessage("INNKEEPER: Both of you
          need to keep it down. If we get
          caught using black magic, we will all
          be hanged!");
      }
    }),
Actions.delay(5),
Actions.addAction(_screenFadeOutAction),
Actions.delay(3),
```

Here, we display the dialog as the characters communicate, making sure to add a
`DelayAction` so that the player has time to read the dialog (in our case, five to seven
seconds of delay seems to be appropriate):

```
Actions.addAction(_setupScene02),
Actions.addAction(_screenFadeInAction),
Actions.delay(3),
Actions.run(
  new Runnable() {
    @Override
    public void run() {
      showMessage("BLACKSMITH: Now, let's get on
        with this. I don't like the cemeteries
        very much...");
    }
  }
),
Actions.delay(7),
```

```
Actions.run(
  new Runnable() {
    @Override
    public void run() {
      showMessage("MAGE: I told you, we can't rush
        the spell. Bringing someone back to life
        isn't simple!");
    }
  }
),
Actions.delay(7),
Actions.run(
  new Runnable() {
    @Override
    public void run() {
      showMessage("INNKEEPER: I know you loved
        your daughter, but this just isn't
        right...");
    }
  }
),
Actions.delay(7),
Actions.run(
  new Runnable() {
    @Override
    public void run() {
      showMessage("BLACKSMITH: You have never had
        a child of your own. You just don't
        understand!");
    }
  }
),
Actions.delay(7),
Actions.run(
  new Runnable() {
    @Override
    public void run() {
      showMessage("MAGE: You both need to
        concentrate, wait...Oh no, something is
        wrong!!");
    }
  }
),
Actions.delay(7),
```

We fade out of scene 1 and fade into scene 2. We then display some dialog between the characters. The previous sequence of Action objects for scene 2 is represented in the following screenshot (*Figure 6*):

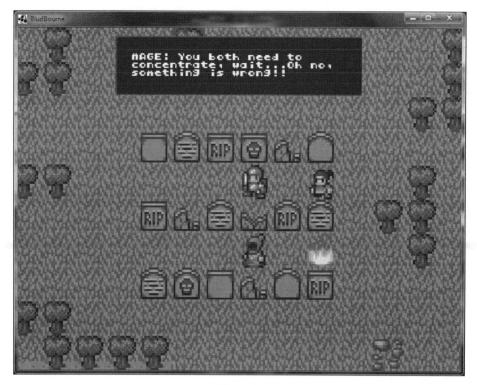

Figure 6

Consider the following code snippet:

```
Actions.addAction(_setupScene03),
Actions.addAction(Actions.fadeOut(2), _animDemon),
Actions.delay(2),
Actions.addAction(Actions.fadeIn(2), _animDemon),
Actions.delay(2),
Actions.addAction(Actions.fadeOut(2), _animDemon),
Actions.delay(2),
Actions.addAction(Actions.fadeIn(2), _animDemon),
Actions.delay(2),
Actions.addAction(Actions.fadeOut(2), _animDemon),
Actions.delay(2),
Actions.addAction(Actions.fadeIn(2), _animDemon),
Actions.delay(2),
Actions.addAction(Actions.scaleBy(40, 40, 5,
```

```
            Interpolation.linear), _animDemon),
    Actions.delay(5),
    Actions.addAction(Actions.moveBy(20, 0),
      _animDemon),
    Actions.delay(2),
    Actions.run(
      new Runnable() {
        @Override
        public void run() {
          showMessage("BLACKSMITH: What...What have we
            done...");
        }
      }
    ),
    Actions.delay(3),
```

The setup for scene 3 animates the demon `Actor` with a sequence of fade-in and fade-out actions and then scales the demon `Actor` to simulate the `Actor` flying toward the camera and flying out of the frame. The following screenshot represents scene 3 when the demon `Actor` first appears (*Figure 7*):

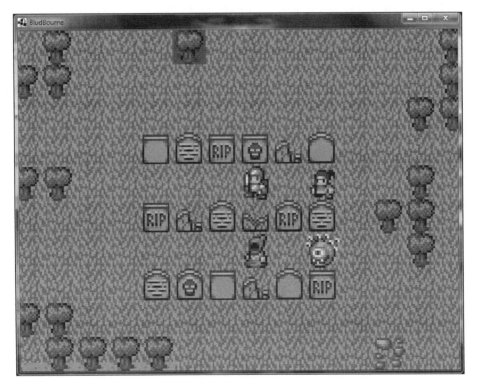

Figure 7

Consider the following code snippet:

```
Actions.addAction(_screenFadeOutAction),
Actions.delay(3),
Actions.addAction(_setupScene04),
Actions.addAction(_screenFadeInAction),
Actions.addAction(Actions.moveTo(54, 65, 13,
    Interpolation.linear), _animDemon),
Actions.delay(10),
Actions.addAction(_screenFadeOutAction),
Actions.delay(3),
Actions.addAction(_screenFadeInAction),
```

We now set up scene 4 where the demon `Actor` will be flying over the world on its way to the castle where it will begin its master plan for utter annihilation of the inhabitants of *BludBourne*. We set the destination of the demon `Actor` and include a linear interpolation so that the demon `Actor` object looks like it is flying over the land. The following screenshot represents this scene (*Figure 8*):

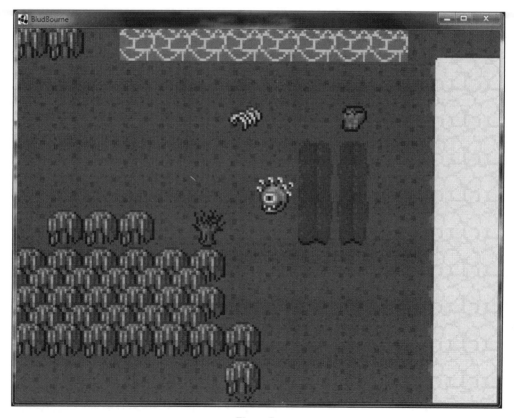

Figure 8

Consider the following code snippet:

```
Actions.addAction(_setupScene05),
Actions.addAction(Actions.moveTo(15, 76, 15,
   Interpolation.linear), _animDemon),
Actions.delay(15),
Actions.run(
  new Runnable() {
    @Override
    public void run() {
      showMessage("DEMON: I will now send my
        legions of demons to destroy these sacks
        of meat!");
          }
      }
  ),
Actions.delay(5),
```

In the final scene, scene 5, we now have the demon Actor flying towards its final resting place, on the throne of the Castle of Doom. The following screenshot shows the final scene (*Figure 9*):

Figure 9

Consider the following code snippet:

```
                Actions.addAction(_screenFadeOutAction),
                Actions.delay(5),
                Actions.after(_switchScreenAction)
        );
    }
```

The final `Action` object is used to switch to the Main Menu when the cutscene completes:

```
    private AnimatedImage getAnimatedImage(
        EntityFactory.EntityName entityName){

        Entity entity = EntityFactory.getInstance().
            getEntityByName(entityName);
        return setEntityAnimation(entity);
    }

    private AnimatedImage getAnimatedImage(
        MonsterFactory.MonsterEntityType entityName){

        Entity entity = MonsterFactory.getInstance().
            getMonster(entityName);
         return setEntityAnimation(entity);
    }

    private AnimatedImage setEntityAnimation(Entity entity){
        final AnimatedImage animEntity = new AnimatedImage();
        animEntity.setEntity(entity);
        animEntity.setSize(animEntity.getWidth() * Map.UNIT_SCALE,
            animEntity.getHeight() * Map.UNIT_SCALE);
        return animEntity;
    }
```

These overloaded `getAnimatedImage()` methods are convenience methods to get an `Entity` object by name and return a newly constructed `AnimatedImage`. The `setEntityAnimation()` method is called by both of these methods in order to load the animation for the `Entity` object and set the default size:

```
    public void followActor(Actor actor){
        _followingActor = actor;
        _isCameraFixed = false;
    }
```

```
public void setCameraPosition(float x, float y){
    _camera.position.set(x, y, 0f);
    _isCameraFixed = true;
}
```

Both `followActor()` and `setCameraPosition()` are used in the operation of the stage camera. If `followActor()` is set, then the camera will update its position relative to the position of the `Actor` object, essentially locked to a specific `Actor`. If `setCameraPosition()` is called instead, then the camera position will remain fixed:

```
public void showMessage(String message){
    _label.setText(message);
    _messageBoxUI.pack();
    _messageBoxUI.setVisible(true);
}

public void hideMessage(){
    _messageBoxUI.setVisible(false);
}
```

These two helper methods are used to show the dialog used throughout the cutscene:

```
@Override
public void render(float delta) {
    Gdx.gl.glClearColor(0, 0, 0, 1);
    Gdx.gl.glClear(GL20.GL_COLOR_BUFFER_BIT);

    _mapRenderer.setView(_camera);

    _mapRenderer.getBatch().enableBlending();
    _mapRenderer.getBatch().setBlendFunction(
        GL20.GL_SRC_ALPHA, GL20.GL_ONE_MINUS_SRC_ALPHA);

    if( _mapMgr.hasMapChanged() ){
        _mapRenderer.setMap(_mapMgr.getCurrentTiledMap());
        _mapMgr.setMapChanged(false);
    }

    _mapRenderer.render();

    if( !_isCameraFixed ){
        _camera.position.set(_followingActor.getX(),
            _followingActor.getY(), 0f);
    }
```

```
        _camera.update();

        _UIStage.act(delta);
        _UIStage.draw();

        _stage.act(delta);
        _stage.draw();
    }
```

The render() method overrides the base render() implementation from MainGameScreen. Here, we update the map rendering information first. We then check whether we need to update the camera coordinates based on whether we have a fixed camera or one following an Actor object. Finally, we update the UI Stage object and the Stage with all of our Actor objects:

```
@Override
public void show() {
    _introCutSceneAction = getCutsceneAction();
    _stage.addAction(_introCutSceneAction);

    notify(AudioObserver.AudioCommand.MUSIC_STOP_ALL,
        AudioObserver.AudioTypeEvent.NONE);
    notify(AudioObserver.AudioCommand.MUSIC_PLAY_LOOP,
        AudioObserver.AudioTypeEvent.MUSIC_INTRO_CUTSCENE);

    ProfileManager.getInstance().removeAllObservers();
    if( _mapRenderer == null ){
        _mapRenderer = new OrthogonalTiledMapRenderer(
            _mapMgr.getCurrentTiledMap(), Map.UNIT_SCALE);
    }
}
```

The show() method will be called when the CutSceneScreen is displayed. Every time we are about to show the cutscene, we first need to get the Action objects that will play out on the screen and then add them to the Stage object. We then stop all music previously playing and start to play the music specific to this cutscene. Finally, because we are extending from MainGameScreen, we want to make sure we remove any observers that might have been added by the base class. Otherwise, we can end up having updates that we don't want:

```
@Override
public void hide() {
```

```
            notify(AudioObserver.AudioCommand.MUSIC_STOP,
                    AudioObserver.AudioTypeEvent.MUSIC_INTRO_CUTSCENE);
            ProfileManager.getInstance().removeAllObservers();
            Gdx.input.setInputProcessor(null);
        }
    }
```

Finally, when we exit the current `CutSceneScreen`, we make sure to stop the music from playing, remove any observers that may have been added by our base class, and return.

So, in this section, we have seen first-hand the power of the `Action` classes and how they can be used to create an engaging cutscene that adds drama to our game.

Summary

In this chapter, we explored the LibGDX classes, `Music` and `Sound`, for playing audio. We learned how the observer pattern can be used in a different way, with `AudioSubject` and `AudioObserver`. We also implemented the `AudioManager` class to manage the `AudioObserver` notifications from all the `AudioSubject` objects. Finally, we learned about the `Action` objects and how these tasks can be used to create cutscenes as implemented in `CutSceneScreen`.

In the next chapter, we will wrap up the last of the features for our game, including a shake camera, static lighting, particle effects, screen transitions, and a day-night cycle.

Time to Set the Mood

9

With all the features that have been implemented for *BludBourne*, arriving at a point in the development where we can add the finishing details and special effects is definitely exciting. In this chapter, we will discuss assorted topics that will give your game the extra attention to detail, which will add to the experience for the player. First, we will implement screen fade transitions between changing map locations and cutscene transitions. Second, we will implement a nice special effect where the UI and enemy will shake when hit. When coupled with the sound effects from *Chapter 8, Oh, No! Looks Like Drama!*, the shaking when hit will really make the blows feel impactful. Third, we will explore the static lighting model and how we can implement it for the light sources in *BludBourne*. Fourth, we will add a nice transitions in-game between the different points in the day based on the current time. Finally, we will discuss the addition of particle effects and how they can really make a scene stand out with minimal effort.

So, we will cover the following topics in this chapter:

- Screen transitions
- Shake camera
- Static lighting
- Day-to-night cycle
- Particle effects

Screen transitions

One simple but effective effect is to have a nice transition when the player travels from one location to another. Sometimes, just appearing in another location can be a jarring experience for the player. The following class diagram (*Figure 1*) shows the relationships for the two classes we will develop for this transition effect, ScreenTransitionActor and ScreenTransitionAction:

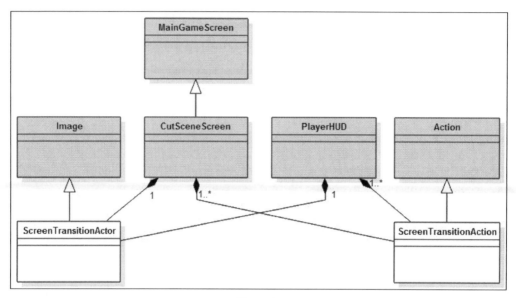

Figure 1

In order to develop ScreenTransitionActor and ScreenTransitionAction, we will need to do a little refactoring from *Chapter 8, Oh, No! Looks Like Drama!*, and move some of the core logic used in the cutscene transition into its logical component class. The ScreenTransitionActor class derives from the Image class and will essentially represent a black screen-sized transition. The ScreenTransitionAction class derives from the Action class and will be used during the animation frame cycle to update the ScreenTransitionActor object in order to display a nice smooth transition for the player. A ScreenTransitionActor object will live in the CutSceneScreen class for transitions between scenes as well as the PlayerHUD for transitions between location changes and battle screens. Static method calls will be made to the ScreenTransitionAction class to animate the transitions during those events.

The ScreenTransitionActor class

The following source for ScreenTransitionActor can be found in core\src\com\
packtpub\libgdx\bludbourne\sfx\:

```
package com.packtpub.libgdx.bludbourne.sfx;

import com.badlogic.gdx.graphics.Color;
import com.badlogic.gdx.graphics.Pixmap;
import com.badlogic.gdx.graphics.Texture;
import com.badlogic.gdx.graphics.g2d.TextureRegion;
import com.badlogic.gdx.scenes.scene2d.Touchable;
import com.badlogic.gdx.scenes.scene2d.ui.Image;
import com.badlogic.gdx.scenes.scene2d.utils.
        TextureRegionDrawable;

public class ScreenTransitionActor extends Image {
```

The ScreenTransitionActor class extends from the Image class in order to satisfy
two requirements. First, an Actor needs to live in the Stage object of each relevant
class in order to take advantage of proper size and positioning on the screen as well
as frame updates. Second, we want to have a drawable type surface to render to the
screen during transitions:

```
private Color _transitionColor = Color.BLACK;
```

This configurable Color object represents the color that the transition screen will be
during the transitions:

```
public ScreenTransitionActor(){
    init();
}

public ScreenTransitionActor(Color color){
    this._transitionColor = color;
    init();
}
```

Here, we have an overloaded constructor, ScreenTransitionActor(), for passing
in the default Color object during construction instead of setting the value later:

```
private void init(){
    toFront();
    setFillParent(true);
```

```
Pixmap pixmap = new Pixmap(1, 1, Pixmap.Format.RGBA8888);
pixmap.setColor(_transitionColor);
pixmap.fill();
setDrawable(new TextureRegionDrawable(
        new TextureRegion(new Texture(pixmap))));
clearListeners();
setTouchable(Touchable.disabled);
}
```

In general, for ScreenTransitionActor to be effective, it should be added to the Stage at the end, in order to have a higher z-order, so that the transition screen appears in front of all the other Actor objects, effectively occluding them. In the init() method, we will first call toFront() to make sure that this object is added in the correct order. We also want this Actor to fill the entire screen, so we make sure to flag this behavior when updating the geometries in the layout for the Stage objects by setting setFillParent() to true.

As stated in the previous chapter, we programmatically create an image with a width and height of one pixel. We then set the Pixmap object's color to specified transition color defined for our class, fill the pixel, and then fill our object with said color. This gives us a Texture that we can use to update the Drawable of our class. Finally, we clear any listeners and disable the Touchable attribute so that the user cannot interact with the transition screen:

```
public Color getTransitionColor() {
    return _transitionColor;
}

public void setTransitionColor(Color transitionColor) {
    this._transitionColor = transitionColor;
}
}
```

Finally, we define the getter and setter accessor methods for the transition color, getTransitionColor() and setTransitionColor(), respectively.

Once we define the ScreenTransitionActor, we need to implement the second component in order to animate the transitions of the Actor, the ScreenTransitionAction class.

The ScreenTransitionAction class

The following source for `ScreenTransitionAction.java` can be found in `core\src\com\packtpub\libgdx\bludbourne\sfx\`:

```
package com.packtpub.libgdx.bludbourne.sfx;

import com.badlogic.gdx.scenes.scene2d.Action;
import com.badlogic.gdx.scenes.scene2d.Actor;
import com.badlogic.gdx.scenes.scene2d.actions.Actions;
import com.badlogic.gdx.scenes.scene2d.actions.SequenceAction;

public class ScreenTransitionAction extends Action {
```

We want to take advantage of the autonomous tasks, called `Action` objects, which we referred to in *Chapter 8, Oh, No! Looks Like Drama!*. We derive from the `Action` class so that we can take advantage of this functionality:

```
public static enum ScreenTransitionType{
    FADE_IN,
    FADE_OUT,
    NONE
}
```

In the `ScreenTransitionType` enum, we define the two primary effects, `FADE_IN` and `FADE_OUT`. We will use these to fade into a scene and fade out of a scene, respectively:

```
private ScreenTransitionType _transitionType =
                            ScreenTransitionType.NONE;
private float _transitionDuration = 3;
```

Here, we define two member variables that affect the animation. The first member variable is the `ScreenTransitionType` enum that we just defined, and we set it to a known default, `ScreenTransitionType.NONE`. The second member variable is a `float` value that defines the total length of the transition effect, in order to correctly update the interpolation values across frames:

```
public ScreenTransitionAction(){
}

public ScreenTransitionAction(ScreenTransitionType type,
                            float duration){
    this._transitionType = type;
    this._transitionDuration = duration;
}
```

Here, we overload the ScreenTransitionAction constructor with the two attributes defined for this class, the ScreenTransitionType enum value and the corresponding duration of time:

```
@Override
public boolean act(float delta) {
    Actor actor = getTarget();
    if ( actor == null ) return false;
    switch(_transitionType){
        case FADE_IN:
            SequenceAction fadeIn = Actions.sequence(
                    Actions.alpha(1),
                    Actions.fadeOut(_transitionDuration));
            actor.addAction(fadeIn);
            break;
        case FADE_OUT:
            SequenceAction fadeOut = Actions.sequence(
                    Actions.alpha(0),
                    Actions.fadeIn(_transitionDuration));
            actor.addAction(fadeOut);
            break;
        case NONE:
            break;
        default:
            break;
    }
    return true;
}
```

We override the act() method of the base class Action in order to implement our transition effect based upon the ScreenTransitionType type and duration. As previously discussed in *Chapter 8, Oh, No! Looks Like Drama!*, the ScreenTransitionType enum type, FADE_IN, will transition the ScreenTransitionActor target from filled to transparent. This will simulate the effect of the screen fading from the target object's color over the transition duration length to the scene. The ScreenTransitionType enum type, FADE_OUT, will transition the ScreenTransitionActor target from transparent to filled. This will simulate the effect of screen fading to the target object's color over the transition duration length:

```
public static ScreenTransitionAction transition (
            ScreenTransitionType type, float duration) {
    ScreenTransitionAction action =
        Actions.action(ScreenTransitionAction.class);
```

```
        action.setTransitionType(type);
        action.setTransitionDuration(duration);
        return action;
    }
```

We define a static accessor here for the `ScreenTransitionAction` object in order to take advantage of the object pool of `Action` objects. This helps us avoid the performance hit of having to continually construct new single-use `Action` objects, as well as the issues related to resetting previously used `Action` objects (as discussed in *Chapter 8, Oh, No! Looks Like Drama!*). We grab the object from the pool and make sure to update the two attributes, type and duration, before passing it back:

```
    public ScreenTransitionType getTransitionType() {
        return _transitionType;
    }

    public void setTransitionType(
                    ScreenTransitionType transitionType) {
        this._transitionType = transitionType;
    }

    public float getTransitionDuration() {
        return _transitionDuration;
    }

    public void setTransitionDuration(float transitionDuration) {
        this._transitionDuration = transitionDuration;
    }
}
```

Here, we define the getter and setter accessor methods for the two attributes of this class, `ScreenTransitionType` and `float` for duration.

The PlayerHUD class

The final piece is how these two classes fit into the other classes in order to be used appropriately. The next code snippet shows how these classes are used in the `PlayerHUD` class in order to transition the player from one map change to another:

```
    ...
    public class PlayerHUD {
    ...
        private ScreenTransitionActor _transitionActor;
```

```
        public PlayerHUD(Camera camera, Entity player,
                    MapManager mapMgr) {
            _transitionActor = new ScreenTransitionActor();
            ...
            _stage.addActor(_transitionActor);
            _transitionActor.setVisible(false);
        }
```

In the `PlayerHUD` class, we define and initialize the `ScreenTransitionActor`
(default color is black). We then make sure that we add this object to the stage
at the end:

```
        public void addTransitionToScreen(){
            _transitionActor.setVisible(true);
            _stage.addAction(
            Actions.sequence(
                Actions.addAction(ScreenTransitionAction.transition(
                        ScreenTransitionAction.
                        ScreenTransitionType.FADE_IN, 1),
                    _transitionActor)));
            }
        ...
        }
```

In the `addTransitionToScreen()` method, we first make sure our
`ScreenTransitionActor` object is visible. Then, we add a `ScreenTransitionAction`
to our stage, with the `ScreenTransitionActor` as our target. We define the two
attributes of this action, a `FADE_IN` effect and a total duration of one second.

The MainGameScreen class

The final code snippet is from the `MainGameScreen` class:

```
    ...
    public class MainGameScreen {
    ...
        public void render(float delta) {
        ...
            if( _mapMgr.hasMapChanged() ){
            ...
                _playerHUD.addTransitionToScreen();
            }
        }
    }
```

Finally, in the `MainGameScreen` class, every time the current map changes to another one, we simply call `addTransitionToScreen()` on the `_playerHUD` object and the transition effect will be rendered on the next frame.

Camera shake

The next effect deals with making the blows dealt and received in the game more impactful. Sound effects definitely help, but some visual cues also can really add to this effect. The `ShakeCamera` class will generate random coordinates based on a starting position. At the beginning of a shake cycle, these positional changes will be significant, but over time, these positional changes will get smaller until we reach some defined threshold. These positional changes give the illusion that the target is shaking on the screen.

The following class diagram (*Figure 2*) shows where the `ShakeCamera` class is primarily used:

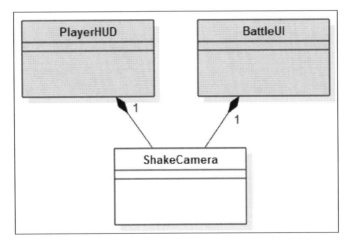

Figure 2

In *BludBourne*, the `ShakeCamera` class is used in two areas. The first area in which the `ShakeCamera` class is used is in the `PlayerHUD` class, when the player has sustained damage from an enemy during battle. The UI will shake for a specified amount of time, signaling to the player that they have been hit. The second area in which the `ShakeCamera` class is used is in the `BattleUI` class, when the enemy has sustained damage from the player during battle. The enemy will shake for a specified amount of time, signaling to the player that they have successfully hit and damaged the enemy.

The basic idea behind the illusion of shaking is that the change in position will happen around a hidden axis, with the positions changing based on a circular positional offset. This not only allows us to see an object shake on the screen, but gives us flexibility in controlling the area that the shaking will take place as well as duration.

In order to better understand the source code for ShakeCamera, we will first review some of the theory before diving into the implementation. This starts with some trigonometry, specifically, *SOHCAHTOA*. *SOHCAHTOA* is a helpful mnemonic for remembering the functions for calculating the sine, cosine, and tangent values for an angle. *SOH* stands for the sine of an angle equal to the value of the opposite leg over the hypotenuse of the triangle. *CAH* stands for the cosine of an angle equal to the adjacent leg over the hypotenuse of the triangle. *TOA* stands for the tangent of an angle equal to the opposite leg over the adjacent leg of a triangle. The following formulas formally define these properties:

$$\sin \theta = \frac{opposite}{hypotenuse}$$

$$\cos \theta = \frac{adjacent}{hypotenuse}$$

$$\tan \theta = \frac{opposite}{adjacent}$$

Why would we want to use these properties? Well, we have a position on the screen defined by the coordinates x and y. We want to get random offsets to these values, but in a circular pattern (to simulate the shaking). The easiest method for getting these random offset values in a circular pattern is to map the values taken from a circle (using Polar coordinates) to the coordinates on the screen (Cartesian coordinates). The sine of the angle gives you a value that represents the rise above the x axis, or a change in y. The cosine of the angle gives you a value that represents the run along the x axis, or a change in x. In order to get the proper length from the sine and cosine functions, we multiply by the radius in order to give us the arc length. This arc length is the actual value we use to offset the current position coordinates. This length will gradually get smaller as we decrease the length of the radius in each iteration until we finally reach a threshold.

The following diagram (*Figure 3*) shows a first iteration of the ShakeCamera, which has already seeded some initial values:

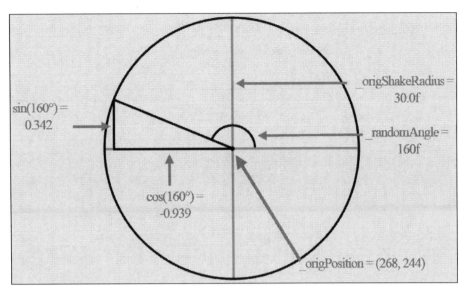

Figure 3

In this example, we start off with a value of 30 for the _origShakeRadius. This value affects the magnitude of the shakes. The larger the radius value, the larger the area on the screen that the shakes will affect. The _randomAngle value is updated with a new random value every iteration (or per shake). This guarantees that the shaking appears random every time. The _origPosition value represents the coordinates of the first position before the shaking starts. This is important because when the shaking stops, we want to reset the position to the original position.

Also, in this example, we have already seeded a random angle value, 160. After calculating the trig functions, we get a value of -0.939 for the *x* coordinate (*cos(160)*) and we get a value of 0.342 for the *y* coordinate (*sin(160)*). We multiply these values by the current radius (30) in order to get the arc length, or the offset in position. The *x* offset is -28.17 (*-0.939 * 30*) and the *y* offset is 10.26 (*0.342 * 30*). This gives us a new position (after adding these offsets to the current position of (268, 244)) of 239.83 for *x* and 254.26 for *y*.

The following diagram (*Figure 4*) shows how this example would map to the screen during a battle:

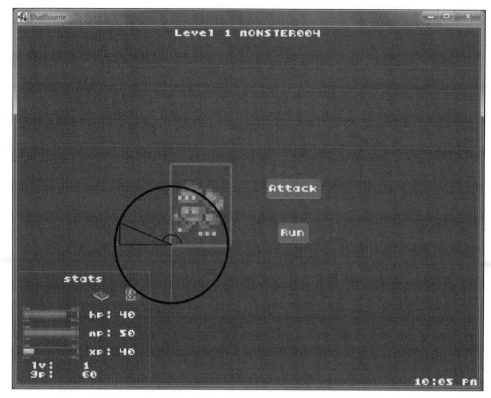

Figure 4

Here, we superimpose *Figure 3* onto an example battle in order to get an idea of how the first calculation is accomplished when the shaking starts. We use the first position (bottom-left corner) of the `AnimatedImage` object as the original position (268,244). From *Figure 3*, we already seeded a random angle of 160, and when we start shaking, based on this example, the next position will be (239.83, 254.26). This means on the next cycle of the shake, the position will be updated, moving about 28 pixels to the left, and 10 pixels up.

The next example (*Figure 5*) demonstrates a sample run of five shakes (excluding the start position, this gives us five changes in position):

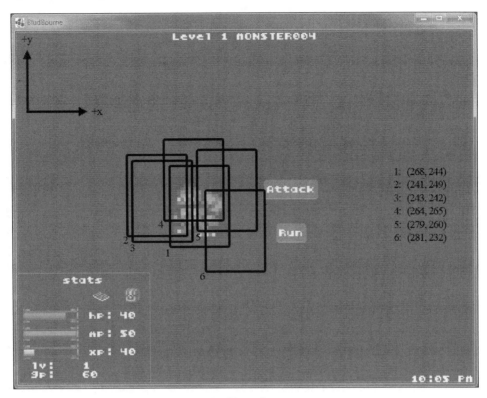

Figure 5

Each of the numbers in *Figure 5* represents a different position for `AnimatedImage`, depending on which iteration we are in during the shaking cycle. As we can see, the movement pattern roughly follows different locations around a hidden circle, which gives us the illusion of random shaking.

Now that we have a better idea of the theory behind `ShakeCamera`, we can now look at the source code located at `core\src\com\packtpub\libgdx\bludbourne\sfx\ShakeCamera.java`:

```
package com.packtpub.libgdx.bludbourne.sfx;

import com.badlogic.gdx.Gdx;
import com.badlogic.gdx.math.MathUtils;
import com.badlogic.gdx.math.Vector2;
```

```
public class ShakeCamera {
   private static final String TAG =
                          ShakeCamera.class.getSimpleName();

   private boolean _isShaking = false;
   private float _origShakeRadius = 30.0f;
   private float _shakeRadius;
   private float _randomAngle;
   private Vector2 _offset;
   private Vector2 _currentPosition;
   private Vector2 _origPosition;
```

We need to update the `ShakeCamera` object in every frame while it is calculating the next change in position. The boolean member variable, `_isShaking`, is set to `true` when the shaking starts and is set to `false` once the `ShakeCamera` object reaches a certain threshold. Once we reach this threshold, we can stop calculating the next change in position. The `_origShakeRadius` is a `float` value that represents the initial radius of the circle when the shaking starts. The larger the radius value, the greater the magnitude of the shakes. The `_shakeRadius` is a `float` type which is updated every iteration of the cycle, getting smaller with each consecutive shake. The `_randomAngle` is a `float` type which represents a new angle of the circle and is updated in every iteration of the shake cycle.

The `_offset` member variable is a `Vector2` type, which is updated every iteration of the shake cycle with the calculated changes in position from the previous iteration. The `_currentPosition` member variable is a `Vector2` type, which is also updated every iteration of the shake cycle and includes the newly calculated offset values. The `_origPosition` member variable is a `Vector2` type, which contains the original start position of the target before the shake cycle started. This is used to reset the target once the shaking has stopped:

```
public ShakeCamera(float x, float y, float shakeRadius){
   this._origPosition = new Vector2(x,y);
   this._shakeRadius = shakeRadius;
   this._origShakeRadius = shakeRadius;
   this._offset = new Vector2();
   this._currentPosition = new Vector2();
   reset();
}
```

In the `ShakeCamera()` constructor, we initialize the member variables and call `reset()` in order to seed the first set of values:

```java
public boolean isCameraShaking(){
  return _isShaking;
}

public void startShaking(){
  _isShaking = true;
}
```

The `isCameraShaking()` is a simple accessor method that returns `true` if the camera is still processing shake values, or `false` if it has exceeded the minimal threshold and stopped processing shake values. The `startShaking()` method starts the next round of the shaking cycle:

```java
private void seedRandomAngle(){
  _randomAngle = MathUtils.random(1, 360);
}
```

The `seedRandomAngle()` method sets a random angle based on the circumference of a circle:

```java
private void computeCameraOffset(){
  float sine = MathUtils.sinDeg(_randomAngle);
  float cosine = MathUtils.cosDeg(_randomAngle);

  _offset.x =  cosine * _shakeRadius;
  _offset.y =  sine * _shakeRadius;
}
```

Here, the `computeCameraOffset()` calculates the offset values to be added to the current position using the calculations described in *Figure 3*:

```java
private void computeCurrentPosition(){
  _currentPosition.x = _origPosition.x + _offset.x;
  _currentPosition.y = _origPosition.y + _offset.y;
}
```

The `computeCurrentPosition()` adds the offset values to the original position values in order to get the new current position:

```
private void diminishShake(){
  if( _shakeRadius < 2.0 ){
    reset();
    return;
  }

  _isShaking = true;
  _shakeRadius *= .9f;

  _randomAngle = MathUtils.random(1, 360);
}
```

The `diminishShake()` method is used to check to see if we have reached the minimum threshold for shaking. If we haven't, then we update values by reducing the magnitude of the next shake and return. Here, our threshold for stopping the shaking is `_shakeRadius` with a value less than 2. In each iteration of the shake cycle, we reduce the current radius by 10% (multiply by 0.9) and eventually we will be below our minimum threshold value of length 2. Finally, we seed another random angle for the next iteration:

```
public void reset(){
  _shakeRadius = _origShakeRadius;
  _isShaking = false;
  seedRandomAngle();
  _currentPosition.x = _origPosition.x;
  _currentPosition.y = _origPosition.y;
}
```

The `reset()` method should be called every time a shake cycle ends. This resets the current radius to the starting radius length. This method also seeds a new starting angle for the next cycle, and resets the current positions to the starting points:

```
public Vector2 getNewShakePosition(){
  computeCameraOffset();
  computeCurrentPosition();
  diminishShake();
  return _currentPosition;
}
}
```

The `getNewShakePosition()` method will calculate the offsets, set the new position values, check whether we have met the minimum threshold of shaking, and finally return with the updated values.

Static lighting

An effect that really enhances the mood of any video game is some lighting model, either static or dynamic. Static lighting deals specifically with pre-rendered lightmap layers which, when blended with the map layers, can produce a very nice effect of having light sources baked into the rendered textures. Dynamic lighting gives nice shadow effects to objects as well as light sources that are calculated every frame. Dynamic lighting is much more involved than static lighting, dealing with writing shaders (code segments) that are sent to the rendering pipeline and eventually rasterized in the framebuffer. Due to the extra computation overhead as well as additional complexity involved, we will focus in this section simply on implementing a simple static lighting model that gives you the biggest gains for minimum amount of work.

The following screenshot (*Figure 6*) shows three separate screens representing the different parts of the process when implementing static lighting:

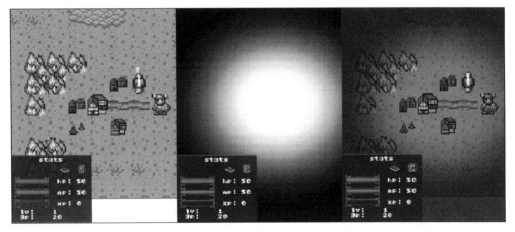

Figure 6

The first part on the left is a scene on the TOP_WORLD map of *BludBourne* right outside the town. The second part in the middle represents a zoomed in section of the lightmap for the same location of the TOP_WORLD map. The third part on the right is a scene where the first and second part of the image are blended together to create the illusion of a light source at night.

There are two primary parts to this process. The first part involves creating the lightmaps themselves for each of the maps. The second part involves calling a method for the individual lightmap layers, and then calling a blend method when rendering. The blend method discussed here will respect the alpha channel and blend the map layer with the lightmap layer accordingly.

Lightmap creation

The first part of the process is creating the lightmaps. First, you will need a reference layer when creating the lightmap. In Tiled, you will first want to open the map you want to create the lightmap for, and then export a copy of the map which will act as a reference layer. Go to **File | Save As Image**. In the **Save As Image** dialog box, the only option that should be checked is **Only include visible layers** as you just want the background, ground, and decoration layers.

Then, open up your favorite paint program and load the reference layer of the map exported from the previous step. Change the opacity to show just enough of the details, and create a layer above this reference layer. Fill this layer with a color that best represents the night in your game. For *BludBourne*, I chose a shade of dark blue that gives a nice effect at night. Then, change the output opacity to something subtle. For *BludBourne*, I set the lightmap layer opacity to 85%, which blended nicely with the underlying map in the game.

Place filled oval shapes over all the different light sources on the reference map. Choose fill colors for the ovals that best represent the lighting, such as white for most candles, and a yellow-orange for lava pits. Finally, after all the oval shapes are placed, add an effect, such as a Gaussian blur, to make the lighting more natural and soft when blended with the underlying map. Finally, when you have finished, export just this layer as your lightmap layer.

The following (*Figure 7*) screenshot shows the lightmap selected in Tiled:

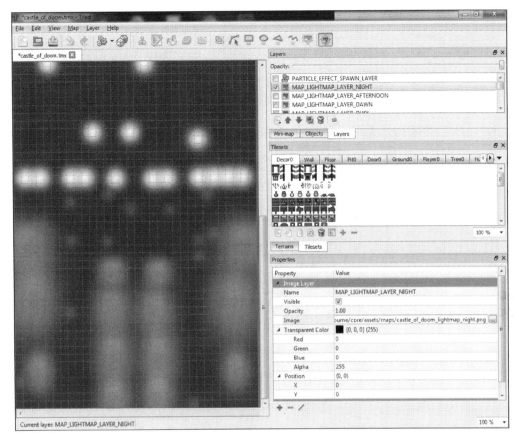

Figure 7

In order to use the lightmap layer in your game, you need to create an **Image Layer** by clicking on the **Add New** layer icon under **Layers**, and selecting **Add Image Layer**. Name this particular lightmap layer MAP_LIGHTMAP_LAYER_NIGHT. Go to **Properties | Image Layer**, and add your newly created lightmap image (exported from the previous step) by selecting the location on disk. Save the map with the added lightmap.

The following screenshot represents the three lightmaps created for *BludBourne*:

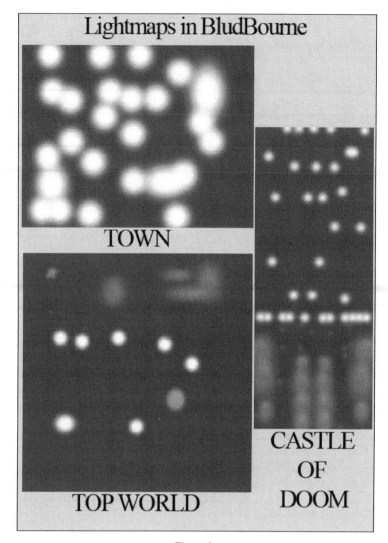

Figure 8

All three of the lightmaps in *Figure 8* have an opacity setting (when exported from Photoshop) of 85%. The lightmap for TOWN represents all of the candles on the walls, and the lantern lights on the ground at night. The lightmap for TOP_WORLD represents white light sources for the lanterns on the ground, a blue area that gives the cemetery an eerie feeling, several reddish spots that represent the lit skulls on the ground, yellow-orange spots for the lava pits, and finally a greenish spot that represents a special spot for a specific kind of enemy spawn. Finally, the CASTLE_OF_DOOM lightmap has light sources for candles, lava pits, and the skulls on the ground.

The Map class

The second part of adding static lighting to your game involves a few areas in the source involved with rendering the lightmaps. The first source we will need to update is in the Map class:

```
    ...
public abstract class Map {
    ...
    public final static String LIGHTMAP_NIGHT_LAYER =
                                "MAP_LIGHTMAP_LAYER_NIGHT";
    protected MapLayer _lightMapNightLayer = null;

    Map( MapFactory.MapType mapType, String fullMapPath){
        _lightMapNightLayer =
            _currentMap.getLayers().get(LIGHTMAP_NIGHT_LAYER);

        if( _lightMapNightLayer == null ){
            Gdx.app.debug(TAG, "No night lightmap layer found!");
        }
    }

    public MapLayer getLightMapNightLayer(){
        return _lightMapNightLayer;
    }
}
```

We define the layer that we named in the Tiled editor as MAP_LIGHTMAP_LAYER_
NIGHT. We then load the layer during construction of the Map class. Finally, we provide an accessor method to access this layer.

The MapManager class

The following source shows the changes that need to be made to the MapManager class:

```
    ...
public class MapManager {
    ...
    public MapLayer getCurrentLightMapLayer(){
        return _currentMap.getLightMapNightLayer();
    }
}
```

We need to get the lightmap layer from the current map, so we create a wrapper for this method call in `MapManager`. This part will make a little more sense when we implement the day-to-night cycle in the next section, and the current lightmap could be one of four different types.

The MainGameScreen class

The final piece that we have to add is a call to the render method for the lightmap layer in the `MainGameScreen` class. In order to properly blend the lightmap with the game map, we need to separate out the render calls in order to guarantee a specific order. The following source snippet shows the changes that need to be made to the `MainGameScreen` class:

```
public class MainGameScreen {
...
  public void render(float delta) {

    TiledMapImageLayer lightMap = (TiledMapImageLayer)_mapMgr.
                       getCurrentLightMapLayer();

    if( lightMap != null) {
      _mapRenderer.getBatch().begin();
      TiledMapTileLayer backgroundMapLayer =
                       (TiledMapTileLayer)_mapMgr.
                         getCurrentTiledMap().getLayers()
                         .get(Map.BACKGROUND_LAYER);

        if( backgroundMapLayer != null ){
        _mapRenderer.renderTileLayer(backgroundMapLayer);
      }

      TiledMapTileLayer groundMapLayer =
                       (TiledMapTileLayer)_mapMgr.
                         getCurrentTiledMap().getLayers().
                         get(Map.GROUND_LAYER);

      if( groundMapLayer != null ){
        _mapRenderer.renderTileLayer(groundMapLayer);
      }

      TiledMapTileLayer decorationMapLayer =
                       (TiledMapTileLayer)_mapMgr.
                         getCurrentTiledMap().getLayers().
                         get(Map.DECORATION_LAYER);

      if( decorationMapLayer != null ){
        _mapRenderer.renderTileLayer(decorationMapLayer);
```

```
        }

        _mapRenderer.getBatch().end();

        _mapMgr.updateCurrentMapEntities(_mapMgr,
            _mapRenderer.getBatch(),delta);
        _player.update(_mapMgr, _mapRenderer.getBatch(), delta);

        _mapRenderer.getBatch().begin();

            _mapRenderer.getBatch().setBlendFunction(
                GL20.GL_DST_COLOR, GL20.GL_ONE_MINUS_SRC_ALPHA);
        _mapRenderer.renderImageLayer(lightMap);

            _mapRenderer.getBatch().setBlendFunction(
                GL20.GL_SRC_ALPHA, GL20.GL_ONE_MINUS_SRC_ALPHA);
        _mapRenderer.getBatch().end();
        }
    }
}
```

First, we want to draw the three layers of our game maps (background layer, ground layer, and decoration layer) using the renderTileLayer() method. After this, we draw all the map entities, as well as the player character. Finally, we render the lightmap layer. As mentioned in *Chapter 2, Welcome to the Land of BludBourne*, we use the getBatch() call when we have numerous objects to draw. By drawing in a batch update, starting with a begin() and completing with an end() method, the overhead of updating the textures will be minimized. The GPU will consume all the texture updates at one time (batching the updates) instead of constantly throttling between updating and rendering separate textures.

The method that makes all the magic happen with these lightmap layers is setBlendFunction(). LibGDX wraps the OpenGL functions with a cleaner interface abstracting away the underlying details. When we pass source and destination values to setBlendFunction(), we are passing in integer values that map to specific constant values. These constants define the parameters of the pixel arithmetic that is calculated when blending the RGBA pixels to produce the desired color value. The first parameter of setBlendFunction() is the source factor which represents the incoming RGBA values, or in our case, the lightmap pixel values. The second parameter of setBlendFunction() is the destination factor, which represents the RGBA values already in the frame buffer, or in our case, the background, ground, and decoration layers of the map.

The primary blending functions that we will use (defined in the LibGDX GL20 interface for OpenGL ES 2.0 support) are GL_ZERO, GL_ONE, GL_DST_COLOR, GL_ONE_MINUS_DST_COLOR, GL_SRC_ALPHA, and GL_ONE_MINUS_SRC_ALPHA.

When dealing with textures without an alpha layer such as a lightmap, we set the blend function to the following:

```
_mapRenderer.getBatch().setBlendFunction(
    GL20.GL_SRC_ALPHA, GL20.GL_ONE_MINUS_SRC_ALPHA);
```

When blending a specific lightmap with an alpha layer, we want to set the blend function to the following:

```
_mapRenderer.getBatch().setBlendFunction(
    GL20.GL_DST_COLOR, GL20.GL_ONE_MINUS_SRC_COLOR);
```

Then, set the blend function back to the primary source and destination factors after rendering.

The following figure (*Figure 9*) outlines the various combinations of source and destination factors, and it includes the final output image after the blending:

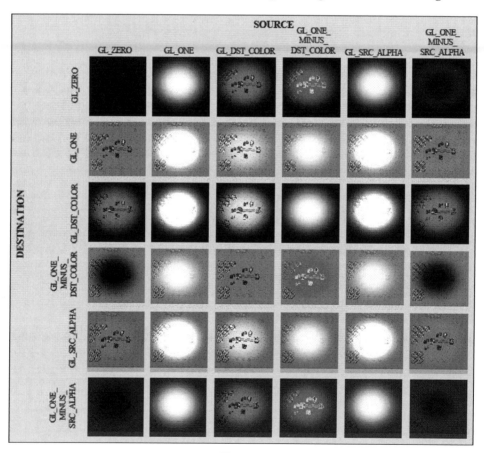

Figure 9

Day-to-night cycle

The day-to-night effect really helps add a sense of passage of time. The day-to-night cycle is one in which, as the player plays your game, the environment changes depending on the time of day. The first part of developing this feature is to have some internal reference point for the time of day built into the game because in most games, the passage of time is independent of the real world time. The second part of this feature is to add some additional lightmaps that make the world feel as if it is occurring at a specific time of day, such as a dark lightmap with light sources we learned in the previous section, which gives the player the illusion of night.

The ClockActor class

The following class diagram (*Figure 10*) describes the class that we will implement for the first part of this feature:

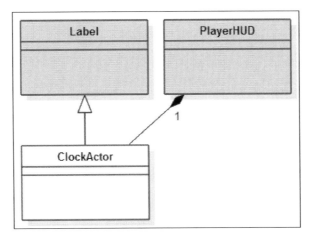

Figure 10

The ClockActor class derives from Label so that we get the benefits of using a Label object in a Stage. We only need one ClockActor object and this object will live in the PlayerHUD, since the clock time will be shown at all times to signal to the player the specific time of day in the game.

Here's the source of ClockActor and it can be found at core\src\com\packtpub\libgdx\bludbourne\sfx\ClockActor.java:

```
package com.packtpub.libgdx.bludbourne.sfx;

import com.badlogic.gdx.graphics.Color;
import com.badlogic.gdx.math.MathUtils;
```

```
import com.badlogic.gdx.scenes.scene2d.ui.Label;
import com.badlogic.gdx.scenes.scene2d.ui.Skin;

public class ClockActor extends Label {

    public static enum TimeOfDay {
        DAWN,
        AFTERNOON,
        DUSK,
        NIGHT
    }
```

The TimeOfDay enum defines all of the different parts of a day in the world of
BludBourne, starting with DAWN for the morning, AFTERNOON for mid-day, DUSK for
when the sun starts to go down, and finally NIGHT for when the lights come on and
the monsters come out:

```
    private float _totalTime = 0;
    private float _rateOfTime = 1;
    private static String PM = "PM";
    private static String AM = "AM";
    private static String FORMAT = "%02d:%02d %s";
    private boolean _isAfternoon = false;
```

The first member variable is _totalTime, which is a float value that acts as an
accumulator of the time in seconds from when the player first starts playing the
game. This is the value that we will persist to the save game profile as well, as all
other time values can be calculated from this one. The next member variable is
_rateOfTime, which is a float type that represents the speed at which you want
time in the game to advance. For instance, a value of 1 would have the game running
at the normal speed, where 60 minutes in real time equals 60 minutes in game time.
A _rateOfTime value of 60 has a multiplier effect with the game running at a faster
rate, where 60 minutes in real time equals 3600 minutes (or 60 hours) in game time.
The PM and AM String values are simply constants we use to define which half of the
day we are currently in. The FORMAT String value is used as a template in how we
wish to display the time of day on the screen. We use two decimal places to represent
both the hour and minutes with a String value of AM or PM after it. Finally, we
have a simple boolean value, _isAfternoon, that designates whether we are in the
morning or afternoon half of the day:

```
    public ClockActor(CharSequence text, Skin skin) {
        super(text, skin);
        init();
    }
```

```
        public ClockActor(CharSequence text, Skin skin,
                            String styleName) {
            super(text, skin, styleName);
            init();
        }


        public ClockActor(CharSequence text, Skin skin,
                            String fontName, Color color) {
            super(text, skin, fontName, color);
            init();
        }


        public ClockActor(CharSequence text, Skin skin,
                            String fontName, String colorName) {
            super(text, skin, fontName, colorName);
            init();
        }


        public ClockActor(CharSequence text, LabelStyle style) {
            super(text, style);
            init();
        }
```

Here, we make sure to overload all the constructors for the Label class we are deriving from:

```
        private void init(){
            String time = String.format(FORMAT, 0, 0,
                                    _isAfternoon?PM:AM);
            this.setText(time);
            this.pack();
        }
```

The init() method, used in the constructors for the ClockActor class, initializes the String value to be displayed on the screen, sets it to be the current text for the Label, and then packs the object so that the label correctly recalculates the geometries:

```
        public float getTotalTime() {
            return _totalTime;
        }


        public void setTotalTime(float totalTime) {
            this._totalTime = totalTime;
```

```
}

public float getRateOfTime() {
    return _rateOfTime;
}

public void setRateOfTime(float rateOfTime) {
    this._rateOfTime = rateOfTime;
}
```

The getTotalTime() and setTotalTime() methods are simple accessor methods for getting and setting the total time (in seconds) that has transpired since the current profile game has started. The getRateOfTime() and setRateOfTime() methods are accessor methods for getting and setting the rate of time for how quickly or slowly the in-game time moves relative to the real-world time:

```
public TimeOfDay getCurrentTimeOfDay(){
    int hours = getCurrentTimeHours();
    if( hours >= 7 && hours <= 9 ){
        return TimeOfDay.DAWN;
    }else if( hours >= 10 && hours <=16 ){
        return TimeOfDay.AFTERNOON;
    }else if( hours >= 17 && hours <= 19 ){
        return TimeOfDay.DUSK;
    }else{
        return TimeOfDay.NIGHT;
    }
}
```

The getCurrentTimeOfDay() method is a convenience method that provides a way to query which part of the day is currently running in-game. We first call a helper method to calculate the current time in a 24-hour format. From here, we partition out the different parts of the day, starting with DAWN in the hours of 7 AM to 10 AM in the morning. Then AFTERNOON is in the hours of 10 PM to 5 PM. DUSK is defined as the time of day from 5 PM to 8 PM. Finally, NIGHT is in the hours of 8 PM to 7 AM:

```
@Override
public void act(float delta){
    _totalTime += (delta * _rateOfTime);

    int seconds = getCurrentTimeSeconds();
    int minutes = getCurrentTimeMinutes();
    int hours = getCurrentTimeHours();
```

```
        if ( hours == 24 || (hours/12) == 0 ){
            _isAfternoon = false;
        }else{
            _isAfternoon = true;
        }

        hours = hours % 12;

        if ( hours == 0 ){
            hours = 12;
        }

        String time = String.format(FORMAT, hours, minutes,
                                _isAfternoon ? PM : AM);
        this.setText(time);
    }
```

Here, we override the `act()` method for `ClockActor`, which will be called by the `Stage` during a frame update. We first add the current difference between frames to the current total time, making sure to multiply by the current rate of time. We segment out the different components of the current time by seconds, minutes, and hours. We then check to see which half of the day we are currently in to determine the meridiem. Then, we mod the current hours (which are in 24-hour format) by 12 since we are using a 12-hour format for the display clock. Finally, we format the time for the `ClockActor` object with the current in-game time and set the new value:

```
    public int getCurrentTimeSeconds(){
        return MathUtils.floor(_totalTime % 60);
    }

    public int getCurrentTimeMinutes(){
        return MathUtils.floor((_totalTime / 60) % 60);
    }

    public int getCurrentTimeHours(){
        int hours = MathUtils.floor((_totalTime / 3600) % 24);

        if ( hours == 0 ){
            hours = 24;
        }

        return hours;
    }
}
```

The `getCurrentTimeSeconds()`, `getCurrentTimeMinutes()`, and `getCurrentTimeHours()` helper methods calculate their respective values based on the current `_totalTime` member variable.

The MapManager class

The last piece of this section is how we take advantage of the time of day in the game. For each time of day, we create a separate lightmap layer for each map. For *BludBourne*, `TimeOfDay.DAWN` has a filled yellow lightmap, `TimeOfDay.AFTERNOON` has a filled white lightmap, `TimeOfDay.DUSK` has a filled orange lightmap, and finally, `TimeOfDay.NIGHT` has a lightmap with a dark color and the assorted light sources. These additional layers are added to each Tiled map, just as we did for the `NIGHT` lightmap. After creating accessors for these `MapLayer` objects, we can now create a method in `MapManager` that will be called every frame update. The following source from `MapManager` outlines that method:

```
...
public class MapManager {
...
    private MapLayer _currentLightMap = null;
    private MapLayer _previousLightMap = null;
    private ClockActor.TimeOfDay _timeOfDay = null;
    private float _currentLightMapOpacity = 0;
    private float _previousLightMapOpacity = 1;
    private boolean _timeOfDayChanged = false;
...
```

In order to have a nice transition between the change in the time of day in *BludBourne*, we set the new lightmap opacity to 0 so that it is fully translucent, and set the previous lightmap (before the change) opacity to 1 so that it is fully opaque. Then, over a period of time, we gradually bring up the current lightmap's opacity until it reaches 1, and in parallel, gradually bring down the previous lightmap's opacity until it reaches 0:

```
public void updateLightMaps(ClockActor.TimeOfDay timeOfDay){
    if( _timeOfDay != timeOfDay ){
        _currentLightMapOpacity = 0;
        _previousLightMapOpacity = 1;
        _timeOfDay = timeOfDay;
        _timeOfDayChanged = true;
        _previousLightMap = _currentLightMap;
    }
```

In the `updateLightMaps()` method, if the current time of day does not match the value passed in, then we know that the time of day has changed. During a time of day change, we will want to reset our member variables that maintain the transition state, including the `_currentLightMapOpacity` and `_previousLightMapOpacity` values:

```
switch(timeOfDay){
    case DAWN:
        _currentLightMap =
            _currentMap.getLightMapDawnLayer();
        break;
    case AFTERNOON:
        _currentLightMap =
            _currentMap.getLightMapAfternoonLayer();
        break;
    case DUSK:
        _currentLightMap =
            _currentMap.getLightMapDuskLayer();
        break;
    case NIGHT:
        _currentLightMap =
            _currentMap.getLightMapNightLayer();
        break;
    default:
        _currentLightMap =
            _currentMap.getLightMapAfternoonLayer();
        break;
}
```

Previously, we copied the current lightmap to the previous lightmap member variable. Now, we get the current lightmap based on the change in the time of day:

```
if( _timeOfDayChanged ){
  if( _previousLightMap != null &&
      _previousLightMapOpacity != 0 ){

    _previousLightMap.setOpacity(_previousLightMapOpacity);
    _previousLightMapOpacity = MathUtils.clamp(
        _previousLightMapOpacity -= .05, 0, 1);

    if( _previousLightMapOpacity == 0 ){
      _previousLightMap = null;
    }
  }
}
```

```
    if( _currentLightMap != null &&
        _currentLightMapOpacity != 1 ) {

    _currentLightMap.setOpacity(_currentLightMapOpacity);
    _currentLightMapOpacity = MathUtils.clamp(
        _currentLightMapOpacity += .01, 0, 1);
    }
}else{
    _timeOfDayChanged = false;
}
```

Here, if there has been a change in the time of day, then we decrease the opacity of the previous lightmap. At the same time, we increase the opacity of the new, current lightmap.

Particle effects

The final effect that we will explore in this chapter really adds some nice special effects to the game world, such as smoke, explosions, fire, and spell casts. Particle effects are a very powerful tool in your toolbox. With a little effort and without tons of experience as an artist, a developer can create nice special effects which add a certain level of polish to a game. These particle effects are composed of numerous particles, or small sprites, that have their own lifetimes and react to their environment based on certain properties. The real power of particle effects becomes apparent when you start to combine different sets of particle emitters to create a composite particle effect.

There are two main parts to using particle effects. The first part is creating the particle effect itself, and the second part is instantiating and rendering the particle in the game.

Particle Editor

Luckily, LibGDX has a very nice particle effects editor that comes with the installation of LibGDX. A nice, detailed reference for creating particle effects in the editor can be found at http://github.com/libgdx/libgdx/wiki/2D-Particle-Editor.

To use the Particle Editor application, you will need to first search for gdx-tools-1.5.5.jar from your library home in your project path. From the top level of the JAR, you will be able to find the Particle Editor at com\badlogic\gdx\tools\particleeditor\. The main entry point for the editor is called ParticleEditor.class. After running this class in your IDE (for IntelliJ, you can right-click and select **Run**), the editor will launch, as shown the following screenshot(*Figure 11*):

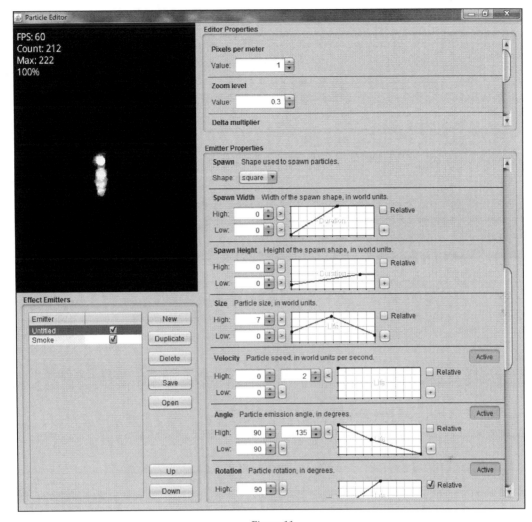

Figure 11

There are four primary panels in the Particle Editor application. The first panel in the top-left corner represents the final render of the current particle effect settings in real time, in a preview window. Every time a new property is updated, this window will update with the new values so that you can instantly view the changes that you made. There is also some nice debug output so that you can better ascertain whether the current particle effect is adversely affecting the frame rate, as well as the number of particles available.

The second panel in the bottom-left corner is named **Effect Emitters**, and it displays the current emitters used for the currently loaded particle effect. Emitters represent the source of the particles, where the particles start from at the beginning of their lifetime. One use case for using different emitters would be a torch fire that has smoke emanating at different speeds from the fire. One emitter controls the fire based particles that create the flame, and a second emitter controls the white smoke coming from the flame.

The third panel in the top-right corner is named **Editor Properties**, and it controls the top-level project properties of the current rendered particle effect (the preview window). Those properties are as follows:

- **Pixels per meter**: This value translates between pixel units to world space units making the particle effect easier to view details.

- **Zoom level**: This value affects how close or how far the render window camera is relative to the particle effect.

- **Delta multiplier**: This value affects the delta time between frame renders in the render window. The larger the value, the faster the render as the value has a multiplicative effect. The smaller the value, the slower the render. A value of 0.25 renders at a quarter the normal time, allowing one to see small details in a particle effect render, for instance.

- **Background color**: These values control the background color of the render window.

The fourth panel in the bottom-right section is named **Emitter Properties**, and it controls all of the attributes that can affect the particle effect. These attributes are listed as follows:

- **Image**: This property is the actual `Sprite` image that represents one particle in a particle effect. There are two images under `core\assets\sfx` that can be used. The first image, `particle.png`, will render the particles as soft, circular shapes. The second image, `particle_square.png`, will render the particles as soft, square shapes, giving a slightly more pixel-like style to the effects.

- **Count**: There are two values for this property which represent the range in the number of particles to can be rendered at any one time, from the minimum amount to the maximum. This property is important as the more particle effects rendered on a screen, the more computation and memory required adversely affecting the render times per frame.

- **Delay**: This is the length of time, in milliseconds, from when the effect is first rendered to when the emitters will start generating particles for the particle effect. This can be useful, for instance, when trying to sync different emitters at the same time.

- **Duration**: This is the length of time, in milliseconds, from when the emitter first starts generating particles to when the emitter finishes generating particles.
- **Emission**: This is the amount of particles that will be generated by the emitter every second. You can set the minimum and maximum values that will be used to select a random value in that range. The chart is used to control the amount of particles over time relative to the duration of the emitter.
- **Life**: This is the length of time, in milliseconds, in which one particle will live (as a candidate for rendering during a frame update). You can set the minimum and maximum values that will be used to select a random value in that range.
- **Life Offset**: This offset is the length of time, in milliseconds, that one particle's life will be consumed when first generated. You can set the minimum and maximum values that will be used to select a random value in that range.
- **X Offset**: This offset is used to calculate the starting x coordinate position, in world units, of the particle.
- **Y Offset**: This offset is used to calculate the starting y coordinate position, in world units, of the particle.
- **Spawn**: This is the starting shape that the emitter will use when spawning particles.
- **Spawn Width**: This is the starting shape width, in world units, that the emitter will use when spawning particles. You can set the minimum and maximum values that will be used to select a random value in that range. The chart is used to control the starting shape width of the particles over time relative to the duration of the emitter.
- **Spawn Height**: This is the starting shape height, in world units, that the emitter will use when spawning particles. You can set the minimum and maximum values that will be used to select a random value in that range. The chart is used to control the starting shape height of the particles over time relative to the duration of the emitter.
- **Size**: This value is the particle size in world units. You can set the minimum and maximum values that will be used to select a random value in that range. The chart is used to control the size of a particle over the duration of its lifetime.

- **Velocity**: This value is the particle speed in world units per second. You can set the minimum and maximum values that will be used to select a random value in that range. The chart is used to control the speed of a particle over the duration of its lifetime.

- **Angle**: This value is the particle's direction of travel, in degrees, relative to the emitter. You can set the minimum and maximum values which will be used to select a random value in that range. The chart is used to control the direction of a particle over the duration of its lifetime.

- **Rotation**: This value is the particle's rotation in degrees. You can set the minimum and maximum values that will be used to select a random value in that range. The chart is used to control the rotation of a particle over the duration of its lifetime.

- **Wind**: This value represents the wind strength force, in world units per second, applied to the particles along the x axis. You can set the minimum and maximum values that will be used to select a random value in that range. The chart is used to control the amount of wind force on a particle over the duration of the particle's lifetime.

- **Gravity**: This value represents the gravity strength force, in world units per second, applied to the particles along the y axis. You can set the minimum and maximum values that will be used to select a random value in that range. The chart is used to control the amount of gravity force on a particle over the duration of the particle's lifetime.

- **Tint**: This property changes the particle's color. You can drag the slider on the color bar to select the specific color. If you want to have a blended range of colors, you can set the range of colors that you want with the two sliders under the color bar.

- **Transparency**: This property changes the alpha value, or transparency, of the particle over the duration of its lifetime.

In the **Options** section, we have a few more options that are applied over the entire particle effect:

- **Additive**: When checked, this option enables additive blending. When multiple colors are combined, adding up their RGB components in order to get a final resultant color is known as additive blending. This is equivalent to setting the blend function (discussed in the *Static lighting* section of this chapter) with a source factor of GL_SRC_ALPHA and a destination factor of GL_ONE.

- **Attached**: When checked, this option sets the positions of the particles in the particle effect to be updated relative to the position of the emitter.

- **Continuous**: When checked, this option enables the emitters to restart and continue generating particles automatically after its duration has expired.
- **Aligned**: When checked, this option enables the particle's angle to be added to the rotation. This will line up the particle's image with the direction of travel.
- **Behind**: When checked, this option enables the current particle effect emitter to be queried later in order to determine if the particle effect should be drawn over or behind another sprite.
- **Premultiplied Alpha**: When checked, this option enables a mixture of both alpha and additive blending modes. This option overrides the **Additive** option and will effectively ignore it. This is equivalent to setting the blend function (discussed in the *Static lighting* section of this chapter) with a source factor of GL_ONE and a destination factor of GL_ONE_MINUS_SRC_ALPHA.

In order to get an idea of how certain combinations of properties can affect a particle effect, you can access the particle effects for *BludBourne* and load them into the editor from core\assets\sfx. Once the particle effect has been created, click on **Save**.

The ParticleEffectFactory class

After we have created and saved the particle effect, we can now move onto the final part: instantiating and rendering the particle effect in our game. The following class diagram (*Figure 12*) describes the relationships with the ParticleEffectFactory class that we will need to implement:

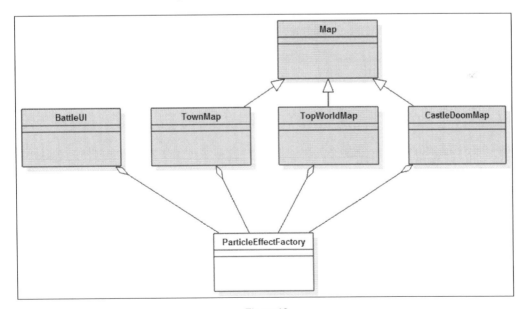

Figure 12

In this class diagram, the `ParticleEffectFactory` class is used to create `ParticleEffect` objects for the environments of the `Map` objects, such as torch fire and lava pit smoke. The `ParticleEffectFactory` class also creates single-use `ParticleEffect` objects, such as a successful wand attack when the player damages an enemy in the `BattleUI`.

Here's the source for the `ParticleEffectFactory` class:

```
package com.packtpub.libgdx.bludbourne.sfx;

import com.badlogic.gdx.Gdx;
import com.badlogic.gdx.graphics.g2d.ParticleEffect;
import com.badlogic.gdx.math.Vector2;

public class ParticleEffectFactory {

    private static String SFX_ROOT_DIR = "sfx";

    public static enum ParticleEffectType{
        CANDLE_FIRE("sfx/candle.p"),
        LANTERN_FIRE("sfx/candle.p"),
        LAVA_SMOKE("sfx/smoke.p"),
        WAND_ATTACK("sfx/magic_attack.p"),
        NONE("");

        private String _fullFilePath;

        ParticleEffectType(String fullFilePath){
            this._fullFilePath = fullFilePath;
        }

        public String getValue(){
            return _fullFilePath;
        }
    }
```

Here, we define a `ParticleEffectType` enum type that represents all the different types of particle effects that can be used in *BludBourne*. We pass into the constructor of these enum types a `String` value, which represents the relative path to the specific particle effect file in our project. The CANDLE_FIRE type is used for all locations on the maps where there are candles burning, such as wall candles or desk candles. The LANTERN_FIRE type is used for all locations on the maps where there are lanterns anchored to the ground. The LAVA_SMOKE type is used for all locations on the maps where there are active lava pits spewing toxins into the air. Finally, we have the WAND_ATTACK type, which is used as a special effect when the player strikes an enemy with a magic attack using the wand:

```
private static ParticleEffectFactory _instance = null;

private ParticleEffectFactory(){
}

public static ParticleEffectFactory getInstance() {
    if (_instance == null) {
        _instance = new ParticleEffectFactory();
    }

    return _instance;
}
```

The `getInstance()` method is a static method used to access the single static instance of the `ParticleEffectFactory` class so that it can only be accessed as a Singleton:

```
public static ParticleEffect getParticleEffect(
    ParticleEffectType particleEffectType,float positionX,
    float positionY){

    ParticleEffect effect = new ParticleEffect();

    effect.load(Gdx.files.internal(
        particleEffectType.getValue()),
        Gdx.files.internal(SFX_ROOT_DIR));

    effect.setPosition(positionX, positionY);

    switch(particleEffectType){
        case CANDLE_FIRE:
            effect.scaleEffect(.04f);
            break;
        case LANTERN_FIRE:
            effect.scaleEffect(.02f);
            break;
        case LAVA_SMOKE:
            effect.scaleEffect(.04f);
            break;
        case WAND_ATTACK:
            effect.scaleEffect(1.0f);
            break;
        default:
            break;
    }
```

```
        effect.start();
        return effect;
    }
```

The `getParticleEffect()` method is a static method that returns a single `ParticleEffect` instance based upon the `ParticleEffectType` passed in. The first step is to instantiate a new `ParticleEffect` object, load the effect file from disk specified by the `ParticleEffectType`, and then set the position based on values passed in. Then, based on the `ParticleEffectType`, we can make additional changes to the `ParticleEffect` object. The `ParticleEffect` object is enabled by calling `start()`, and then returned:

```
    public static ParticleEffect getParticleEffect(
        ParticleEffectType particleEffectType, Vector2 position){
        return getParticleEffect(particleEffectType, position.x,
                                 position.y);
    }
}
```

Finally, the `getParticleEffect()` method is an overloaded method that takes a `Vector2` object for the position instead of two `float` values.

The BattleUI class

The following code snippet is from `BattleUI` and demonstrates the use of `ParticleEffectFactory` as well as management of the resultant `ParticleEffect` object:

```
...
public class BattleUI {
...

    private Array<ParticleEffect> _effects;

    public BattleUI(){
        _effects = new Array<ParticleEffect>();
    }
```

In the `BattleUI` class, we will first keep an `Array` container of `ParticleEffect` objects, as they need to be updated and rendered every frame and periodically checked and removed if not active:

```
    @Override
    public void onNotify(Entity entity, BattleEvent event) {
      switch(event){
        ...
```

```
    case PLAYER_USED_MAGIC:
      float x = _currentImagePosition.x + (_enemyWidth/2);
      float y = _currentImagePosition.y + (_enemyHeight/2);
        _effects.add(ParticleEffectFactory.getParticleEffect(
          ParticleEffectFactory.ParticleEffectType.WAND_ATTACK,
          x,y));
      break;
    default:
      break;
  }
 }
```

In the onNotify() method, if we have received a BattleEvent event named
PLAYER_USED_MAGIC, then we need to render a magic attack, ParticleEffectType.
WAND_ATTACK, for the player. We first get the position values for where we want
the ParticleEffect to be rendered, making sure to offset the position so that the
ParticleEffect is rendered in the center of the enemy. We pass these values to
the ParticleEffectFactory and then add the instantiated ParticleEffect to our
Array container:

```
@Override
public void act(float delta){
    for( int i = 0; i < _effects.size; i++){
        ParticleEffect effect = _effects.get(i);

        if( effect == null ) continue;

        if( effect.isComplete() ){
            _effects.removeIndex(i);
            effect.dispose();
        }else{
            effect.update(delta);
        }
    }
}
```

Since the ParticleEffect objects need to be updated every frame, we need
to override the act() method. We iterate over the entire Array container of
ParticleEffect objects. If one of the objects has finished, we remove it from the
container and call dispose() so that the memory can be flagged for reclamation. If
the ParticleEffect is still running, then we update the object:

```
@Override
  public void draw(Batch batch, float parentAlpha){
      super.draw(batch, parentAlpha);
```

```
        //Draw the particles last
        for( int i = 0; i < _effects.size; i++){
            ParticleEffect effect = _effects.get(i);
            if( effect == null ) continue;
            effect.draw(batch);
        }
    }
}
```

Here, the draw() method is also overridden so we can guarantee that the ParticleEffect objects will be rendered in the correct draw order. First, we call the base class draw method making sure to pass in the appropriate parameters. Then, we iterate over the Array container of ParticleEffect objects, calling the appropriate draw() method.

The following screenshots (*Figure 13* and *Figure 14*) show how the finished product of using lightmaps with particle effects can really set the mood in your game:

Figure 13

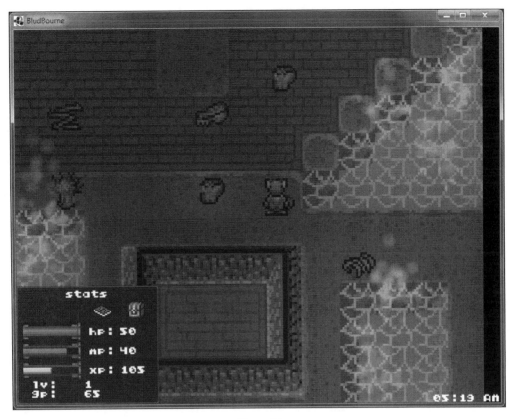

Figure 14

Summary

In this chapter, we delved into some special effects that can really make your game stand out. We implemented ScreenTransitionActor and ScreenTransitionAction for screen fade transitions when changing map locations. Then, we implemented ShakeCamera to make various on-screen objects shake. Next, we explored and implemented a static lighting model. We then took this lighting model a step further and after implementing the ClockActor class, we were able to show nice transitions across a typical day in *BludBourne*. The final topic we covered was the addition of particle effects and how we were able to easily use them in *BludBourne* by implementing the ParticleEffectFactory class.

In the next chapter, we will be wrapping up our journey with some deployment tips for our game, and see what lies before us on the next adventure.

10
Prophecy Fulfilled, Our Hero Awaits the Next Adventure

In our final chapter, we will first look at platform options for the digital distribution of your game. We will also look at the different options for generating the final package ready for distribution. We will then look at various security measures you can use, from encoding save game profiles to obfuscating the final package ready for distribution. We will also learn a few easy techniques for debugging these builds, and also some simple techniques a developer can use to test their final builds.

In summary, we will cover the following topics in this chapter:

- Digital distribution platforms
- Obfuscating the save game profiles
- Creating an executable JAR
- Native launchers
- Obfuscating the packaged JAR
- Debugging tips
- Testing builds before release

Digital distribution platforms

After completing your game, the final step is to package it up and deploy it to the various digital distribution channels. The different distribution channels will typically take a certain percentage of the sale price of your game for each unit sold (revenue sharing model), such as Valve's Steam platform (`http://store.steampowered.com/`). The model applies to other platforms as well, including the mobile app space such as Apple's App Store (`http://itunes.apple.com/us/genre/ios/id36?mt=8`) and Google's Play store (`http://play.google.com/store?hl=en`). Some distribution channels (such as Apple) will require you to go through a certification process, and others (such as Google) will allow you to upload right away. One of the biggest challenges with a video game release will be overcoming the discoverability issue, but being on one of these platforms will help to some degree.

As part of your marketing ramp-up plan for release, each of these distribution platforms will need to be evaluated, in order to better estimate your marketing budget. Some of the platforms require a specific process in order to be accepted and released on their platform. For instance, Steam requires a small upfront fee, but then, in order to be released, your game will need to be voted on by the users of their platform, under a community-based release process called GreenLight.

Since we have focused primarily on the Windows PC platform for this book, your first release will most likely be on one of the desktop-based release platforms. The following is a short list of the current PC-based digital distribution platforms:

- Steam (`http://steamcommunity.com/greenlight/`); a helpful FAQ is listed at `http://steamcommunity.com/workshop/about/?appid=765&section=faq#developers`

- GOG.com (`http://www.gog.com/indie`)

- The Humblestore (`http://www.humblebundle.com/developer`)

- Green Man Gaming (`http://www.greenmangaming.com/`); for publishing or selling your game, click on the **Support** link

- itch.io (`http://itch.io/`)

Obfuscating the save game profiles

One aspect of security when releasing your title is specific to the save game profiles. When we first implemented the save game profiles, we had the JSON serialize output from the `ObjectMap` object to a nice, readable format. This was intentional so that you could easily modify the save game state in order to test out edge cases, simplifying the process for duplicating bugs. For final release though, we will want to make the save game profile more difficult to edit, thus making it more difficult for a player to exploit the game.

Again, LibGDX makes this extremely easy with a few method calls using the `Base64Coder` class. The `Base64Coder` class encodes and decodes `String` objects using the Base64 format. The Base64 format is an encoding scheme where we take some binary data and translate it into its numerical Base64 representation. The following is a source snippet from `ProfileManager.java` with the changes:

```
import com.badlogic.gdx.utils.Base64Coder;
...
public class ProfileManager extends ProfileSubject {
...
    public void writeProfileToStorage(String profileName,
                    String fileData, boolean overwrite){

        String fullFilename = profileName+SAVEGAME_SUFFIX;

        boolean localFileExists =
                    Gdx.files.local(fullFilename).exists();

        //If we cannot overwrite and the file exists, exit
        if( localFileExists && !overwrite ){
            return;
        }

        FileHandle file =  null;

        if( Gdx.files.isLocalStorageAvailable() ) {
            file = Gdx.files.local(fullFilename);
            String encodedString =
                    Base64Coder.encodeString(fileData);
            file.writeString(encodedString, !overwrite);
        }

        _profiles.put(profileName, file);
    }
```

Here, in the `writeProfileToStorage()` method, we encode the string by calling the static method `encodeString()` from `Base64Coder` in order to translate the string that we are going to write out to the save game profile:

```
    . . .
    public void loadProfile(){
            if( _isNewProfile ){
                notify(this, ProfileObserver.ProfileEvent.
                        CLEAR_CURRENT_PROFILE);
                saveProfile();
            }

            String fullProfileFileName = _profileName+SAVEGAME_SUFFIX;

            boolean doesProfileFileExist =
                        Gdx.files.local(fullProfileFileName).exists();

            if( !doesProfileFileExist ){
                return;
            }

            FileHandle encodedFile = _profiles.get(_profileName);
            String s = encodedFile.readString();

            String decodedFile = Base64Coder.decodeString(s);

            _profileProperties = _json.fromJson(ObjectMap.class,
                                                decodedFile);
            notify(this, ProfileObserver.ProfileEvent.PROFILE_LOADED);
            _isNewProfile = false;
        }
    }
```

Finally, in `loadProfile()`, we make sure to read the save game profile as a string. We then decode this string using the static method, `decodeString()`, from the `Base64Coder` class. Finally, we load the decoded string into the JSON parser and update the property values in our `ObjectMap` object.

Logging levels

A final item to note is that, in a final release, you may want to limit the debug information that is output to standard out. This is one more area of security to minimize the code paths that your game processes so that someone can't easily develop a memory profile of your game state.

For internal debugging, and even for a beta group, you may want to keep the logging level at `LOG_DEBUG`. The following is a source snapshot for `DesktopLauncher.java` located at `desktop\src\com\packtpub\libgdx\bludbourne\desktop`:

```
public class DesktopLauncher {
  public static void main (String[] arg) {
    ...
  Gdx.app.setLogLevel(Application.LOG_DEBUG);
  }
}
```

For a final build of your game, you may want to update the logging level to `LOG_INFO` instead:

```
public class DesktopLauncher {
  public static void main (String[] arg) {
    ...
  Gdx.app.setLogLevel(Application.LOG_INFO);
  }
}
```

Unfortunately, Java does not support conditional compilation where a different segment of code would be compiled based on some external value. We could do a workaround by defining a static `String` constant or static `boolean` type in a file and set the variable to a different value, depending on the directory where it is located. The release build target would only pick up the source from one directory and a debug build target would pick up the other one.

Creating an executable JAR

Java archives are referred to as JAR files. These JAR files are the packages that contain the final bytecode generated from compiling the original source. There is a type of JAR file, called an executable JAR, which can be run by simply double clicking on the file as if it were any other Windows executable. The executable JAR contains a manifest file that describes the main entry point of the application, and it usually includes dependent libraries.

There are two primary methods for generating an executable JAR: using a Gradle target or creating an artifact with IntelliJ's IDEA IDE.

Gradle

The first method, using a Gradle target, can be implemented with the following steps:

1. Open up a command window and navigate to your project root directory where the `gradlew.bat` file lives. In Windows, holding down the left *Shift* key while pressing the right mouse button will add an option, **Open Command Window Here**, to the context window that pops up.

2. Execute the following command in the command prompt:

    ```
    C:\BludBourne>gradlew desktop:dist
    ```

    This command will build the distribution JAR for the desktop target.

3. The final JAR archive will be placed in `desktop\build\libs` relative to the project root directory. Navigate to this directory for the next step.

4. You can execute this JAR using one of two different ways. The first is by running the following command at the command prompt:

    ```
    C:\BludBourne\desktop\build\libs\java –jar desktop-1.0.jar
    ```

    The second way is to double click on the JAR file, `desktop-1.0.jar`, from a Windows Explorer window.

IntelliJ IDEA

The second option is to create an artifact with IntelliJ's IDEA IDE. In IDEA, an artifact is a compilation output, consisting of source code, binaries, libraries, and resources, for a specific module packaged as a JAR. This JAR will be deployment-ready, meaning that the JAR is suitable for deployment on whichever target is specified.

The second method can be implemented with the following steps:

1. Navigate to your project root directory, using Windows Explorer, where the `BludBourne.ipr` file lives.

2. Double-click on the IPR file in order to load the *BludBourne* project into the IDEA IDE.

3. In the **Project** pane, make sure the top-level element of the project, named **BludBourne**, is selected.

4. In the menu, select the **File | Project Structure** option.

5. In the **Project Structure** window, select **Artifacts**.

6. To add a new artifact, click on the **+** option in the middle pane.

7. In the **New** pop-up window, select **Jar | From modules with dependencies....** The resulting window is shown in the following screenshot (*Figure 1*):

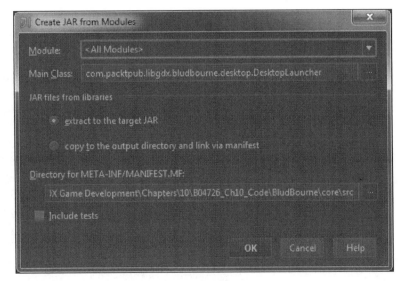

Figure 1

8. In the **Create JAR from Modules** dialog window, select **All Modules** from the **Module** section.

9. For the **Main Class** section, select the **com.packtpub.libgdx.bludbourne. desktop.DesktopLauncher** class.

10. For the **JAR files from libraries** section, select the **extract to the target JAR** option.

11. For the **Directory for META-INF/MANIFEST.MF** section, choose a path where the manifest will reside. The recommended path is `core\build\resources\main\META-INF`. The `manifest.mf` file will be generated here, so verify that the directory is empty. This path also solves a possible error with a `manifest.mf` file being overwritten, which causes a `no main manifest attribute, in BludBourne.jar` error at execution.

12. Click on **OK**. We should now have an artifact called `BludBourne.jar` set up in the window. Make note of the **Output directory** location. Using the default path should suffice.

13. Under the **Output Layout** tab, make sure that the artifact project, **BludBourne.jar**, (top-level) is selected.

14. Select the **+ | Directory Content** option to add a copy of our assets folder.

15. In the **Select Path** dialog, select the root directory for all our project resources, `core\assets`, and click on **OK**.

16. In the **Project Structure** window, you should have a configured build that looks similar to the following screenshot (*Figure 2*):

Figure 2

17. Click on **Apply** and then on **OK** in the **Project Structure** window.

18. Now we can build the artifact by selecting the **Build | Build Artifacts...** option.

19. In the **Build Artifact** pop-up window, select **BludBourne.jar**.

20. In the **Action** popup window, select **Build**.

21. Using Windows Explorer, navigate to the output directory (relative to the project root), which is `out\artifacts\BludBourne_jar`.

22. You can execute this JAR using one of two different ways. The first is by running the following command in the command prompt:

```
C:\BludBourne\out\artifacts\BludBourne_jar\java -jar BludBourne.
jar
```

The second way is to double click on the JAR file, `BludBourne.jar`, from the Windows Explorer window.

Native launchers

Generally, when distributing software, you will need to use an installer product to create a package executable that will be installed by the user. Installer software will generate a dependency graph while compiling the dependencies. A set of rules (defined by you) will be used as checks to successfully generate the installer. The use of an installer is beyond the scope of this chapter, but typically the various digital distribution systems will provide the tools necessary for the final packaging.

One item for your game to always keep in mind is that injecting dependencies directly into the final executable is usually preferable at the expense of a larger file size. Making assumptions about the player's system, or at least, posting the requirements for specific software dependencies can be a burdensome process for the player. The file size of the final executable is more of a primary concern of systems with limited space, such as mobile devices. For a Window's PC platform, file size is not as large of a concern, and since a Java-based executable JAR will run in its own JVM sandbox, we do not have to be concerned about dependency conflicts with system resources.

When looking at distributing your game, one consideration to keep in mind is the ease of use for the player to install your game. The player should not have to worry about all the various resources related to your game. One tool that we can use to create our final package for distribution is called **Packr**.

Packr

The tool we will use next with our executable JAR (created in the last section) is named Packr (http://github.com/libgdx/packr). In the last section, we used either a Gradle target or an IntelliJ artifact to create an executable JAR. The problem with the executable JAR is that it still requires the hosting system to have a Java runtime installed. Packr adds the Java runtime as part of the final build so that the player does not need to install or upgrade their own Java runtime.

The following steps demonstrate how to use Packr:

1. First, download the latest stable build JAR, typically copied to `packr.jar` for distribution from http://libgdx.badlogicgames.com/packr.

2. Copy the `packr.jar` file to the build directory where the `BludBourne.jar` file is located.

3. Open up a command window and navigate to where your `packr.jar` file lives. In Windows, holding down the left *Shift* key while pressing the right mouse button will add an option, **Open Command Window Here**, to the context window that pops up.

4. Execute the following command at the command prompt:

```
C:\BludBourne\build>java -jar packr.jar \
-platform windows \
-jdk https://bitbucket.org/alexkasko/openjdk-unofficial- \
    builds/downloads/openjdk-1.7.0-u80-unofficial-windows-i586- \
    image.zip \
-executable BludBourne \
-appjar BludBourne.jar \
-mainclass "com/packtpub/libgdx/bludbourne/desktop/
DesktopLauncher" \
-vmargs "-Xmx1G" \
-minimizejre "soft" \
-outdir out
```

5. After the build, navigate to the `out` directory specified by the `-outdir` parameter.

6. You can now run the native launcher, designated as `BludBourne.exe`, without the need to have a Java runtime installed.

The files included in the `out` directory are as follows:

```
C:.
|   BludBourne.exe
|   BludBourne.jar
|   config.json
|   tmp.txt
|
└──jre
```

The native launcher that the user can just execute is `BludBourne.exe`. The dependent JAR with all the bytecode and assets, `BludBourne.jar`, is located at the same level. The `config.json` file allows some runtime configuration in how the application is launched. Finally, the `JRE` directory contains the properly licensed OpenJDK package that is used for the execution of the native launcher.

The following describes the parameters used with Packr in a little more detail:

- `platform`: This is the target platform for the build. Valid targets are `windows` (only 32-bit for now), `linux32`, `linux64`, or `mac`.
- `jdk`: This is the path to a zipped version of or the URL to OpenJDK (license allows redistribution with applications). Builds can be found at `http://github.com/alexkasko/openjdk-unofficial-builds`.
- `executable`: This is the name you want for the final executable file (without the extension).
- `appjar`: This is the file path for the executable JAR needed for the final native launcher.
- `mainclass`: This is the fully qualified path for the entry point of the application (the value used in the `manifest.mf` file). A forward slash is currently used in between the package names instead of the dots.
- `vmargs`: These are all arguments that will be passed to the JVM during runtime.
- `outdir`: This is the final output directory of the native launcher when finished.
- `resources`: This is an optional parameter (not used in our example because all the files are included in the JAR) for a list of files (and directories) to be packaged next to the native executable.
- `minimizejre`: This parameter minimizes the memory footprint of the JRE by removing the specified directories and files.

Obfuscating the packaged JAR

Another consideration is the security of your game executable to prevent people, or at the least, make the process more difficult for the player to exploit your game code. A common technique used in the industry is to rename class member variables and class names, or obfuscate the compiled bytecode of the distribution JARs. There is a tool I have used in the past for obfuscating Android-based games, but can also be applied to the desktop version of your game. **Proguard** (v5.2.1) still seems to be the golden standard because it is configurable, relatively effective, and open source. The main website for Proguard is `http://proguard.sourceforge.net/`.

The following steps demonstrate how to use Proguard:

1. Navigate to where the current build distribution JAR, `BludBourne.jar`, is located.

2. Rename this JAR to `BludBourne_ORIG.jar`.

3. Download the latest Proguard zip file from `http://sourceforge.net/projects/proguard/files` and unzip the archive.

4. Navigate into the unzipped archive to the root directory (which contains the `README` file) and down into the `bin` directory.

5. Double-click on the `proguardgui.bat` batch file to execute the GUI tool on Windows.

6. You should see the following splash screen after Proguard loads:

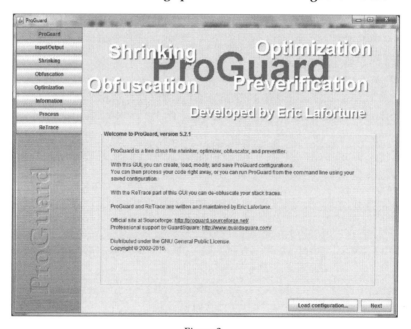

Figure 3

7. Load the predefined configuration file, `proguard.cfg`, from the root directory of the project, under `BludBourne/`. We discuss the specifics of the configuration file later in this section.

8. Click on the **Input/Output** button on the left pane.

9. Click on the **Add input...** button, navigate to where the current distribution JAR is located, and select the source JAR file, in our case `BludBourne_ORIG.jar`.

10. Click on the **Add output...** button, navigate to where the current source distribution JAR is located (`BludBourne_ORIG.jar`), and type in `BludBourne.jar`.

11. In the bottom pane, if you have chosen to use Packr, you will have external dependencies (JRE) that will need to be added. Click on **Add...** and select the `jre` directory (OpenJDK binaries) that is included with your distribution.

12. Click on the **Process** button on the left pane.

13. Click on the **Process!** button on the bottom-right of the **Process** window.

14. The target obfuscated distribution JAR, `BludBourne.jar`, will be located in the output directory.

The proguard.cfg file

An explanation of all the configuration options is available at `http://proguard.sourceforge.net/index.html#manual/usage.html`. The following is the `proguard.cfg` file used for generating the final obfuscated distribution jar for *BludBourne*:

```
-optimizationpasses 5
-verbose

-renamesourcefileattribute SourceFile
-keepattributes SourceFile,LineNumberTable,Signature

-dontwarn com.badlogic.gdx.jnigen.**
-dontwarn java.awt.**
-dontwarn com.badlogic.**
-dontwarn org.lwjgl.**

-dontnote java.awt.**
-dontnote com.badlogic.**
-dontnote org.lwjgl.**
```

```
-keep class org.lwjgl.** { *; }
-keep class com.badlogic.** { *; }
-keep class * implements com.badlogic.gdx.utils.Json*

-keepnames class * implements java.io.Serializable

-keepclassmembers class * implements java.io.Serializable {
    static final long serialVersionUID;
    private static final java.io.ObjectStreamField[]
      serialPersistentFields;
    !static !transient <fields>;
    private void writeObject(java.io.ObjectOutputStream);
    private void readObject(java.io.ObjectInputStream);
    java.lang.Object writeReplace();
    java.lang.Object readResolve();
}


-keepclasseswithmembernames class * {
    native <methods>;
}


-keepclassmembers enum * {
    public static **[] values();
    public static ** valueOf(java.lang.String);
}


#BludBourne specific
-keep public class com.packtpub.libgdx.bludbourne.
   desktop.DesktopLauncher{
  public static void main(java.lang.String[]);
}


-keepclassmembers class com.packtpub.libgdx.bludbourne.
   EntityConfig{ *; }
-keepclassmembers class com.packtpub.libgdx.bludbourne.
   EntityConfig$AnimationConfig{ *; }
-keepclassmembers class com.packtpub.libgdx.bludbourne.
   dialog.ConversationGraph{ *; }
-keepclassmembers class com.packtpub.libgdx.bludbourne.
   quest.QuestGraph{ *; }
```

```
-keepclassmembers class com.packtpub.libgdx.bludbourne.
    battle.LevelTable{ *; }
-keepclassmembers class com.packtpub.libgdx.bludbourne.
    battle.MonsterZone{ *; }
-keepclassmembers class com.packtpub.libgdx.bludbourne.
    InventoryItem{ *; }

-keep class com.packtpub.libgdx.bludbourne.
    dialog.ConversationChoice{ *; }
-keep class com.packtpub.libgdx.bludbourne.dialog.Conversation{ *;
    }
-keep class com.packtpub.libgdx.bludbourne.quest.QuestTask{ *; }
-keep class com.packtpub.libgdx.bludbourne.
    quest.QuestTaskDependency{ *; }
```

Most of the options here are standard for configurations involving LibGDX on the desktop. The items to note are the ones that relate to *BludBourne*. Specifically, we need to make sure that we keep the entry point for *BludBourne* so that it doesn't get obfuscated. Otherwise, Proguard will not know how to map from the obfuscated classes back to their original names.

The other classes that we have to keep from being obfuscated, specifically deal with JSON. The reason is that when reading our JSON-based script files from disk, the JSON parser cannot resolve the types inferred from the field names. Since we have obfuscated the POJO class names and members, the parser will fail because the field names do not match up with their POJO representations. This issue with obfuscation is also only caught at runtime when the JSON parser is actually used.

Debugging tips

Sometimes, when first creating the executable JAR, there will be times when the game will simply not execute. This is typically related to packaging issues; when your game is trying to load resources and they cannot be found. Other times, there may be issues with obfuscation and another rule will need to be added to the `proguard.cfg` file. The following are a few tips for resolving these issues.

The command line

We will want to run the binary from the command prompt using the following command:

```
java -jar BludBourne.jar
```

This allows us to view any stack trace generated when an exception was thrown during execution. I used this debugging method to find an issue with the initial executable JAR created for *BludBourne*. When running *BludBourne* from the IDE on Windows, the paths (and files) get resolved correctly because we are searching the project paths on the filesystem, which is case-insensitive. However, when run from the JAR, these same paths (and files) are resolved with case sensitivity in mind (for portability reasons). I hand edited the TMX map files so that all the paths were lower case; thus, matching up with the paths in the JAR and fixing the issue.

Attach to the running process

Another option is to attach to the running process in order to remote debug the JAR. The following steps will demonstrate how to do this using IDEA:

1. Make sure the project is loaded in IDEA associated with the executable JAR that you want to debug.

2. Select **Run | Edit Configurations...** from the menu.

3. In the **Run/Debug Configurations** window, click on the + symbol to add a new configuration and select **Remote**.

4. The defaults for the remote configuration should be sufficient. Just make sure to note all the options under **Command line arguments for running remote JVM** and copy them.

5. Click on **Apply** and **OK**.

6. Now launch the executable JAR from the command line with the following command (which adds the arguments copied from step 4):

```
java

-agentlib:jdwp=transport=dt_socket,server=y,suspend=n,
address=5005

-jar desktop-1.0.jar
```

7. In IDEA, to attach to the running instance, select **Run | Debug <Remote target>**.

Testing builds before release

The final component in the verification step of your final release package is to run some tests as a sanity check. These are standard tests that even developers should do, before handing off to your quality assurance group, when checking in bug fixes or after adding a new feature.

A smoke test

The first test, a smoke test, deals with a relatively straightforward and fast series of steps for covering as much of the game mechanics and features as possible without a lengthy review process.

BludBourne start and main menu

1. Verify we have a Proguard-processed archive `BludBourne.jar`.
2. Verify we have a Packr-generated native executable `BludBourne.exe` that references the Proguard-processed archive.
3. Start *BludBourne* by running the native executable, `BludBourne.exe`.
4. Verify that the main menu is presented with the appropriate choices.
5. Verify music is playing at the main menu.
6. Select **Exit**.
7. Verify that *BludBourne* shuts down correctly.
8. Start *BludBourne* by running the native executable, `BludBourne.exe`.
9. Select **Credits**.
10. Verify that the credits run until the end.
11. Verify that you can navigate back to the main menu by clicking on the screen.

Cutscene

12. Click on **Watch Intro**.
13. Verify that the introduction cutscene plays through correctly, including music, text, and graphics (~2 minutes).
14. Verify that when the cutscene fades out at the end, we are back at the main menu.
15. Verify music is playing at the main menu.

New game

16. Select **New Game**.

17. Enter a profile name `quicktest` and click on **Start**.

18. Verify that we are starting at the TOWN map and the time on the clock is around 12:00 pm.

19. Verify that your character has 50 HP, 50 MP, 0 XP, Level 1, and 20 GP.

20. Verify that the music is playing for the TOWN map.

Inventory

21. Click on your inventory and verify that you have the default starting gear.

22. Verify that as you hover over inventory items, you can see tooltip information.

23. Verify that you can drag and drop inventory items into your equip slots (add armor and a sword).

24. Verify that the defense and attack points are updated.

25. Verify that you can stack your MP potions and HP scrolls.

26. Exit the inventory.

Town NPCs

27. Verify that there are NPCs walking around.

28. Verify that the lanterns and torch particle effects are active.

29. Select TOWN_FOLK10 and walk away far enough to verify that the selection is gone.

Conversation

30. Start a conversation with TOWN_FOLK10.

31. Verify that you can go through the four options, one for each cardinal direction.

32. Verify that you can exit the conversation by clicking on the **Exit** button.

Quest

33. Select TOWN_FOLK2 and accept the quest.

34. Verify that the quest shows up in your **Quest Log**.

35. Verify the child spawns and that you can safely place the child in your inventory.

36. Verify the child is in your inventory.

37. Return the child and finish quest.

38. Verify that the quest reward music plays.

39. Verify you receive money and experience.

Item purchase

40. Visit TOWN_BLACKSMITH and verify that you can see his items.

41. Drag and drop the cheapest shield and select **BUY**.

42. Verify that your GP has updated and that the coin sound effect is played.

43. Verify that you have received the item after exiting.

44. Exit TOWN.

Battle

45. Walk around and find a battle with a monster.

46. Click on **RUN** until you can successfully evade the monster.

47. Walk around and find a battle with a monster.

48. Attack the monster.

49. Verify that they shake when struck and the damage appears above their head.

50. After defeating the monster, verify your experience has gone up.

Game over

51. Remove all items of defense from your equip slots.

52. Walk around and find a battle with a monster.

53. Verify that you receive damage and that the UI shakes.

54. Repeat the battles until you die.

55. Verify that you see a game over screen.

56. Select **Continue**.

57. Load quicktest.

58. Verify that you are starting in the TOP_WORLD map.

Consuming items

59. Open your inventory and eat your scrolls for health.

60. Verify that your health goes up.

61. Verify that the scrolls in the inventory are removed.

62. Verify that you hear the sound effects when using the items.

Wand attack

63. Equip yourself with all defense and the wand.

64. Verify that when you attack, you see the particle effect.

65. Verify that your MP goes down.

Lightmaps and day-to-night cycle

66. Now, go back to TOWN until nightfall.

67. Verify that the lightmap in TOWN is enabled.

68. Quit the game.

Save game profiles

69. Open up the `quicktest.sav` save game profile in a text editor.

70. Verify that the file is not readable.

71. Start *BludBourne* by running the native executable, `BludBourne.exe`.

72. Select **Load Game** and `quicktest`.

73. Verify that the profile loads correctly.

74. Quit the game.

The burn-in test

Another test to run is one that involves running the game for a prolonged period of time. This is a stress test or burn-in test that evaluates the overall stability of a build. For a more detailed analysis of your game, you can run a memory profiler to pinpoint the specific areas that may be causing issues. The steps for this test is as follows:

1. Start *BludBourne* by running the native executable, `BludBourne.exe`.

2. Select **New Game**.

3. Enter a profile name `burnintest` and click on **Start**.

4. Verify that we are starting at TOWN and that the time on the clock is around 12:00 pm.

5. Launch the process explorer on the desktop and make a note of the current memory footprint of the `BludBourne.exe` executable.

6. Let the game run without interruption for a specific length of time, depending on your requirements.

7. Make a note of the current memory footprint and calculate the difference from the initial size.

8. This measurement will tell you if you have serious memory leaks or if the build is relatively stable with minimal memory overhead.

Summary

In this chapter, we first explored different options for digital distribution platforms to host your game. We then addressed a few topics to minimize exploits of your game code, including obfuscating the save game profiles using the `Base64Encoder` class and minimizing the logging chatter output to standard out. Next, we looked at the final packaging steps for generating an executable JAR and also native launchers, using Packr, to eliminate third-party dependencies for the player. We then looked at an additional layer of security by obfuscating our final package with Proguard. There were some general debugging tips that can be useful during these different steps in the process. Finally, we reviewed some tests used during the development of *BludBourne* that, hopefully, can be helpful for you during your deployment phases.

This is where the road ends for our journey in the world of *BludBourne*. We have learned much during our travels together, and I hope that you are armed with some new knowledge that will aid you in your future adventures.

Index

A

Action objects
defining 302
Android SDK Tools
URL 147
animation
player character, implementing with 82
application program interfaces (APIs) 10
App Store, Apple
URL 368
App store, Google
URL 368
artificial intelligence (AI) 8
asset management
implementing, with loading textures 58
implementing, with tile-based maps 58
assets module 23
Audacity (version 2.0.3)
about 290
URL 290
AudioCommand enum type
list, defining 293, 294

B

backend modules
about 20, 21
Application.java interface 20
Audio.java interface 21
Files.java interface 21
Graphics.java interface 21
Input.java interface 21
Net.java interface 21
Preferences.java interface 21

BattleState class
BattleObserver 255-257
BattleSubject 255
defining 254, 255
InventorySubject 257-259
MonsterFactory 262, 263
MonsterZone 265-272
options, defining 256-258
battle system
implementing 252-254
BattleUI class
about 273, 274
AnimatedImage class 275-280
BludBourne
reviewing 57, 58
starter classes, implementing 54, 55
BludBourne project
executing 43, 44
build environment 35
builds
burn-in test 386
smoke test 383
testing, before release 383
URL 377
burn-in test 386

C

class diagram
defining 288, 289
class hierarchy
ConversationChoice class 188
Conversation class 187, 188
ConversationGraph class 190-195
ConversationGraphObserver class 189, 190

T

technologies, role-playing game
about 8
budget, planning 11-13
commercial game, versus technology
demo 8
game framework, versus game engine 9
target platforms 9
third-party extension, Gradle
URL 36
tide
URL 48
tile-based maps
creating 47-53
editing 47-53
tilemap editors, LibGDX
tide 48
tiled 48
tooltip
using 169, 170
TrueType font (TTF) file 23

U

UIs
developing, with LibGDX 143
UI structure
defining 196-201

UIs, with LibGDX
9-patch 147, 148
defining 143
skins 149
texture atlas 144-146
UI summary, developing 149
widget styles 144
unitScale attribute
benefits 69
user interface (UI) 7
Utility class
defining 59-63
utils module 23

V

version control system (VCS) 41, 42

W

**What you see is what you get (WYSIWYG)
tool 147**

Thank you for buying
Mastering LibGDX Game Development

About Packt Publishing

Packt, pronounced 'packed', published its first book, *Mastering phpMyAdmin for Effective MySQL Management*, in April 2004, and subsequently continued to specialize in publishing highly focused books on specific technologies and solutions.

Our books and publications share the experiences of your fellow IT professionals in adapting and customizing today's systems, applications, and frameworks. Our solution-based books give you the knowledge and power to customize the software and technologies you're using to get the job done. Packt books are more specific and less general than the IT books you have seen in the past. Our unique business model allows us to bring you more focused information, giving you more of what you need to know, and less of what you don't.

Packt is a modern yet unique publishing company that focuses on producing quality, cutting-edge books for communities of developers, administrators, and newbies alike. For more information, please visit our website at www.packtpub.com.

About Packt Open Source

In 2010, Packt launched two new brands, Packt Open Source and Packt Enterprise, in order to continue its focus on specialization. This book is part of the Packt Open Source brand, home to books published on software built around open source licenses, and offering information to anybody from advanced developers to budding web designers. The Open Source brand also runs Packt's Open Source Royalty Scheme, by which Packt gives a royalty to each open source project about whose software a book is sold.

Writing for Packt

We welcome all inquiries from people who are interested in authoring. Book proposals should be sent to author@packtpub.com. If your book idea is still at an early stage and you would like to discuss it first before writing a formal book proposal, then please contact us; one of our commissioning editors will get in touch with you.

We're not just looking for published authors; if you have strong technical skills but no writing experience, our experienced editors can help you develop a writing career, or simply get some additional reward for your expertise.

Learning LibGDX Game Development

Second Edition

ISBN: 978-1-78355-477-5   Paperback: 478 pages

Wield the power of the LibGDX framework to create a cross-platform game

1. Write your game code once and run it on a multitude of platforms using LibGDX.

2. Learn about the key features of LibGDX that will ease and speed up your development cycles.

3. An easy-to-follow, comprehensive guide that will help you develop games in LibGDX successfully.

LibGDX Game Development Essentials

ISBN: 978-1-78439-929-0   Paperback: 216 pages

Make the most of game development features powered by LibGDX and create a side-scrolling action game, Thrust Copter

1. Utilize the robust features of LibGDX to easily create and publish cross-platform 2D and 3D games that involve complicated physics.

2. Be the best cross-platform game developer with the ability to create rich interactive applications on all the leading platforms.

3. Develop a 2D side scrolling game, Thrust Copter, add physics, and try to convert it to 3D while working on interesting LibGDX experiments.

Please check **www.PacktPub.com** for information on our titles

Libgdx Cross-platform Game Development Cookbook

ISBN: 978-1-78328-729-1   Paperback: 516 pages

Over 75 practical recipes to help you master cross-platform 2D game development using the powerful Libgdx framework

1. Gain an in-depth understanding of every Libgdx subsystem, including 2D graphics, input, audio, file extensions, and third-party libraries.

2. Write once and deploy to Windows, Linux, Mac, Android, iOS, and browsers.

3. Full of uniquely structured recipes that help you get the most out of Libgdx.

Learning Libgdx Game Development

ISBN: 978-1-78216-604-7   Paperback: 388 pages

Walk through a complete game development cycle with practical examples and build cross-platform games with Libgdx

1. Create a libGDX multi-platform game from start to finish.

2. Learn about the key features of libGDX that will ease and speed up your development cycles.

3. Write your game code once and run it on a multitude of platforms using libGDX.

4. An easy-to-follow guide that will help you develop games in libGDX successfully.

Please check **www.PacktPub.com** for information on our titles

66714541R00233

Made in the USA
Lexington, KY
21 August 2017